Python for Bioinformatics

Using machine learning for drug discovery, cluster analysis, and phylogenetics

Dr. Parul Verma

Dr. Shahnaz Fatima

www.bpbonline.com

First Edition 2025

Copyright © BPB Publications, India

ISBN: 978-93-65897-760

All Rights Reserved. No part of this publication may be reproduced, distributed or transmitted in any form or by any means or stored in a database or retrieval system, without the prior written permission of the publisher with the exception to the program listings which may be entered, stored and executed in a computer system, but they can not be reproduced by the means of publication, photocopy, recording, or by any electronic and mechanical means.

LIMITS OF LIABILITY AND DISCLAIMER OF WARRANTY

The information contained in this book is true to correct and the best of author's and publisher's knowledge. The author has made every effort to ensure the accuracy of these publications, but publisher cannot be held responsible for any loss or damage arising from any information in this book.

All trademarks referred to in the book are acknowledged as properties of their respective owners but BPB Publications cannot guarantee the accuracy of this information.

To View Complete
BPB Publications Catalogue
Scan the QR Code:

www.bpbonline.com

Dedicated to

Family and Friends

About the Authors

- **Dr. Parul Verma** has been working as a faculty member at Amity Institute of Information Technology, Amity University, Uttar Pradesh, Lucknow. Her research interests are natural language processing, web mining, deep mining, Semantic Web, Edge and IoT. She has published and presented almost 50 papers in Scopus and other indexed National and International Journals and Conferences. She has been actively involved in research being as a supervisor to Research Scholars and Post Graduate students. She has also edited a book titled Artificial Intelligence and Machine Learning for Edge Computing published by Elsevier. She has been nominated as a member of Technical Program Committee and Organizing Committee of many International Conferences. She is also a member of many International and National bodies like Association for Computing Machinery (ACM), International Association of Engineers (IAENG), International Association of Computer Science and Information Technology (IACSIT), Internet Society.

- **Dr. Shahnaz Fatima** is a faculty member at the Amity Institute of Information Technology, Amity University, Uttar Pradesh, Lucknow. Her research interests are human-computer interaction, data mining, deep learning, the Semantic Web, and Edge computing in IoT. She is actively involved in supervising both Doctorate Research Scholars and postgraduate students. She has authored numerous impactful research papers published in Scopus-indexed journals, as well as various national and international conferences. Additionally, she edited the book Distributed Computing to Blockchain: Architecture, Technology, and Applications, published by Elsevier and also indexed by Scopus. She is a member of the International Association of Computer Science and Information Technology (IACSIT) and the International Association of Engineers (IAENG).

About the Reviewers

❖ **Vinoth Nageshwaran** is a seasoned data engineering leader with over 16 years of experience specializing in designing and implementing scalable data architectures using modern technologies such as Snowflake, AWS, Google Cloud, and DBT. He has a strong foundation in managing containerized applications with Kubernetes and utilizing Looker for advanced data analytics and visualization. Vinoth's expertise extends to integrating Python for data manipulation and leveraging OpenAI's capabilities to enhance data-driven decision-making processes.

As a member of IEEE and ACM, he has contributed significantly to the field of data engineering and AI/ML, showcasing his proficiency in establishing robust data governance frameworks and ensuring data integrity across multiple platforms. His extensive experience includes leading cross-functional teams to foster innovation, collaboration, and the successful deployment of data solutions. Vinoth is also actively involved in education, volunteering to teach SQL sessions and sharing his knowledge through guest lectures and technical reviews.

His commitment to continuous learning and passion for technology ensures that he stays at the forefront of industry trends, making him a valuable contributor to this book. His insights as a reviewer have provided a critical perspective on the application of computational techniques in bioinformatics, bridging the gap between data science and biology.

❖ **Satish Prahalad Gururajan** is a passionate solutions architect with extensive professional experience in application development using Java technologies. He has great experience in various roles as developer, architect, product owner, and designer in career spanning close to two decades. He is a holder of multiple industry certifications in SAFe® Product Owner/Product Manager, Product Owner CSPO® and Scrum Master CSM®.

Satish specializes in problem-solving and loves presenting complex topics in simple manner.

Acknowledgements

We want to express our deepest gratitude to our families and friends for their unwavering support and encouragement throughout this book's writing.

We are immensely grateful to BPB and the editorial team for their belief in this book and for guiding us through the publication process. Your professionalism and attention to detail have helped transform this manuscript into its final form.

Finally, to the readers and the scientific community, we are deeply thankful for your interest in this work. We hope that this book will contribute meaningfully to your research and understanding of the application of Python in Bioinformatics.

Thank you all for making this journey possible.

Preface

The rapid evolution of biological research, coupled with advancements in data generation technologies, has resulted in an overwhelming amount of biological data that is too vast and complex to analyze manually. In response, bioinformatics has emerged as a critical field, blending biology, computer science, and mathematics to interpret and analyze this vast data. At the core of bioinformatics lies programming, and Python has become the go-to language for bioinformaticians due to its simplicity, versatility, and vast libraries designed for biological data analysis.

This book, "Python for Bioinformatics", aims to bridge the gap between biology and computational science, providing a comprehensive introduction to Python programming with a focus on its application in bioinformatics. Whether you are a biologist looking to learn programming to analyze your data, a computer scientist aiming to enter the field of bioinformatics, or a student with a passion for both biology and coding, this book is designed to equip you with the knowledge and tools necessary to succeed by covering the following topics:

Chapter 1: Introduction to Bioinformatics and its Applications – This chapter covers Bioinformatics, which is an interdisciplinary field that merges biology, computer science, and information technology to analyze and interpret biological data. It emerged as a response to the growing amount of biological information generated by genomic research and other fields. Bioinformatics has become an essential field, underpinning modern biological research and providing the computational tools necessary to make sense of complex biological data. This chapter introduces the foundational concepts of bioinformatics and its broad range of applications across various scientific disciplines.

Chapter 2: Bioinformatics and its Use Cases – This chapter covers Bioinformatics as a multidisciplinary field that plays a crucial role in analyzing and interpreting biological data. Its use spans various areas of life sciences from genomics to drug discovery. Bioinformatics has revolutionized the biological sciences by providing computational tools for data analysis, prediction, and integration. Its wide range of applications from basic research to clinical and industrial use has made it an indispensable tool for advancing science and improving health outcomes. This chapter explores different applications of bioinformatics in scientific research and healthcare.

Chapter 3: Introduction to Python and Basic Programming - This chapter covers the introduction to the basics of Python language, its installation, modes of working, the basic syntax of Python programming, various keywords and operators, and the formation of expressions. By the end of this chapter, readers will be familiar with Python and its environment. The chapter also covers the concept of basic programming constructs as well.

Chapter 4: String Handling, Modular Programming, and Data Structures - This chapter covers the concept of handling strings in Python. It provides a basic understanding of the library functions and user-defined functions. It will also focus on how to create functions and the various ways in which they can be utilized. The chapter also elaborates on the concept of modules, explaining how to create them, as well as how to import specific functions from a module or import an entire module. Additionally, it covers different data structures such as lists, tuples, and dictionaries, providing a thorough understanding of these concepts as well.

Chapter 5: File Handling and Object Oriented Concept – This chapter covers file handling, it is a crucial aspect of many applications, as files serve as a means for permanent data storage. Python allows you to read and write various types of files, including flat files, .csv files, and binary files. This chapter will explore basic input-output operations across different file types. Additionally, Python offers features that enable programmers to adopt an object-oriented approach. The chapter aims to help you understand fundamental concepts of object-oriented programming, such as classes, inheritance, polymorphism, and their implementation in Python.

Chapter 6: Basic Concepts of Biopython Module- This chapter covers the Biopython module, which gives the facility to deal with various types of sequences like RNA, DNA, and protein sequences. The module offers a range of functions designed to support tasks related to bioinformatics applications. Sequences serve as the fundamental units in these applications. They can perform various operations typical of biological sequences, such as transcription, complementing, and translation, to name a few. This chapter will discuss both basic and advanced concepts related to the Biopython module and sequences.

Chapter 7: Pattern Matching with Regular Expression – This chapter covers pattern matching, which is a crucial component of bioinformatics applications. It serves as a valuable tool for extracting information from large datasets. Regular expressions are particularly useful for pattern matching, as they simplify the coding process by providing a concise way to search for specific data within vast amounts of information. This chapter aims to help readers understand the concept of pattern matching in the context of bioinformatics applications, using the Python programming language.

Chapter 8: Data Handling and Visualization in Bioinformatics– This chapter covers Information Visualization (IV) techniques, which involve computerized methods for selecting, transforming, and representing data visually. This visual representation allows individuals to interact with the data, facilitating exploration and understanding. The primary goals of data visualization techniques are twofold. First, they enable users to view large volumes of data simultaneously, something that would not be feasible otherwise. Second, these techniques help identify patterns and trends, which aids in extracting valuable insights from extensive datasets. This chapter discusses the main Python libraries used for data visualization.

Chapter 9: Mini Applications in Bioinformatics– This chapter covers the small applications of bioinformatics to help readers understand the use of Python and the Biopython module. It demonstrates simple projects using the Biopython module to provide a basic understanding of the module and related libraries.

Chapter 10: Mini Projects on Bioinformatics - This chapter covers mini projects that will enable readers to implement the concepts they have learned. Integrating and implementing isolated concepts through projects enhances learning. The projects described may assist readers in understanding how to create small Bioinformatics applications.

Code Bundle and Coloured Images

Please follow the link to download the
Code Bundle and the *Coloured Images* of the book:

https://rebrand.ly/fo9zg48

The code bundle for the book is also hosted on GitHub at **https://github.com/bpbpublications/Python-for-Bioinformatics**.
In case there's an update to the code, it will be updated on the existing GitHub repository.

We have code bundles from our rich catalogue of books and videos available at **https://github.com/bpbpublications**. Check them out!

Errata

We take immense pride in our work at BPB Publications and follow best practices to ensure the accuracy of our content to provide with an indulging reading experience to our subscribers. Our readers are our mirrors, and we use their inputs to reflect and improve upon human errors, if any, that may have occurred during the publishing processes involved. To let us maintain the quality and help us reach out to any readers who might be having difficulties due to any unforeseen errors, please write to us at :

errata@bpbonline.com

Your support, suggestions and feedbacks are highly appreciated by the BPB Publications' Family.

Did you know that BPB offers eBook versions of every book published, with PDF and ePub files available? You can upgrade to the eBook version at www.bpbonline.com and as a print book customer, you are entitled to a discount on the eBook copy. Get in touch with us at :

business@bpbonline.com for more details.

At **www.bpbonline.com**, you can also read a collection of free technical articles, sign up for a range of free newsletters, and receive exclusive discounts and offers on BPB books and eBooks.

Piracy

If you come across any illegal copies of our works in any form on the internet, we would be grateful if you would provide us with the location address or website name. Please contact us at **business@bpbonline.com** with a link to the material.

If you are interested in becoming an author

If there is a topic that you have expertise in, and you are interested in either writing or contributing to a book, please visit **www.bpbonline.com**. We have worked with thousands of developers and tech professionals, just like you, to help them share their insights with the global tech community. You can make a general application, apply for a specific hot topic that we are recruiting an author for, or submit your own idea.

Reviews

Please leave a review. Once you have read and used this book, why not leave a review on the site that you purchased it from? Potential readers can then see and use your unbiased opinion to make purchase decisions. We at BPB can understand what you think about our products, and our authors can see your feedback on their book. Thank you!

For more information about BPB, please visit **www.bpbonline.com**.

Join our book's Discord space

Join the book's Discord Workspace for Latest updates, Offers, Tech happenings around the world, New Release and Sessions with the Authors:

https://discord.bpbonline.com

Table of Contents

1. Introduction to Bioinformatics and its Applications 1
    Introduction 1
    Structure 1
    Objectives 2
    Applications of bioinformatics 2
    Bioinformatics and its data structures 4
    Bioinformatics and its structural databases 6
    Tools and techniques of bioinformatics 8
    Conclusion 10

2. Bioinformatics and its Use Cases 11
    Introduction 11
    Structure 12
    Objectives 12
    Gene therapy 12
        Viral vectors 13
        Non-viral vectors 14
    Stem cell therapy 15
    Drug discovery 18
    Genomic data analysis 20
    Transcriptomics 23
    Proteomics 25
    Metagenomics 27
    Clinical genomics 29
    Agricultural genomics 31
    Systems biology 33
    Conclusion 35

3. Introduction to Python and Basic Programming 37
    Introduction 37

Structure	37
Objectives	38
History and evolution of Python	38
Features of Python	40
How to download and install Python	41
How Python works	43
Script mode	*44*
Language fundamentals	46
Variables in Python	*46*
Data types in Python	*48*
Text data type	*48*
Numeric data type	*48*
Sequence data type	*50*
Mapping type	*50*
Set type	*51*
Boolean data type	*52*
Binary type	*52*
Expressions	*53*
Type conversion	*53*
Implicit type casting	*54*
Explicit type casting	*55*
Keywords in Python	*55*
Operators in Python	*56*
Comments in Python	*58*
Syntax of docstrings	*59*
Input statement in Python	*60*
Language constructs in Python	60
Indentation in Python	*60*
Conditional statements	*62*
if statement	*62*
if…else statement	*64*
If-elif-else statement	*64*

   Nested if-elif-else statement 65
  Loops in Python 66
   Definite loop 66
   Indefinite loop in Python 68
   Nested loops 68
  Jump statements in Python 70
   Break statement 70
 Conclusion 73

4. String Handling, Modular Programming, and Data Structures 75
 Introduction 75
 Structure 75
 Objectives 75
 String basic in Python 76
  Accessing characters 76
   String length 76
   String concatenation 77
   String slicing 77
  String methods 79
   upper() 79
   lower() 80
   strip() 80
   split() 81
   replace() 81
   find() 81
 Data structures 82
  Lists 82
   Creating a list 82
   Accessing elements 82
   List length 83
  List methods 84
   Tuples 84
   Creating a tuple 85

| *Sets* 87
| *Dictionaries* 87
| *Strings* 88
| Modular programming 88
| *Examples of modular programming in Python* 89
| *Functions* 90
| MODULES 92
| PACKAGES 92
| Conclusion 95

5. File Handling and Object Oriented Concept 97
   Introduction 97
   Structure 97
   Objectives 98
   Opening files 98
       Handling different types of files in Python 100
       Binary files 101
           Opening binary files 101
           Comma-separated values files 103
           FASTA File 105
   Introduction to working with directories 107
   Object-oriented programming concepts 109
   Classes in Python 110
       Defining a class 111
   Inheritance 113
   Polymorphism 115
   Conclusion 117

6. Basic Concept of Biopython Module 119
   Introduction 119
   Structure 119
   Objectives 120
   How to install Biopython 120
   Sequence object in Biopython 121

- Sequence working as a string 121
- Sequence object operations 123
  - *Complement of a sequence* 123
  - *Complement and reverse complement function* 123
  - *Transcription of a sequence* 124
    - Back transcription 124
  - *Translation of a sequence* 125
- Mutable sequence 127
  - *Multiplying mutable sequence* 130
- SequenceRecord object 130
  - *Creating a sequence record object* 130
- Sequence input-output module 131
- Accessing sequences from FASTA and GenBank 132
  - *Sequence iterator for FASTA file* 132
  - *Filtering sequences from the FASTA file* 135
  - *Sequence iterator for GenBank file* 136
- Conclusion 137

7. Pattern Matching with Regular Expression 139
- Introduction 139
- Structure 140
- Objectives 140
- Importance of patterns in bioinformatics sequences 140
  - *Searching for a pattern using regular expression* 143
    - Alternation feature of regular expression 144
  - *Character groups in regular expression* 145
  - *Quantifiers in regular expression* 146
  - *Positions in regular expression* 151
    - Group function in regular expression 152
    - Getting a match position using regular expression 153
  - *Finding multiple matches in regular expression* 154
- String splitting using regular expression 155

Conclusion.. 156

8. Data Handling and Visualization in Bioinformatics 157

Introduction... 157

Structure.. 158

Objectives 158

Data handling 158

Data visualization... 159

 Tools for data handling and visualization in bioinformatics................................ 160

Working with NumPy 161

 Arrays in NumPy 161

  Single dimensional array 162

  Multidimensional array 162

  Single dimensional array 162

  Multidimensional array 163

Working with Pandas 165

 Handling datasets and DataFrames through Pandas 165

Working with Matplotlib... 168

 Line plot by Matplotlib... 168

  Basic plot 168

 Line plot with x and y values 169

  Customizing line style and marker 170

  Bar plot... 172

  Histogram plot 174

  Scatter plot 175

Working with ggplot... 176

Conclusion... 178

9. Mini Applications in Bioinformatics 179

Introduction... 179

Structure... 179

Objectives 180

Project 1: Concatenation of DNA sequences 180

    Project 2: Calculating AT content in the sequence 181
    Project 3: Searching for restriction sites/ enzymes in DNA sequences 182
    Project 4: Reading a Swiss-Prot file 183
    Project 5: Reading Swiss-Prot record from ExPASy server 185
    Project 6: Parsing Swiss-Prot keywords list 187
    Project 7: Prosite records parsing 188
    Project 8: Using ExPASy for parsing enzyme records 190
    Project 9: Reading PDB files 191
    Project 10: Reading GenBank file 193
    Project 11: Sequence alignment 193
        Pairwise sequence alignment *195*
            ClustalW *198*
            Basic Local Alignment Search Tool *199*
    Project 12: Retrieving sequence digested by restricted enzymes 202
    Conclusion 204

10. Mini Projects on Bioinformatics 205
    Introduction 205
    Structure 205
    Objectives 206
    Mini project 1: Phylogenetics 206
        Project code - Phylogenetics *208*
        Detailed description of the project *210*
    Mini poject 2: Cluster analysis 213
        Project code: Cluster analysis *214*
        Detailed description of the project *216*
    Mini project 3: Drug discovery 218
        Project code: Drug discovery *220*
        Detailed description of the project *223*
    Conclusion 229

Index **231-237**

Chapter 1
Introduction to Bioinformatics and its Applications

Introduction

The exponential growth in the volume of data is a result of technological advancements and the ability of computer systems to handle large amounts of information. This has led to the development of bioinformatics, which involves using computer processes to acquire, analyze, and interpret biological data related to macromolecules. The integration of computer science and biology has become essential because the structure and behavior of organisms are largely governed by their genetic information. Genes can be seen as virtual repositories of data, containing instructions for the development and functioning of an organism. By analyzing and understanding these genetic instructions, scientists can gain insights into various biological processes.

Structure

The chapter covers the following topics:

- Applications of bioinformatics
- Bioinformatics and its data structures
- Bioinformatics and its databases
- Tools and techniques of bioinformatics

Objectives

It is true that the field of bioinformatics has experienced significant growth and challenges due to the rapid emergence of natural realities and the increasing amount of data being generated. Bioinformatics is an interdisciplinary field that combines biology, computer science, mathematics, and statistics to analyze and interpret biological data, particularly large and complex datasets generated by modern high-throughput technologies. The primary objective of bioinformatics is to extract meaningful information, knowledge, and insights from biological data to advance our understanding of living organisms and improve various aspects of life sciences and medicine. The objective of bioinformatics is to bridge the gap between biology and computational science, enabling researchers to extract valuable insights from biological data that contribute to advancements in various fields, from fundamental biological research to clinical applications and beyond. The objective of the chapter is to introduce the readers to the role of bioinformatics in current scenarios. The chapter will also provide a glimpse of various applications of bioinformatics.

Applications of bioinformatics

Bioinformatics is an interdisciplinary field that combines biology, computer science, and mathematics to analyze and interpret biological data, particularly large datasets generated by high-throughput technologies. The primary goal of bioinformatics is to extract valuable biological insights and knowledge from these data. The following are the applications of bioinformatics:

- **Genome sequencing annotation**: Bioinformatics is instrumental in analyzing and annotating genomes, including identifying genes, regulatory elements, and non-coding regions. It has been pivotal in sequencing various organisms, from bacteria to humans. Genome sequencing and annotation are crucial steps in understanding the genetic information encoded within an organism's DNA. These processes provide valuable insights into an organism's genetic makeup, gene functions, and potential implications for various fields, including medicine, genetics, evolutionary biology, and biotechnology.

- **Comparative genomics**: By comparing the genomes of different species, researchers can gain insights into evolutionary relationships, identify conserved genes, and study genetic variations that underlie species-specific traits. Comparative genomics is a field of biological research that focuses on comparing the genomes of different organisms to understand their evolutionary relationships, identify shared and unique genetic features, and gain insights into the functions and adaptations of genes. This approach allows scientists to study the genetic diversity and evolutionary history of species, providing valuable information about how genes and genomes have evolved over time.

- **Functional genomics**: Bioinformatics tools help elucidate the functions of genes and their products, such as proteins and RNAs, by predicting their roles in cellular processes and pathways. Functional genomics is a branch of genomics that focuses on understanding the functions of genes and non-coding sequences in an organism's genome. It involves studying how genes are regulated, how their products (proteins or RNA molecules) function, and how they contribute to various biological processes. Functional genomics combines experimental techniques, computational analysis, and bioinformatics to decipher the roles and interactions of genes within the context of an entire genome.

- **Proteomics**: Proteomics involves the large-scale study of proteins, and bioinformatics aids in protein identification, structure prediction, and functional analysis. It's critical for drug discovery and understanding disease mechanisms. Proteomics is the branch of molecular biology and biochemistry that focuses on the comprehensive study of proteins, including their structures, functions, interactions, and expression patterns within a biological system. It plays a crucial role in understanding the complex molecular processes that occur within cells, tissues, and organisms.

- **Structural biology**: Structural biology is a branch of molecular biology that focuses on the study of the three-dimensional structures of biological molecules, including proteins, nucleic acids (DNA and RNA), and complexes of macromolecules. Understanding the spatial arrangement of these molecules is crucial for gaining insights into their functions, interactions, and roles in various biological processes. Bioinformatics is used to predict protein structures and study the interactions between proteins and other molecules, such as ligands and drugs. This is valuable in drug design and understanding protein function.

- **Phylogenetics**: Bioinformatics helps in constructing phylogenetic trees to understand the evolutionary relationships between species, populations, and genes. It is essential in fields like evolutionary biology and epidemiology. Phylogenetics is a field of biology that focuses on the study of evolutionary relationships among organisms. It seeks to understand the evolutionary history and ancestry of species by analyzing and comparing their genetic, morphological, and molecular characteristics.

- **Functional annotation of sequences**: Identifying the functions of DNA and protein sequences, such as coding regions, binding sites, and motifs, is crucial for understanding gene regulation and protein function. It is a critical step in genomics and bioinformatics that involves identifying and characterizing the biological functions and features of genes, proteins, or other biological elements within a DNA, RNA, or protein sequence. It helps researchers understand the roles of these sequences in various cellular processes and biological functions.

- **Metagenomics**: This field studies the genetic material recovered directly from environmental samples. Bioinformatics tools are used to analyze metagenomic data, revealing the diversity and functional potential of microbial communities. Metagenomics involves the study of genetic material recovered directly from environmental samples, such as soil, water, air, and various biological habitats, including the human body's microbiome. Unlike traditional genomics, which focuses on the genomes of individual organisms, metagenomics explores the collective genetic material of entire microbial communities, present in each sample.

- **Disease genomics**: Researchers use bioinformatics to identify genetic factors associated with various diseases, from common disorders like diabetes to rare genetic diseases. also known as **medical genomics** or **genomic medicine**, is a branch of genomics that focuses on the study of the genetic basis of diseases. It involves the application of genomic and genetic techniques to understand the genetic factors underlying various diseases, including both common and rare disorders. This information can be used for diagnosis and treatment development.

- **Drug discovery**: Computational methods in bioinformatics are vital in virtual screening, molecular docking, and structure-based drug design, accelerating the discovery of new drugs and predicting their interactions with target proteins. Drug discovery is the complex and highly interdisciplinary process of identifying and developing new medications or therapies to treat diseases and improve human health. It involves a series of stages, from initial target identification to clinical trials and regulatory approval.

- **Vaccine development**: Bioinformatics aids in identifying potential vaccine targets by analyzing pathogen genomes and predicting antigenic epitopes, facilitating the development of vaccines against infectious diseases. Vaccine development is a complex and highly regulated process that involves the creation and testing of vaccines to prevent or mitigate infectious diseases. Vaccines are one of the most effective tools in public health for preventing the spread of contagious diseases and protecting individuals and populations.

- **Environmental genomics**: Bioinformatics helps in studying the genetic diversity of organisms in various ecosystems, contributing to our understanding of biodiversity and ecological processes. It is also known as **ecogenomics** or **environmental metagenomics**, is a scientific field that applies genomics and high-throughput sequencing technologies to study the genetic composition and functional potential of entire microbial communities in various environmental samples. This field enables researchers to explore the diversity, interactions, and functions of microorganisms in natural environments and their roles in ecosystem processes.

Bioinformatics and its data structures

Bioinformatics, a multidisciplinary field relies on various data structures to store, organize, and analyze biological data efficiently. Here are some of the common data structures used in bioinformatics:

- **Sequences:**
    - **Strings**: Sequences of DNA, RNA, or protein are often represented as strings of characters (for example, ACGT for DNA and AUGCU for RNA).
    - **Arrays**: They can be used to store sequences where each element corresponds to a nucleotide or amino acid position.
- **Sequence databases:**
    - **Databases**: Data structures like relational databases (for example, SQL databases) are used to store and manage large collections of biological sequences, annotations, and metadata.
    - **Index structures**: Indexing techniques like *B-trees* and *hash tables* can be used for efficient retrieval of sequences from databases.
- **Graphs:** Graph data structures are used to represent biological networks, such as protein-protein interaction networks, metabolic pathways, and phylogenetic trees.
    - **Directed acyclic graphs (DAGs)**: DAGs are used to represent hierarchical relationships in ontology databases like the **Gene Ontology** (**GO**).
- **Alignment matrices:**
    - **Matrices**: Dynamic programming algorithms for sequence alignment (for example, *Smith-Waterman* and *Needleman-Wunsch*) often use matrices to score and store alignment results.
- **Trees:**
    - **Phylogenetic trees**: Phylogenetic trees are used to represent the evolutionary relationships among species or genes. Common tree data structures include *Newick* and *Nexus* formats.
    - **Suffix trees**: Suffix trees are used for efficient substring searching and pattern matching in DNA or protein sequences.
- **Lists and arrays:**
    - **Lists**: Linked lists and arrays are used to store and manipulate collections of biological data, such as lists of gene names, proteins, or sequence motifs.
    - **Dynamic arrays**: Dynamic arrays, like *Python lists* or *Java ArrayLists*, are used for flexible storage and manipulation of data.
- **Hash tables:** They are used for fast data retrieval based on keys. They are used in bioinformatics for tasks like storing and querying sequence databases or gene annotation data.
- **Stacks and queues:**
    - **Stacks**: Stacks can be used in algorithms for tasks like parsing biological data formats (for example, parentheses matching in secondary structure prediction).

- - **Queues**: Queues are used in various bioinformatics applications, such as sequence alignment algorithms.
- **Graph algorithms:** Various graph algorithms, including **Breadth-First Search (BFS)**, **Depth-First Search (DFS)**, and shortest path algorithms, are applied to analyze biological networks and pathways.
- **Spatial data structures:** Quad trees and k-d trees are used in the analysis of spatial data in structural biology, such as protein structures and genomic data.
- **Priority queues:** They are used in tasks like clustering and sorting based on sequence similarity or other criteria.
- **Dynamic data structures:** Dynamic programming tables are used in algorithms for tasks like multiple sequence alignment and RNA secondary structure prediction.
- **Sparse data structures:** Sparse matrices are used to efficiently store and manipulate large datasets with numerous zero or missing values.

Bioinformatics data structures vary in complexity and are selected based on the specific requirements of the analysis or application. The choice of data structure often influences the efficiency and performance of bioinformatics algorithms and tools.

Bioinformatics and its structural databases

Structural databases in bioinformatics are repositories of **three-dimensional** (**3D**) structural information about biological macromolecules, such as proteins, nucleic acids, and complex molecular assemblies. These databases provide a wealth of information for structural biology research, drug discovery, and understanding the function and interactions of biomolecules. Here are some of the most prominent structural databases in bioinformatics:

- **Protein Data Bank (PDB)**: The PDB is the widely used and comprehensive database of 3D protein structures. It contains experimentally determined structures of proteins, nucleic acids, and other biomolecules. PDB structures are often obtained through X-ray crystallography, NMR spectroscopy, or **cryo-electron microscopy** (**cryo-EM**). PDB also provides tools and resources for structural analysis and visualization. It plays a crucial role in bioinformatics and structural biology by serving as the primary repository for 3D structural information of biological macromolecules, such as proteins, nucleic acids, and complex molecular assemblies. Its significance lies in providing a wealth of structural data that enables researchers to gain insights into biomolecular structure, function, and interactions.
- **Nucleic Acid Database (NDB)**: It is a specialized database dedicated to the storage and retrieval of 3D structures of nucleic acids, including DNA, RNA, and their complexes. It contains structural data obtained through X-ray crystallography, NMR spectroscopy, and other techniques. It is a specialized database that serves

as a repository for 3D structural information about nucleic acids, including DNA, RNA, and their complexes with other molecules, such as proteins and small ligands. It is a valuable resource for researchers in the fields of structural biology, molecular biology, bioinformatics, and computational biology.

- **Protein structure classification databases**: These databases classify protein structures into families or superfamilies based on structural similarities. Examples include class, architecture, topology, homologous superfamily (CATH-Classification of Protein Structure), **Structural Classification of Proteins** (**SCOP**), and superfamily. These databases are specialized repositories that categorize and classify protein structures based on their structural similarities and evolutionary relationships. These databases play a crucial role in structural biology and bioinformatics by providing a systematic framework for organizing and retrieving protein structures.

- **Molecular modeling database**: The databases similar to *SWISS-MODEL* and *ModBase* provide homology-based structural models of proteins when experimental structures are not available. They use comparative modeling techniques to predict protein structures based on known **homologous structures**. Modeling Database (MMDB) typically refers to a digital repository or database that stores information about the three-dimensional structures of molecules, such as proteins, nucleic acids (DNA and RNA), small organic molecules, and more. These databases are essential tools in molecular biology, bioinformatics, chemistry, and drug discovery. Researchers use MMDBs to access, analyze, and visualize structural data, aiding in the understanding of molecular interactions, functions, and properties.

- **Genomics database**: These databases contain structural information generated by structural genomics projects, which aim to determine the structures of a large number of proteins systematically. Examples include the **Structural Genomics Consortium** (**SGC**) and the **Joint Center for Structural Genomics** (**JCSG**). It is a digital repository or database that stores and manages genomic data, which includes information about the complete set of genes and genetic material within an organism, including DNA sequences, gene annotations, variations, gene expression profiles, and other relevant genetic information.

- **Drug-target interaction database**: Databases like *BindingDB* and *DrugBank* include structural information about drug targets (for example, proteins) and their interactions with small molecules or drugs. They help in drug discovery and understanding the mechanisms of drug action. It is a specialized type of bioinformatics database that contains information about the interactions between drugs (or small molecules) and their respective molecular targets. These databases are essential tools in drug discovery and development, as they provide valuable insights into how drugs interact with specific proteins, enzymes, receptors, or nucleic acids within the human body or other organisms.

- **Protein membrane database**: Membrane proteins play critical roles in biology and are often challenging to study. Databases like the **Membrane Protein Data Bank (MPDB)** focus on the structures of membrane proteins.

- **Virus structure database**: Databases such as the *VIPERdb* specialize in storing 3D structures of viruses, including capsids and other viral components.

These structural databases are critical in advancing structural biology, bioinformatics, and molecular biology research. Researchers and scientists can access and analyze the structural data to gain insights into biomolecular functions, drug discovery, and the mechanisms of various biological processes.

Tools and techniques of bioinformatics

Bioinformatics is a rapidly evolving field that relies heavily on various software tools and applications to analyze and interpret biological data. These tools cover a wide range of tasks, from sequence analysis to structural biology and beyond. The following are the tools that are used in bioinformatics:

- **Sequence analysis:** Sequence analysis is a fundamental and critical component of bioinformatics, involving the study of biological sequences, primarily DNA, RNA, and protein sequences. This analysis aims to extract meaningful information, patterns, and insights from these sequences. Various tools support the sequence analysis as follows:
    - Basic Local Alignment Search Tool (BLAST): It is used for sequence similarity searching to find homologous genes or proteins.
    - ClustalW or Clustal Omega: Tools for multiple sequence alignment to identify conserved regions and evolutionary relationships among sequences.

- **Genome assembly and annotation:** These are crucial steps in genomics, allowing researchers to decode the genetic information contained within the DNA of an organism. The following tools may be used for a similar purpose:
    - Genome assemblers: Tools like *SPAdes*, *Velvet*, and *SOAPdenovo* are used to assemble DNA sequences into complete genomes.
    - Gene prediction: Software such as *GeneMark*, *AUGUSTUS*, and *Glimmer* predicts genes and coding regions within genomes.

- **Structural bioinformatics:** It is a subfield of bioinformatics that focuses on the analysis, prediction, and modeling of the three-dimensional structures of biological macromolecules, primarily proteins, nucleic acids (DNA and RNA), and their complexes. Following are the tools used for the analysis and prediction of proteins and nucleic acids.

- o Protein structure prediction: Tools like *Phyre2* and *SWISS-MODEL* predict protein structures based on amino acid sequences.
- o Molecular docking: Software like *AutoDock* and *Vina* are used to predict the binding of small molecules to protein targets.

- **Phylogenetics:** It is the scientific discipline that focuses on the study of evolutionary relationships among organisms. The following tools do support computational phylogenetics:
  - o Phylogenetic tree construction: Programs like *PhyML*, *RAxML*, and *MEGA* construct phylogenetic trees to study evolutionary relationships among species or genes.
  - o Sequence evolution models: Tools like phylogenetic analysis by maximum likelihood (PAML) estimate sequence evolution parameters.

- **Functional annotation:** It is crucial for making sense of genomic and proteomic data, as it transforms raw sequence information into biologically meaningful knowledge. The following tools may be helpful in functional annotations:
  - o Gene Ontology (GO) enrichment analysis: Tools like *DAVID* and *Panther* analyze gene lists to identify enriched biological functions.
  - o Pathway analysis: Software such as *KEGG* and *Reactome* map genes to biological pathways.

- **Metagenomics:** It is a field of genomics that involves the study of genetic material (DNA and, to some extent, RNA) recovered directly from environmental samples containing a mixture of microorganisms. Rather than studying individual organisms in isolation, metagenomics focuses on the collective genetic material of entire microbial communities, including bacteria, archaea, viruses, and other microorganisms.
  - o Metagenome assembly: Tools like *MetaSPAdes* and *MEGAHIT* assemble metagenomic sequences to study microbial communities.
  - o Taxonomic classification: Software like *Kraken* and *MetaPhlAn* classify microbial taxa in metagenomic data.

- **Machine learning and data mining:**
  - o Classification: Algorithms like *Random Forest*, *SVM*, and *neural networks* are applied to biological data for tasks such as disease prediction and protein function prediction.
  - o Clustering: Methods like *k-means* and *hierarchical clustering group* similar data points for various applications, including gene expression analysis.

- **Data visualization:**
  - Heatmaps: Tools like *Heatmapper* and *ComplexHeatmap* visualize gene expression or other biological data.
  - Network analysis: *Cytoscape* and *Gephi* are used to visualize and analyze biological networks.
- **Web resources:** Various online databases and resources like *NCBI*, *Ensembl*, and *UniProt* provide access to biological data and tools for analysis.

The above-mentioned tools and software are available to researchers. The choice of tools depends on the specific research goals and the type of data being analyzed, and the field continues to evolve with the development of new tools and methods. Researchers often use a combination of these tools to perform comprehensive analyses in various areas of biology and bioinformatics.

Conclusion

Computational systems have become major in natural examinations. Initially progressed for the investigation of natural groupings, bioinformatics now incorporates an immense scope of trouble regions comprehensive of primary science, genomics, and quality expression research.

In conclusion, bioinformatics stands at the forefront of scientific advancement, serving as a pivotal bridge between biology and data science. As we have explored in this introduction, it is a multidisciplinary field that harnesses the power of computational tools, algorithms, and data analysis techniques to unlock the mysteries of life at the molecular level. Its applications are far-reaching, touching every facet of biological research, from genomics and proteomics to structural biology, metagenomics, and beyond.

The implications of bioinformatics in our world today are profound. It has revolutionized our understanding of the genetic code, enabling the sequencing of entire genomes, the identification of disease-causing mutations, and exploring complex biological systems. Through sequence analysis, structural bioinformatics, and functional annotation, we have gained insights into the intricate mechanisms governing life, evolution, and health. In the next chapter, we will learn about use cases of bioinformatics.

CHAPTER 2
Bioinformatics and its Use Cases

Introduction

Bioinformatics is one of the streams of computer science where biological information is processed computationally, and various inferences are drawn from it. Bioinformatics is a culmination of two branches: Biology and information technology. The huge volume of biological data is used for research purposes, which is visualized and analyzed with respect to various applications to perform predictions, modeling of chemical reactions, analysis of genes, and study of proteins, to name a few. One can say that Bioinformatics is a collection of multiple streams like biology, information technology, computer science, and chemistry.

The scope of bioinformatics is wide. It is not only restricted to the analysis of huge volumes of biological data; besides that, it is also being used for understanding genome sequencing, analysis of genetic diseases, discovery of drugs, proposing personalized drugs after assessing the medical history of the patient, *gene therapy*, where damaged genes are replaced by new ones. Following are the use cases of bioinformatics: Genomics, transcriptomics, proteomics, metagenomics, systems biology, drug discovery, clinical genomics, structural biology, evolutionary biology, and agricultural genomics. These are just a few examples of the wide-ranging applications of bioinformatics. As biological data continues to grow in scale and complexity, bioinformatics plays a vital role in extracting knowledge and insights from the vast amounts of biological information.

Structure

The chapter covers the following topics:

- Gene therapy
- Stem cell therapy
- Drug discovery
- Genomic data analysis
- Transcriptomics
- Proteomics
- Metagenomics
- Clinical genomics
- Agricultural genomics
- Systems biology

Objectives

The objective of the chapter is to introduce readers to the various use cases or applications of Bioinformatics in diversified areas. The readers will get an insight into the use cases and where they are applicable. Being an interdisciplinary field, bioinformatics has a lot of scope for research and new findings. The chapter will also introduce readers to various research avenues in bioinformatics.

Gene therapy

It is one of the popular biological processes that helps mankind in preventing diseases by making corrections in the genetic structure of the patient. Doctors study the genetic structure of the patients and treat the ailment by alterations in their gene structures instead of using medicines or some surgical solutions. The initial techniques of *gene therapy* were quite different from the current ones, where new genes are added to the patient cells that help them fight disease. In some cases, new genes are copied to the faulty genes to help in patient recovery. Gene therapy is being used by many doctors to treat numerous diseases. Diseases like eye and muscle disorders can be treated well with gene therapy.

Before understanding how gene therapy works, one should understand the role of genes. Genes are a unit inherited from parents to children. They are made up of DNA sequences arranged in a sequence, one after the other, at a specific position in the chromosomes of cells. Genes play an important role in human health. One having defective gene/genes can affect its health. Researchers have been working for a long time to identify ways to modify genes or replace faulty genes with healthy ones to solve the illness in many cases.

Genes are closely related to cells; thousands of genes collectively work as a part of cells. Genes differentiate the working of cells. Cells collectively form various organs, muscles, bones, and tissues, which support different body activities.

The role of gene therapy is to alter the genetic code. Proteins are the power station of cells and also the basic structural component of cells as well. The genetic code guards or instructs protein development for the cells; any violation may affect the production or function of proteins, which in turn may affect how our body works.

The defective gene may lead to many problems for human health. Sometimes, part of a gene is defective, or maybe the whole gene. Even healthy genes do mutate in our lives due to various factors. However, most of these mutations do not cause diseases. In some cases, mutation and intergenomic disorders may lead to fatal diseases. The researchers study the cause behind such diseases and try to find some line of treatment using gene therapy in different ways.

The treatment can be performed by adding, replacing, or maybe removing the defective gene in order to provide treatment for such diseases. To introduce/replace the new gene in a body of humans, researchers use *vectors* as a vehicle to commute. It is a genetically engineered component used to deliver necessary genes for treating diseases.

Vectors are used to deliver genetic material into the cell nucleus. Vectors are of different types. One of them is a virus. Vectors are classified as viral and non-viral. Both of them work differently for the delivery of genetic material into cells. Non-viral vectors adopt physical/chemical methods of gene transmission to a cell. The usage of non-viral vectors is quite effective and safe as well. Popularly used non-viral vectors are: chemical disruption, polymer-based vectors, electroporation, etc.

Viral vectors

Viral vectors are created from the blueprint rather than the actual virus. Nowadays, viral vectors are popularly used by medical researchers in gene therapy. The popular viral vectors used these days in gene therapy are as follows:

- **Adenoviral vectors (ADV)**: This is the first virus used for the purpose of gene therapy. It is the most common virus that causes the common cold. ADVs are considered the prominent virus for the treatment of cancer. Its basic role is to trigger immunity in patients.

- **Lentiviral vectors**: Three special kinds of viruses do fall in the category of retrovirus. Retrovirus uses RNA as its genetic material; when a retrovirus infects a host cell, the RNA is converted into DNA, which is incorporated into the genome of the host cell. The most explored virus is *HIV lentivirus,* which is used to design lentiviral vectors. These are further utilized in gene therapy. Lentivirus does enter the cell and classifies it into stem cells and cardiac cells. It integrates genetic material into the genome which leads to increased durability for the gene expression.

- **Adeno-associated viral vectors (AAVs)**: The category of virus discovered during the research of adenovirus and is considered the standard virus. These categories of viruses are most popularly used in gene therapy. AAVs are further classified based on their usage in different cells, from kidney cells to brain cells.

Non-viral vectors

This virus does not use any blueprint or plan for gene therapy. Non-viral vectors use two basic techniques to deliver genetic material to the cells: Chemical and physical. The chemical method uses natural/synthetic materials compatible with the human body, like lipids, polymers, nanoparticles, etc. For example, **Lipid Nanoparticles** (**LNPs**). It provides one of the methods to deliver genetic material for gene therapy in a protected way. LNPs portray various benefits to researchers in the process of gene therapy, being efficient and scalable in size to be delivered.

Physical methods, on the other hand, directly deliver genetic material to target cells. For example, electroporation is one of the non-viral physical methods. This method uses a pulse of electricity to form temporary pores on a cell membrane. The pores enable the transfer of genes to the cells that can be affected. Gene therapy with a viral vector has set the benchmark and is also successful. It does carry some risk. Sometimes, the virus induces the immune system of the patient. Besides that, the integration of a virus into a chromosome may lead to various health risks as well.

Gene therapy is a therapeutic approach that involves the introduction, modification, or replacement of genes in a patient's cells to treat or prevent diseases. Bioinformatics plays a significant role in gene therapy, from target identification and gene delivery to data analysis in personalized medicine. Overall, bioinformatics plays a vital role in gene therapy by providing computational tools, databases, and analytical methods to support various stages of the gene therapy process.

Gene therapy has made significant strides in recent years, driven by advancements in molecular biology, genomics, and biotechnology. These developments have opened up new possibilities for treating a wide range of genetic disorders, cancers, and other diseases. Following are the recent advancements in gene therapy:

- CRISPR-Cas9 and many other gene editing tools brought a revolution in gene editing. The recent advancements have improved the accuracy, efficiency, and delivery methods, reduced off-target effects, and enabled more complex genetic modifications.

- In vivo gene therapy has made it possible to deliver gene therapies in vivo, directly to the patients, rather than modifying cells outside the body and then reintroducing them.

- **Chimeric antigen receptor** (**CAR**) T-cell therapy, a form of gene therapy, has shown remarkable success in treating certain types of leukemia and lymphoma. Recent advancements have improved the specificity and durability of CAR-T cells, and efforts are underway to expand this approach to solid tumors and other cancers.

Stem cell therapy

This is one of the popular therapies used for the treatment of various diseases in a human being. Before understanding this concept of stem cell therapy, let us understand the concept of stem cells. The stem cells are the raw material from which specialized cells can be generated with specific features. They are used to generate daughter cells in the lab (maintaining the right conditions) or maybe in the body itself. The daughter cells generated either become a stem cell or some other specialized cell that may be a part of blood cells, brain cells, heart muscle, or bone cells. Stem cells of the body only have the capacity to generate new cells naturally.

Stem cells are the interest of researchers for a long time. Researchers evaluated the working of stem cells in order to identify their role and work. Stem cells can be converted into a particular type of cell and are being used for the regeneration and repair of tissues damaged by certain diseases. Stem cell therapy is known to be a beneficial therapy for people with diseases like *Parkinson's*, *Alzheimer's*, and *Spinal cord injury*, to name a few. Stem cells are used in regenerative medicine and also in transplants. Stem cells can also be used to test the effectiveness of any new drug.

Stem cell therapy is a medical treatment that utilizes stem cells to promote tissue repair, regeneration, or replacement in various diseases and conditions. Stem cells are undifferentiated cells that have the potential to develop into different cell types in the body. This is how it works.

Stem cells used in therapy can be derived from different sources. The two primary sources are **embryonic stem cells** (**ESCs**), which are obtained from early-stage embryos, and adult stem cells, which are found in various tissues of the body, such as bone marrow, adipose tissue, or umbilical cord blood. Stem cells are obtained from the selected source. For adult stem cells, they can be harvested through procedures like bone marrow aspiration or adipose tissue extraction. Alternatively, stem cells can be obtained from a donor or a stem cell bank. In the case of ESCs, they are derived from donated embryos with informed consent.

The harvested stem cells may require processing and expansion in the labs to increase their numbers. The purpose of increasing the number is to have a sufficient quantity of cells required for the therapy.

Once the stem cells are prepared, they are introduced into the patient's body through various administration routes depending on the condition being treated. Common methods include intravenous infusion, direct injection into specific tissues or organs, or localized application to the affected area.

After administration, stem cells have the ability to migrate and home to the damaged or diseased tissues. They respond to signals from the surrounding environment and undergo differentiation, transforming into specialized cell types that are needed for tissue repair. For example, in the case of damaged heart tissue, stem cells may differentiate into cardiomyocytes (heart muscle cells) to promote regeneration. Stem cells also exert therapeutic effects through paracrine signaling. They release various bioactive molecules, such as growth factors, cytokines, and chemokines, which promote tissue healing, reduce inflammation, and modulate the immune response. These paracrine effects can stimulate the regeneration of damaged cells, support the growth of blood vessels, and regulate the local microenvironment.

Stem cells may integrate into the existing tissue structure, replacing damaged or dysfunctional cells. They can also promote tissue repair by stimulating endogenous repair mechanisms, enhancing angiogenesis (formation of new blood vessels), and supporting the survival and function of surrounding cells.

Patients undergoing stem cell therapy are closely monitored to assess the treatment's effectiveness, safety, and potential side effects. Follow-up examinations, imaging studies, and functional tests are performed to evaluate the outcomes of the therapy and make any necessary adjustments to the treatment plan.

Bioinformatics plays a significant role in stem cell therapy by contributing to the understanding, characterizing, and optimizing stem cells for therapeutic purposes. Bioinformatics tools are used to analyze large-scale data, such as genomics, transcriptomics, and proteomics, to understand the molecular characteristics of stem cells. These analyses help identify key genes, signaling pathways, and regulatory networks involved in stem cell biology. By comparing different types of stem cells and their differentiation states, bioinformatics aids in defining the unique properties of stem cells used in therapy. Bioinformatics methods are employed to identify biomarkers associated with stem cell properties, including pluripotency, differentiation potential, and cell quality. It plays a role in the development of personalized stem cell therapies. By integrating genomic and clinical data, bioinformatics enables the identification of patient-specific factors that influence the response to stem cell therapy.

Stem cell therapy has been applied in a variety of medical fields with varying degrees of success. Here are some notable case studies that highlight the potential of stem cell therapy:

- **Hematopoietic stem cell transplantation (HSCT) for leukemia:** HSCT has been one of the most successful applications of stem cell therapy, particularly for treating blood cancers such as leukemia, lymphoma, and multiple myeloma. The therapy involves the replacement of diseased or damaged bone marrow with healthy stem cells that can regenerate the entire blood and immune system.
    - **Patient example:** A 40-year-old patient diagnosed with **acute myeloid leukemia (AML)** underwent HSCT after chemotherapy failed to achieve

remission. The patient received stem cells from a matched unrelated donor. Following transplantation, the patient achieved complete remission and showed no signs of relapse after five years.

- o **Outcome**: This case demonstrates the potential of HSCT to cure certain types of blood cancers. However, it also underscores the importance of finding a suitable donor and the risks associated with **graft-versus-host disease (GVHD)**, which can occur when the donor's immune cells attack the recipient's tissues.

- **Spinal cord injury (SCI) treatment with mesenchymal stem cells (MSCs)** : Stem cell therapy for SCI aims to repair damaged neural tissue and restore motor and sensory functions. MSCs are commonly used due to their ability to differentiate into various cell types, including neurons, and their anti-inflammatory properties:

    - o **Patient example**: A 28-year-old male who suffered a complete SCI at the T10 level, resulting in paralysis below the waist, underwent stem cell therapy. MSCs were harvested from the patient's bone marrow, expanded in the lab, and injected into the site of injury. Over the next several months, the patient experienced partial sensory and motor recovery, allowing him to regain some function and improve his quality of life.

    - o **Outcome**: This case illustrates the potential for stem cell therapy to promote functional recovery in SCI patients. However, the extent of recovery varies widely among patients, and more research is needed to optimize treatment protocols and improve outcomes.

- **Treating type 1 diabetes (T1D) with stem cell-derived beta cells:** T1D is an autoimmune disease characterized by the destruction of insulin-producing beta cells in the pancreas. Researchers have explored the use of stem cells to generate new beta cells for transplantation as a potential cure for T1D.

    - o **Patient example**: A clinical trial involved a 22-year-old woman with long-standing T1D who received a transplant of stem cell-derived beta cells encapsulated in a semi-permeable device to protect them from immune attack. The patient showed improved glycemic control and reduced insulin requirements over the course of a year.

    - o **Outcome**: While the patient did not achieve complete insulin independence, the results indicate that stem cell-derived beta cells can function in the human body and improve diabetes management. The challenge remains in achieving long-term survival and function of the transplanted cells, as well as protecting them from immune system rejection.

Drug discovery

It is also one of the applications of bioinformatics. Drug discovery is an extensive and complicated method. Drug discovery is the process of finding new medicines based on the target. Drug designing is highly dependent on the various approaches of bioinformatics in the era of big data. Drug development and discovery involve pre-clinical research as the first step of the whole process.

The requirement is to reduce the cost and time of the drug discovery process. Bioinformatics plays a crucial role in it. Translational drug discovery is highly supported by computational methods. Various Bioinformatics approaches are working nowadays to identify disease-specific drugs with different strategies.

Bioinformatics applications are considered one of the important aspects of translational drug discovery in the pharma industry. The huge volume of data generated by the different phases of drug discovery is a challenge for its processing and analysis. Bioinformatics tools and resources can be an important support system for discovering these drugs.

The usage of bioinformatic applications in drug discovery can be classified into disease-based approaches and drug-based approaches, as explained below:

- **Disease-based bioinformatics approaches:** These approaches are dependent on the type of disease, like cancer or any other disease based on infection. Bioinformatics approaches can be used to identify the crucial drivers of diseases, especially in individual patients. This helps in the development of personalized treatment techniques for individual patients.

- **Drug-based bioinformatics approaches:** These applications for drug discovery involve using computational tools and techniques to analyze biological and chemical data, identifying and developing new drugs more efficiently. It is the application of computational methods and data analysis techniques to the field of drug discovery. It leverages bioinformatics tools to process and interpret vast amounts of biological data to identify potential drug targets, optimize lead compounds, and support clinical trials.

- **Bioinformatics (BI):** It can be a popular mechanism for the discovery of drugs in various infectious diseases as well. The specific gene expression can be populated by the cells bearing any type of viral/bacterial infection. The profile comparison of this gene expression with other diseases and with genetic profiles of others do offer certain changes in the structure of existing drugs.

- **Translational bioinformatics (TBI):** It serves a crucial role in bridging the gap between clinical data and pharma research. TBI techniques are used to fetch feasible information from the huge volume of data for the health improvement of human beings.

The healthcare industry is the fastest-growing one. The advancement in drug discovery has revolutionized the industry. It has changed the way drugs are discovered and how diagnostics is being done for various new diseases. The advancement in the various tools for translational drug discovery and its involvement in every step of drug discovery has opened new avenues for the BI approaches in the drug discovery process. The BI has been actively involved in the various phases of drug discovery. Starting with preclinical research, then clinical trials, and post-launch of the drug as well.

The field of drug discovery is driven by the need to find effective treatments for various diseases and conditions. Traditionally, drug discovery has relied heavily on experimental methods, such as high-throughput screening of chemical compounds. However, with advancements in bioinformatics and computational biology, there is now an increased emphasis on using computational approaches to accelerate the drug discovery process. Bioinformatics plays a crucial role in several stages of the drug discovery pipeline, as explained below:

- **Target identification and validation**: Bioinformatics tools are used to analyze genomic, proteomic, and metabolic data to identify potential drug targets, such as proteins or genes that play a role in disease pathways. Computational methods help validate the relevance and ability to drug of these targets.

- **Virtual screening**: Bioinformatics techniques enable virtual screening of large compound libraries against target structures or models. Molecular docking, molecular dynamics simulations, and other computational methods are used to predict the binding affinity and interactions between potential drug candidates and target proteins.

- **Lead optimization**: Once potential drug candidates are identified, bioinformatics is used to analyze and optimize their chemical structures. This involves **Structure-Activity Relationship (SAR)** analysis, pharmacophore modeling, **Quantitative Structure-Activity Relationship (QSAR)** studies, and other computational techniques to enhance the drug's efficacy, selectivity, and safety profiles.

- **ADMET prediction**: Bioinformatics tools help assess the **absorption, distribution, metabolism, excretion, and toxicity (ADMET)** properties of drug candidates. Computational models are employed to predict the pharmacokinetic and toxicological properties of potential drugs, aiding in the selection of compounds with desirable ADMET profiles.

- **Data integration and analysis**: Bioinformatics facilitates the integration and analysis of diverse data sources, including genomic data, protein structures, chemical databases, and clinical data. By combining and mining these datasets, researchers can uncover insights and patterns to guide the drug discovery process.

By leveraging bioinformatics techniques, drug discovery can be made more efficient, cost-effective, and targeted. It enables researchers to explore a vast chemical space, prioritize promising candidates, and optimize lead compounds before proceeding to experimental validation. Ultimately, bioinformatics in drug discovery aims to accelerate the development of safe and effective therapeutics to address unmet medical needs.

Bioinformatics has played a pivotal role in drug discovery by enabling the analysis of vast amounts of biological data, leading to the identification of new drug targets, the design of new molecules, and the repurposing of existing drugs. Here are some specific examples of drugs discovered or developed with the help of bioinformatics:

- **Imatinib (Gleevec)**: It targets the BCR-ABL fusion protein, a product of the Philadelphia chromosome, which is a hallmark of CML. Bioinformatics tools were crucial in understanding the molecular structure of the BCR-ABL protein and identifying it as a target for inhibition. Structure-based drug design, guided by bioinformatics, enabled the development of Imatinib, which specifically binds to the ATP-binding site of the BCR-ABL kinase, effectively blocking its activity.

- **Dorzolamide (Trusopt)**: It is a carbonic anhydrase inhibitor used to reduce intraocular pressure in glaucoma patients and was developed using bioinformatics techniques. Computational methods were employed to model the enzyme carbonic anhydrase, leading to the design of dorzolamide, which selectively inhibits this enzyme in the eye, reducing fluid production and pressure.

- **Atazanavir (Reyataz)**: It is a protease inhibitor used in the treatment of HIV. Bioinformatics played a crucial role in identifying the structure of the HIV protease enzyme and in designing molecules that could specifically inhibit this enzyme. Structure-based drug design, supported by bioinformatics tools, led to the development of atazanavir, which binds to the active site of the HIV protease, preventing the maturation of the virus and its ability to infect new cells.

- **Aliskiren (Tekturna)**: It is a renin inhibitor used to treat high blood pressure. Bioinformatics and computational chemistry were instrumental in designing Aliskiren by modeling the structure of the renin enzyme and identifying its active site. Aliskiren was developed to specifically bind to this active site, inhibiting renin and thus lowering blood pressure by reducing the production of angiotensin II.

Genomic data analysis

It is the field where researchers try to identify the hidden information in the DNA sequences using various computational methods. The genome is a complete DNA sequence of any organism. The genomic sequence of any organism stores its hereditary information. The genome is like an information repository for building and maintaining an organism. The specific region of the genome contains some specific information about any organism. The deep analysis of the genome is helping in the interpretation of human health and diseases. The genomic data is voluminous in nature. Every cell of the human body consists of two copies of genome which actually reflects 6 billion DNA letters. The researchers are putting their best efforts into understanding the function of the genome and how it affects human health.

Genomic data analysis using bioinformatics is a crucial aspect of modern genetics and genomics research. It involves the application of computational methods, algorithms, and tools to extract meaningful information from large-scale genomic datasets. Following are the use cases for genomic data analysis, where bioinformatics plays an important role:

- **Sequence alignment**: Bioinformatics plays an important role in the alignment and assembling of raw DNA and RNA sequences. Sequence alignment tools, like *BLAST* and *Clustal*, help identify similarities and differences between the two sequences. The following activities are involved in genomic data analysis:

- **Genome annotation**: Bioinformatics tools and methods are used to annotate genomes by characterizing the basic functional elements of genes. The basic motive is to characterize regulatory regions, non-coding RNAs, and repetitive elements. Tools like *GeneMark* and *AUGUSTUS* facilitate gene prediction, functional annotation, and classification as well.

- **Variant calling**: Bioinformatics enables the detection and analysis of genetic variations, including **Single Nucleotide Polymorphisms (SNPs)**, insertions, deletions, and structural variants. Variant calling algorithms, such as *GATK*, *SAMtools* and *FreeBayes* are used to identify variants by comparing sequencing data to a reference genome.

- **Comparative genomics**: Bioinformatics facilitates comparative analysis of the genomes of different species to find out evolutionary relationships, conserved regions, and functional elements.

- **Epigenomics**: Bioinformatics plays a critical role in analyzing epigenetic modifications such as DNA methylation and histone modifications. Tools like *Bismark*, *MACS*, and *Chip-seq pipelines* enable the analysis of DNA methylation patterns.

- **Data integration and visualization**: Bioinformatics helps in integrating genomic data with other clinical data and public databases. Visualization tools, such as *Genome Browser*, *IGV*, and *Circos*, facilitate the visualization of genomic features, gene expression profiles, and variant landscapes.

Bioinformatics leverages data mining and ML techniques to extract patterns, classify samples, and make predictions from genomic datasets. Algorithms like random forests, support vector machines, and deep learning models are applied for tasks like genomic variant classification, cancer subtyping, and drug response prediction.

Genomic data analysis using bioinformatics is fundamental for understanding the structure, function, and regulation of genomes. It enables researchers to gain insights into genetic variations, gene expression patterns, regulatory networks, and disease mechanisms. By combining computational approaches with experimental validation, bioinformatics is pivotal in advancing genomic research and its applications in various fields, including medicine, agriculture, and evolutionary biology. Following are some example case studies that justify the role of Genomic Data Analysis:

- **Case example 1: BRCA1 and BRCA2 genes in breast cancer**
    - **Overview**: Genomic data analysis identified mutations in the **BRCA1 and BRCA2** genes as strong risk factors for breast and ovarian cancers. This discovery was made possible by analyzing genomic sequences of individuals with and without these cancers.
    - **Approach**: Researchers used **linkage analysis** and **whole-genome sequencing (WGS)** to identify regions of the genome associated with higher cancer risk. Further sequencing of these regions pinpointed mutations in BRCA1 and BRCA2.
    - **Impact**: This has led to the development of genetic tests that can identify individuals at high risk for these cancers, enabling preventive measures such as increased surveillance or prophylactic surgery.

- **Case example 2: The Cancer Genome Atlas (TCGA)**
    - **Overview**: The TCGA is a large-scale project that cataloged genetic mutations responsible for various cancers by sequencing the genomes of thousands of tumor samples.
    - **Approach**: TCGA employed **whole-exome sequencing (WES)**, **RNA sequencing (RNA-seq)**, and other genomic techniques to identify mutations, gene expression changes, and other genomic alterations in different cancer types.
    - **Impact**: The findings from TCGA have led to the identification of key driver mutations, such as those in the **TP53**, **KRAS**, and **PIK3CA** genes. This has enabled the development of targeted therapies and personalized treatment plans for cancer patients.

- **Case example 3: The Human Microbiome Project (HMP)**
    - **Overview**: The **Human Microbiome Project** aimed to characterize the microbial communities found in and on the human body and understand their role in health and disease.
    - **Approach**: The project utilized **metagenomic sequencing** to analyze the collective genomes of microbiota in different body sites. Bioinformatics tools were used to classify microbial species and assess their functional potential.
    - **Impact**: The HMP has revealed the complexity of the human microbiome and its association with various health conditions, such as inflammatory bowel disease, obesity, and even mental health disorders. This knowledge is paving the way for microbiome-based therapies.

Transcriptomics

Transcriptomics is a field of study within bioinformatics that focuses on analyzing and understanding the transcriptome of an organism. The transcriptome refers to the complete set of RNA transcripts, including **messenger RNA (mRNA)**, non-coding RNA, and other molecules, produced in a particular cell or tissue at a specific time. Transcriptomics aims to provide insights into gene expression patterns, alternative splicing events, and regulatory mechanisms that occur at the transcriptional level. Here is a general overview of how transcriptomics works:

The first step in transcriptomics is to collect the biological samples of interest, such as cells, tissues, or body fluids. The choice of sample depends on the research question and the biological system under investigation.

RNA molecules are extracted from the collected samples using various extraction methods. This step involves breaking open the cells or tissues and isolating the total RNA or specific RNA fractions, such as mRNA or ncRNA. High-quality RNA extraction is crucial to ensure reliable and accurate downstream analyses.

The extracted RNA is then processed for sequencing using a technique called RNA-Seq. RNA-Seq allows researchers to obtain the nucleotide sequence information of the RNA molecules in the sample. It provides a comprehensive and quantitative profile of the transcriptome, enabling the identification and quantification of individual RNA molecules.

Prior to sequencing, the RNA molecules are converted into **complementary DNA (cDNA)** through reverse transcription. The cDNA is then processed to create a sequencing library, which involves fragmenting the cDNA, adding adapters, and amplifying the fragments to generate sufficient material for sequencing.

The prepared library is subjected to high-throughput sequencing technologies, such as **next-generation sequencing (NGS)**. NGS platforms generate millions of short reads or longer reads depending on the technology used. These reads represent fragments of the RNA molecules and are used for subsequent analysis.

The sequencing data generated from RNA-Seq undergoes bioinformatic analysis to extract meaningful information. This analysis includes the following steps:

1. **Alignment or mapping**: The sequenced reads are aligned or mapped to a reference genome or transcriptome to determine their origin and location within the genome. This step helps identify the genes from which the RNA molecules originated.

2. **Quantification**: The aligned reads are then counted to quantify the expression levels of genes or transcripts. This step provides information about the abundance of different RNA molecules in the sample.

3. **Differential expression analysis**: Statistical methods are applied to compare gene expression levels between different conditions or samples. This analysis helps

identify genes that are differentially expressed, meaning they show significant changes in expression levels under different experimental conditions.

4. **Functional analysis**: The identified differentially expressed genes are further analyzed to gain insights into their biological functions, pathways, and regulatory networks. This step involves various computational approaches and tools, such as gene ontology analysis, pathway enrichment analysis, and network analysis.

The results of transcriptomic analysis are interpreted in the context of the research question and existing knowledge in the field. Visualization techniques, such as heatmaps, scatter plots, and pathway diagrams, are employed to aid in the interpretation and presentation of the findings.

Transcriptomics is crucial in understanding gene expression patterns, regulatory mechanisms, and cellular processes in various biological systems. It enables researchers to identify novel genes, discover alternative splicing events, characterize non-coding RNAs, and explore gene regulatory networks. Transcriptomic analysis provides valuable insights into normal biological processes, disease mechanisms, drug discovery, and personalized medicine.

Bioinformatics plays a crucial role in transcriptomics by developing computational methods, algorithms, and tools to analyze large-scale transcriptome data generated through techniques like RNA sequencing. Transcriptomics analysis in bioinformatics provides valuable insights into gene expression patterns, splicing events, and regulatory mechanisms underlying various biological processes, diseases, and developmental stages. It facilitates the identification of potential biomarkers, drug targets, and pathways for further development. Following are some case studies to understand the role of transcriptomics in the current scenario:

- **Case example 1: Breast cancer subtyping**
    - **Overview**: Transcriptomic analysis helps in classifying breast cancer into molecular subtypes, such as **luminal A**, **luminal B**, **HER2-enriched**, and **basal-like**. Each subtype has distinct gene expression profiles, which influence treatment strategies.
    - **Application**: By analyzing the RNA expression levels of key genes, oncologists can determine the most effective treatment plans for individual patients. For instance, tumors classified as **HER2-positive** may benefit from targeted therapies like *trastuzumab*.
    - **Impact**: This approach enables personalized medicine, where treatments are tailored based on the molecular characteristics of a patient's tumor, improving outcomes and reducing side effects.
- **Case example 2: Assessing drug-induced liver injury (DILI)**
    - Overview: Transcriptomics is used to assess the toxic effects of drugs on the liver by analyzing changes in gene expression profiles in liver cells after drug exposure.

- o Application: By examining the transcriptomic signatures of hepatocytes (liver cells), researchers can identify early markers of liver toxicity before clinical symptoms appear. This can be used to screen drug candidates and predict their safety profiles.
- o Impact: Transcriptomic data helps pharmaceutical companies make informed decisions about the safety and efficacy of drug candidates, potentially reducing the risk of adverse effects in clinical trials.

- **Case example 3: Improving drought resistance in crops**
  - o Overview: Transcriptomics is used to identify genes that are differentially expressed in plants under drought conditions, helping to understand the mechanisms of stress tolerance.
  - o Application: By analyzing the transcriptomes of plants exposed to drought, researchers can identify candidate genes that contribute to drought resistance. These genes can then be targeted in breeding programs or through genetic engineering to develop more resilient crop varieties.
  - o Impact: Transcriptomic data helps in developing crops that can withstand environmental stresses, thereby improving agricultural productivity and food security in the face of climate change.

- **Case example 4: Studying Alzheimer's disease**
  - o Overview: Transcriptomics is used to explore gene expression changes in the brains of individuals with Alzheimer's disease, aiming to uncover the molecular mechanisms underlying neurodegeneration.
  - o Application: By comparing the transcriptomes of healthy brains and those affected by Alzheimer's, researchers can identify dysregulated pathways and potential biomarkers for early diagnosis or therapeutic targets.
  - o Impact: This research contributes to a better understanding of Alzheimer's disease and can lead to the development of new diagnostic tools or treatments to slow or prevent the progression of the disease.

Proteomics

Proteomics is a branch of bioinformatics that focuses on the large-scale study of proteins, including their structure, function, and interactions within biological systems. It involves the identification, quantification, and characterization of proteins. It also involves analysis of protein interactions and post-translation modifications. The basic role of proteomics is to provide insights into the behavior of proteins in various biological processes, disease mechanisms, and drug discovery. Here are some key aspects of proteomics analysis:

- **Protein identification and characterization**: Bioinformatics methods are employed to match experimental mass spectrometry data to protein sequences or databases to identify and characterize proteins. Database search algorithms like Mascot, SEQUEST, or X!Tandem are used to compare experimental spectra with theoretical spectra generated from protein sequences, allowing the identification of proteins present in a sample.

- **Protein quantification**: Bioinformatics tools and statistical methods are used to quantify protein abundance levels in different samples or experimental conditions. Label-free quantification methods, such as spectral counting or intensity-based methods, help estimate protein abundance based on the number of identified peptides or their signal intensities.

- **Protein interaction analysis**: Bioinformatics approaches enable the analysis of protein-protein interactions to understand protein networks and functional modules within biological systems. Interaction prediction methods, such as yeast two-hybrid assays or co-immunoprecipitation coupled with mass spectrometry, generate large-scale protein interaction data that can be analyzed using network analysis algorithms to identify interacting partners and protein complexes.

- **Protein structure analysis**: Methods like homology modeling, protein threading, and structure prediction algorithms contribute to understanding protein folding, structure-function relationships, and the impact of mutations on protein structure and stability.

- **Post-translational modification (PTM) analysis**: Proteomics analysis focuses on the identification and characterization of PTMs, such as phosphorylation, acetylation, ubiquitination, and glycosylation. Bioinformatics tools help annotate PTM sites, predict PTM functions, and understand their roles in protein regulation and signaling pathways.

Proteomics analysis in bioinformatics provides valuable insights into protein structure, function, interactions, and post-translational modifications. It aids in understanding biological processes, disease mechanisms, and drug targets, thereby contributing to fields such as medicine, molecular biology, and drug discovery. Following are some case studies for a better understanding of proteomics:

- **Case example 1: Early detection of cancer**
    o Overview: Proteomics has been instrumental in identifying protein biomarkers that can be used for the early detection and diagnosis of various cancers, such as breast, prostate, and ovarian cancers.
    o Contribution: By analyzing the protein expression profiles of patients and healthy individuals, researchers have identified specific proteins that are differentially expressed in cancer. These proteins can serve as biomarkers, detectable in blood or tissue samples, for early cancer diagnosis.
    o Impact: Early detection through proteomic biomarkers increases the chances of successful treatment and survival, as interventions can be initiated before the disease progresses to advanced stages.

- **Case example 2: COVID-19 vaccine development**
    - Overview: Proteomics has played a crucial role in the rapid development of vaccines for infectious diseases, including the COVID-19 vaccines.
    - Contribution: Proteomic techniques were used to study the structure and function of the SARS-CoV-2 spike protein, which is essential for viral entry into human cells. This knowledge facilitated the design of vaccines that target the spike protein, eliciting an immune response that protects against the virus.
    - Impact: The success of mRNA vaccines, such as those developed by Pfizer-BioNTech and Moderna, is partly due to the detailed protein structure and function information provided by proteomics.

- **Case example 3: Kinase inhibitors for cancer**
    - Overview: Proteomics has accelerated drug discovery by identifying protein targets and understanding their roles in disease, particularly in cancer.
    - Contribution: The identification of kinases (proteins that add phosphate groups to other proteins) as key regulators of cell signaling pathways in cancer have led to the development of kinase inhibitors, such as **imatinib (Gleevec)** for chronic myeloid leukemia.
    - Impact: Proteomics-guided drug discovery has resulted in the development of targeted therapies that are more effective and have fewer side effects than traditional chemotherapies.

- **Case example 4: Cardiovascular diseases**
    - Overview: Proteomics has been applied to understand the molecular basis of chronic diseases, such as cardiovascular diseases, by identifying protein biomarkers and pathways involved in disease progression.
    - Contribution: In cardiovascular research, proteomics has identified proteins involved in inflammation, oxidative stress, and lipid metabolism that are linked to heart disease. These proteins can serve as biomarkers for early detection or targets for new therapies.
    - Impact: Proteomics-based insights into cardiovascular diseases have the potential to improve risk assessment, diagnosis, and the development of more effective treatments.

Metagenomics

Metagenomics is a field of study within bioinformatics that focuses on analyzing genetic material directly extracted from environmental samples, such as soil, water, or the human microbiome. It involves the sequencing, assembly, and analysis of the collective genomes of microbial communities present in these samples, without the need for isolating and culturing individual organisms. Metagenomics provides insights into the diversity, functional potential, and ecological roles of microorganisms in various ecosystems.

Bioinformatics plays a crucial role in metagenomics by developing computational methods, algorithms, and tools to analyze and interpret the vast amount of data generated from metagenomic sequencing. The steps involved in the process are as follows:

- **Taxonomic classification**: Metagenomic sequences are compared to reference databases, such as the NCBI's non-redundant database, or specialized databases like *SILVA* or *Greengenes*, to assign taxonomic identities to the microbial sequences. Bioinformatics tools, such as *Kraken*, *MetaPhlAn*, or *MEGAN*, use sequence similarity or marker genes to infer the taxonomic composition of the microbial community.

- **Functional annotation**: Metagenomic sequences are annotated to identify functional genes and pathways within the microbial community. Bioinformatics tools, such as *BLAST*, *HMMER*, or *DIAMOND*, compare metagenomic sequences to protein databases, such as *NCBI's RefSeq* or *UniProt*, to assign functional annotations and predict protein functions.

- **Gene prediction and annotation**: Bioinformatics methods enable the prediction and annotation of genes within metagenomic sequences. Gene prediction tools, such as *Prodigal* or *MetaGeneMark*, identify **open reading frames** (**ORFs**) representing potential protein-coding genes. These predicted genes can be functionally annotated using databases.

- **Metagenomic assembly**: Metagenomic sequences can be assembled into longer contiguous sequences (contigs) to reconstruct microbial genomes or gain insights into the genomic potential of the community. Assembly tools, such as *MEGAHIT*, *SPAdes*, or *MetaSPAdes*, are specifically designed for metagenomic data to handle complexity and diversity.

Metagenomic analysis in bioinformatics enables researchers to explore and understand the genetic diversity, functional potential, and ecological roles of microbial communities in various environments. It provides insights into microbial ecology, biogeochemical cycles, and interactions between microorganisms and their hosts. Metagenomics has applications in environmental science, agriculture, human health, and biotechnology, contributing to fields like microbial ecology, microbial biotechnology, and personalized medicine. Refer to the following case studies for a better understanding:

- **Case example 1: Antibiotic resistance in soil microbes**
    - Overview: Metagenomic studies have uncovered a vast reservoir of **antibiotic resistance genes** (**ARGs**) in soil and other environments, revealing the natural origins and spread of resistance.
    - Discovery: By analyzing soil samples from various environments, researchers discovered numerous ARGs that were previously unknown. These genes

can potentially transfer to pathogenic bacteria, posing a threat to human health.
- o Impact: This discovery has heightened awareness of the environmental factors contributing to antibiotic resistance and has informed strategies to monitor and control the spread of resistance in clinical and agricultural settings.

- **Case example 2: Gut microbiome and obesity**
  - o Overview: Metagenomic analysis of the human gut microbiome has uncovered its significant role in health and disease, including its influence on obesity, diabetes, and other metabolic disorders.
  - o Discovery: Studies have shown that individuals with obesity have distinct gut microbiomes compared to lean individuals, with specific microbial species associated with energy metabolism and fat storage.
  - o Impact: This discovery has led to the development of microbiome-targeted therapies and dietary interventions aimed at modulating the gut microbiome to prevent or treat obesity and related metabolic disorders.

- **Case example 3: Identifying novel viruses**
  - o Overview: Metagenomics has been used to identify emerging viral pathogens in both human and animal populations, aiding in early detection and response efforts.
  - o Discovery: For example, metagenomic sequencing of samples from bats and other wildlife has led to the identification of novel coronaviruses and other viruses with zoonotic potential (capable of crossing from animals to humans).
  - o Impact: Early detection of these pathogens through metagenomics has been critical in monitoring potential outbreaks and developing preventive measures, such as vaccines and antiviral therapies.

Clinical genomics

Clinical genomics is a field within bioinformatics that focuses on the application of genomic information in clinical practice, particularly in the diagnosis, treatment, and management of diseases. It involves the analysis, interpretation, and integration of genomic data with clinical and phenotypic information to provide personalized and precision healthcare solutions.

Bioinformatics plays a crucial role in clinical genomics by developing computational methods, algorithms, and tools to analyze and interpret genomic data generated through techniques like **next-generation sequencing** (**NGS**) or microarrays. Here are some key aspects of clinical genomics in bioinformatics:

- **Genomic data analysis**: Bioinformatics tools and pipelines are used to process and analyze genomic data, including raw sequence reads or microarray intensities. This involves steps such as read alignment, variant calling, annotation, and prioritization of genetic variants. Various algorithms and software tools, such as *BWA*, *GATK*, and *ANNOVAR*, are employed to handle large-scale genomic data and identify genetic variants.

- **Variant interpretation**: Bioinformatics resources and databases, such as *dbSNP*, *ClinVar*, or *OMIM*, provide information on genetic variants and their associations with diseases. These databases help in variant annotation, classification, and interpretation, enabling clinicians and geneticists to understand the clinical significance and potential impact of genetic variants on disease development, progression, and treatment response.

- **Genotype-phenotype correlation**: Clinical genomics aims to establish correlations between genetic variations and clinical phenotypes. Bioinformatics methods facilitate the integration and analysis of genomic data with clinical and phenotypic information from electronic health records, patient histories, and other relevant sources. This helps identify genotype-phenotype associations, uncover disease-causing mutations, and guide clinical decision-making.

- **Pharmacogenomics**: Bioinformatics analysis in clinical genomics plays a crucial role in pharmacogenomics, which focuses on how genetic variations influence an individual's response to medications. By integrating genomic data with knowledge about drug metabolism and pharmacology, bioinformatics tools and databases aid in identifying genetic variants that affect drug efficacy, toxicity, and dosage requirements. This information assists clinicians in prescribing personalized medications and optimizing treatment strategies based on a patient's genetic profile.

- **Clinical reporting**: Bioinformatics tools contribute to generating clinical reports based on genomic data analysis. These reports provide a summary of identified genetic variants, their clinical significance, and relevant therapeutic implications. They assist clinicians in interpreting genomic findings and making informed decisions regarding patient management, including disease diagnosis, treatment selection, and genetic counseling.

- **Data privacy and security**: Bioinformatics in clinical genomics addresses the challenges of data privacy and security. Robust computational methods, encryption techniques, and secure data storage are employed to ensure the confidentiality and protection of sensitive genomic and clinical information.

Clinical genomics in bioinformatics has transformative potential in healthcare. It enables the identification of disease-causing genetic variants, disease risk prediction, early diagnosis of genetic disorders, and personalized treatment approaches. By integrating genomic information into clinical practice, clinical genomics aims to improve patient outcomes, optimize therapeutic interventions, and advance precision medicine. Refer to the following case studies for a better understanding:

- **Case example 1: Targeted therapy in non-small cell lung cancer (NSCLC)**
    - Overview: Clinical genomics has enabled the identification of specific genetic mutations in tumors, leading to targeted therapies that are more effective and have fewer side effects.
    - Outcome: For example, patients with NSCLC who have mutations in the **EGFR** gene can be treated with EGFR inhibitors like *erlotinib* or *gefitinib*. These targeted therapies have shown better response rates and progression-free survival compared to traditional chemotherapy.
    - Impact: Patients receive treatments tailored to their tumor's genetic profile, improving treatment efficacy and reducing unnecessary exposure to toxic chemotherapy.
- **Case example 2: HIV treatment**
    - Overview: Genomic testing has been applied to tailor treatment regimens for infectious diseases, ensuring optimal efficacy and minimizing resistance.
    - Outcome: In HIV treatment, genomic testing for the virus's genetic variations, such as drug resistance mutations, helps in selecting the most effective **antiretroviral therapy** (**ART**) regimen for each patient.
    - Impact: Personalized ART based on genomic insights has led to better viral suppression, reduced transmission rates, and improved long-term health outcomes for people living with HIV.

Agricultural genomics

Agricultural genomics, also known as **agri-genomics**, is a field within bioinformatics that focuses on the application of genomic technologies and bioinformatics methods in agricultural research and crop improvement. It involves the analysis, interpretation, and utilization of genomic information to enhance crop productivity, disease resistance, nutritional quality, and overall agricultural sustainability.

Bioinformatics plays a vital role in agricultural genomics by developing computational tools, algorithms, and databases to analyze and interpret large-scale genomic data generated from crop plants and agricultural organisms. Here are some key aspects of agricultural genomics in bioinformatics:

- **Crop genomic data analysis**: Bioinformatics tools and pipelines are used to analyze crop genomic data, including genome sequencing, transcriptomics (RNA-seq), epigenomics, and metagenomics data. These tools facilitate tasks such as sequence alignment, variant calling, gene expression quantification, functional annotation, and comparative genomics analysis.

- **Crop genome assembly and annotation**: Bioinformatics methods are employed to assemble and annotate crop genomes, which involves reconstructing the complete DNA sequence of a crop species and identifying genes, regulatory elements, and other genomic features. Assembly algorithms, such as *SOAPdenovo*, *ABySS*, or *SPAdes*, are used to piece together short DNA fragments into longer contiguous sequences (contigs), while annotation tools, such as *AUGUSTUS* or *MAKER*, help identify genes and functional elements within the genome.

- **Genomic selection**: Bioinformatics approaches enable genomic selection in crop breeding, which involves predicting the performance and breeding value of crops based on their genomic profiles. Genomic prediction models are developed using machine learning algorithms and statistical methods to integrate genomic data with phenotypic and environmental data. These models help breeders select superior individuals for breeding programs, accelerating the development of improved crop varieties.

- **Functional genomics**: Bioinformatics analysis facilitates the study of gene functions and regulatory networks in crop plants. Tools and databases, such as **Gene ontology** (**GO**), KEGG pathways, or PlantTFDB, provide annotations and functional information about genes, proteins, and metabolic pathways. This information helps us understand the biological processes and mechanisms underlying agronomically important traits.

- **Crop disease resistance**: Bioinformatics contributes to the identification and characterization of genes involved in crop disease resistance. Comparative genomics, transcriptomics, and proteomics analysis aid in understanding plant-pathogen interactions and identifying genes associated with resistance. This information helps breeders develop disease-resistant crop varieties through genetic engineering or marker-assisted breeding.

- **Crop metabolomics**: Bioinformatics methods are used in crop metabolomics, which involves the study of the metabolic profiles and pathways in crops. Metabolomics data analysis tools, such as *MetaboAnalyst* or *XCMS*, enable the identification and quantification of metabolites and help elucidate the metabolic pathways underlying agronomically important traits, nutritional quality, and stress responses.

Agricultural genomics in bioinformatics has significant implications for crop improvement, sustainable agriculture, and food security. Integrating genomic information with phenotypic and environmental data enables the development of improved crop varieties with enhanced yield, quality, and resilience to biotic and abiotic stresses. Agricultural genomics contributes to advancing precision agriculture, optimizing resource utilization, and addressing global challenges in food production and sustainability.

Bioinformatics has significantly contributed to advancements in crop improvement by providing tools and techniques for analyzing genetic data, identifying desirable traits, and accelerating breeding processes. Refer to the following case studies for a better understanding:

- **Case example 1: Development of blast-resistant varieties**
    - Overview: Rice blast disease, caused by the fungus *Magnaporthe oryzae*, is a major threat to rice production.
    - Bioinformatics contribution: Bioinformatics tools were used to analyze the rice genome and identify genes associated with resistance to blast disease. Researchers identified and characterized key resistance genes such as *Pi54* and *Pi25*.
    - Outcome: Using this information, scientists developed blast-resistant rice varieties through **marker-assisted selection (MAS)**, enhancing yields and reducing crop losses.

- **Case example 2: Identification of drought-resistant genes**
    - Overview: Drought is a significant factor affecting wheat production worldwide.
    - Bioinformatics contribution: Researchers used **genome-wide association studies (GWAS)** and bioinformatics tools to identify genes associated with drought tolerance in wheat. Genes such as *TaDREB3* and *TaMYB* were found to play crucial roles in stress response.
    - Outcome: The identified genes were incorporated into breeding programs, leading to the development of drought-resistant wheat varieties that perform better under water-scarce conditions.

- **Case example 3: Development of salt-tolerant varieties**
    - Overview: Soil salinity limits tomato production in many regions.
    - Bioinformatics contribution: Researchers employed comparative genomics and bioinformatics analyses to identify salt-tolerance genes in tomatoes, such as *SlSOS1* and *SlNHX1*.
    - Outcome: The identified genes were used to breed tomato varieties with enhanced salt tolerance, allowing cultivation in saline-prone areas and improving overall yield.

Systems biology

Systems biology is an interdisciplinary field that combines biology, bioinformatics, computational modeling, and experimental techniques to study and understand biological systems as integrated and interconnected networks of molecules, cells, and organisms. It aims to unravel the complex interactions and dynamics of biological components to gain insights into the behavior and function of biological systems.

Systems biology is an interdisciplinary field that aims to understand biological systems as a whole by integrating experimental data, computational modeling, and theoretical analysis. It seeks to unravel the complex interactions and dynamics of biological components, such as genes, proteins, cells, and organisms, to gain insights into their functioning and behavior. Systems biology involves various activities, as mentioned below:

- **Data acquisition**: Systems biology relies on the collection of various types of data from biological systems. This can include experimental data from techniques like genomics, transcriptomics, proteomics, and metabolomics, as well as data from imaging, physiological measurements, and clinical studies. Data can also be obtained from public databases as well.

- **Data integration**: The acquired data is integrated to build comprehensive datasets that capture the different levels of biological information, such as genomic sequences, gene expression profiles, protein-protein interactions, and metabolic pathways. Integration involves standardization, normalization, and annotation of data to ensure compatibility.

- **Computational modeling**: They are developed to represent the biological system of interest. These models can range from simple mathematical equations to complex computational simulations. The models incorporate biological knowledge, experimental data, and mathematical algorithms to describe the interactions, dynamics, and behavior of the system.

- **Model simulation and analysis**: The developed models are simulated and analyzed using computational techniques. Simulations involve running the model under different conditions, perturbations, or parameter settings to understand how the system responds and behaves. Analysis methods, such as sensitivity analysis, parameter estimation, and statistical tests, are applied to validate the models and refine their predictions.

- **Predictions and hypothesis generation**: Based on simulations and analysis, systems biology generates predictions and hypotheses about the behavior and mechanisms of the biological system. These predictions can be used to guide further experiments, design targeted interventions, or make novel discoveries. Systems biology emphasizes iterative cycles of modeling, experimentation, and refinement to improve the understanding of the system continually.

- **Validation**: The predictions and hypotheses generated by systems biology are experimentally tested to validate their accuracy and relevance. Experiments can involve genetic manipulations, perturbations, knockdowns, or targeted interventions to validate the model predictions and provide additional insights into the system.

- **Refinement**: Systems biology is an iterative process that involves refining the models and hypotheses based on experimental validation and new data. The models are updated and expanded to incorporate new biological knowledge and improve their predictive power. This iterative refinement allows for an increasingly accurate representation of the biological system and enhances the understanding of its behavior and regulation.

Systems biology provides a holistic and quantitative approach to studying biological systems, allowing for a deeper understanding of their complexity, emergent properties, and dysregulation in diseases. It enables the discovery of novel biological principles, the identification of therapeutic targets, and the development of personalized medicine strategies. By integrating experimental data, computational modeling, and theoretical analysis, systems biology offers a powerful framework.

Conclusion

Bioinformatics is a rapidly growing field with a wide range of applications across the various areas of life sciences and healthcare. Bioinformatics is in the stage of advancements in diversified research areas. It will continue to be at the forefront of scientific discoveries in the coming years. Bioinformatics, offers vast potential for future advancements. These advancements are expected to transform various aspects of biological research, medicine, agriculture, and more.

Join our book's Discord space

Join the book's Discord Workspace for Latest updates, Offers, Tech happenings around the world, New Release and Sessions with the Authors:

https://discord.bpbonline.com

CHAPTER 3
Introduction to Python and Basic Programming

Introduction

Python is an advanced scripting language and is the most popular one used to develop versatile applications in different domains. It is one of the languages which is in high demand by people working in different domains. IT professionals are not the only ones who are using Python and reaping its benefits. Besides that, professionals working in the finance domain/ bioinformatics domain, or business analyst all are being benefitted from the advanced features of Python. The rich set of libraries and easy-to-use syntax are important factors that make Python popular among professionals.

Structure

The chapter covers the following topics:

- History and evolution of Python
- Features of Python
- How to download and install Python
- How Python works
- Language fundamentals
- Language constructs

Objectives

The objective of the chapter is to provide detailed knowledge about the basic concepts of Python programming language. The chapter will give detailed knowledge about the various aspects of programming like variables, data types, keywords, operators, decision-making constructs, and looping constructs with the help of example programs.

History and evolution of Python

Python is a general-purpose scripting language used to develop highly diversified applications. The language was developed by *Guido van Rossum* in the year 1991. He coined the term *Python* for the language as it is unique and motivated by the BBC comedy series *Monty Python's Flying Circus*.

It is an open-source programming language and since its inception, many versions have been introduced. The latest version of Python is 3.12. Being an open source, the users can contribute to the libraries of Python. The language can be used for the development of versatile applications, like Desktop applications, web applications, games, AI-based applications, and mobile apps to name a few.

The evolution of Python versions reflects the language's growth and adaptation to the needs of its users, incorporating new features, syntax changes, optimizations, and libraries. Here is a brief overview of Python's major versions and their key milestones:

- **Python 1.x series:**
    - **Python 1.0 (January 1994)**: The first official release, including the core data types (strings, lists, etc.), modules, exception handling, functions, and basic libraries.
    - **Python 1.5 (December 1997)**: Introduced significant standard libraries, such as the **re** module for regular expressions.
    - **Python 1.6 (September 2000)**: Last of the 1.x series; added new features like Unicode support and improvements to the standard library.
- **Python 2.x series:**
    - **Python 2.0 (October 2000)**: Introduced list comprehensions, garbage collection via reference counting, and the **zip** function. This version laid the groundwork for many modern Python features.
    - **Python 2.1 to 2.6 (2001–2008)**: Gradual introduction of new features like iterators, generators, yield keywords, set data type, the with statement for context managers, and support for the ternary conditional operator.
    - **Python 2.7 (July 2010)**: Considered the final release of the 2.x series, it backported several features from Python 3.x, such as the new syntax for

print functions, dictionary comprehensions, and better Unicode support. Python 2.7 was actively supported until January 1, 2020, marking the end of life for the 2.x branch.

- **Python 3.x series:**
    - **Python 3.0 (December 2008)**: A major overhaul, designed to rectify fundamental design flaws and make Python more consistent and easier to use. Introduced significant changes like the `print()` function (replacing the print statement), `str` type for Unicode, the removal of old-style classes, and better integer division handling (`//` for floor division).
    - **Python 3.1 to 3.4 (2009–2014)**: Incremental improvements, including the addition of ordered dictionaries, asyncio for asynchronous programming, and enhancements to the standard library.
    - **Python 3.5 (September 2015)**: Introduced async and await keywords for asynchronous programming, type hinting (PEP 484), and the matrix multiplication operator (`@`).
    - **Python 3.6 (December 2016)**: Added formatted string literals (f-strings), underscores in numeric literals for readability, dictionary key ordering as an implementation detail, and more.
    - **Python 3.7 (June 2018)**: Introduced data classes, postponed evaluation of type annotations, and further improvements to asyncio and the standard library.
    - **Python 3.8 (October 2019)**: Introduced the assignment expression (walrus operator: =), positional-only parameters, and performance optimizations.
    - **Python 3.9 (October 2020)**: Added support for new string methods, dictionary union operators (`|`), and type hinting generics.
    - **Python 3.10 (October 2021)**: Introduced structural pattern matching (match statement), parameter specification variables, and numerous standard library enhancements.
    - **Python 3.11 (October 2022)**: Focused on performance improvements, achieving up to a 10–60% speed boost, along with more precise error messages and refined exception handling.
    - **Python 3.12 (October 2023)**: Added new features like subinterpreters, Pythonic data classes, more flexible f-strings, and continuous optimizations for performance and code execution.

Python continues to evolve with a focus on improving performance, adding modern features, enhancing security, and expanding its applicability in areas like data science, machine learning, web development, and system scripting.

Features of Python

Python is the most popular language nowadays. The popularity of the language is not only because of its rich set of libraries but besides that, many other features of Python language do make it popular, some are mentioned below:

- **Simple and easy to understand:** The simple syntax of python programming language helps the naïve users to understand the logical aspect of programming rather than putting more effort into understanding the syntax of the language.

- **Open source:** It is an open-source language where the copyright holder grants the right to the end-user to use, study, distribute, and make changes to its source code. **Open-Source Software (OSS)** grows collaboratively.

- **High-level language:** Python is a high-level language hence the user need not bother about low-level details such as managing the memory used by our program.

- **Portable:** Due to its open-source nature Python can work on many platforms. All your Python programs will work on any of these platforms without requiring any changes at all. However, you must be careful enough to avoid any system-dependent features. Python can be used on *Linux, Windows, Macintosh, Solaris,* and the like.

- **Object oriented:** Python does support both procedural and object-oriented ways of programming as well. In procedure-oriented languages, the program is built around procedures or functions which are nothing but reusable pieces of program. However, in object-oriented programming systems, the whole development revolves around the classes and objects. Procedural programming is a top-down approach and object-oriented programming is the bottom-up approach of development.

- **Extensive libraries:** The Python standard library is huge indeed. It can help you to do various things involving regular expressions, document generation, unit testing, threading, databases, and GUI.

- **Dynamically typed:** It is a dynamically typed language where data type is decided at runtime. No data type declaration at the time of the variable declaration.

- **Extensible:** If the user needs a critical piece of code to run very fast, you can achieve this by writing that piece of code in C programming language, and then combining that with your Python program. This supports Python to extend its efficiency by adding code written in C language.

- **Embeddable:** You can embed Python script within your C/C++ programs to give scripting capabilities for your program's users.

How to download and install Python

One can download Python from **www.python.org** site. You may download the latest version of Python. Click on **Download Python 3.11.0 (www.python.org/downloads)**, as illustrated in *Figure 3.1*:

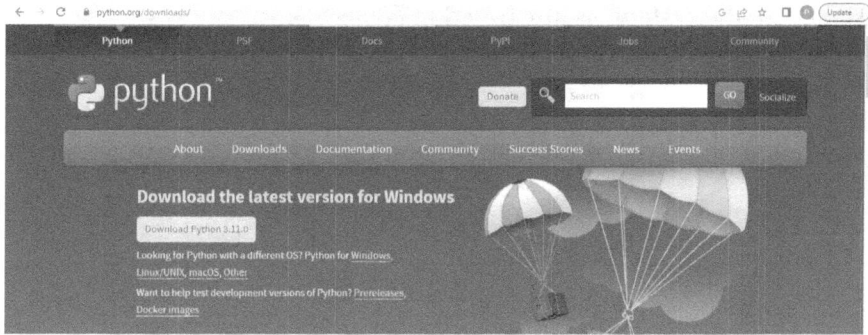

Figure 3.1: Downlaod Python latest version from the site python.org

After downloading you may get the `.exe` file in the `Downloads` folder. Execute the file, as illustrated in *Figure 3.2*:

Figure 3.2: Installation Window of Python

Now, click on the `Install Now` option, which will start the installation process. Follow the steps given below for installation. There are two checkboxes visible in *Figure 3.2*.

1. **Use admin privileges when installing py.exe:** The checkbox allows every user on the machine to access the py.exe launcher.

2. **Add python.exe to PATH:** The checkbox will allow you to add Python to the system's PATH which is an essential step when working with Python, as it allows you to run Python scripts and access Python packages from any directory in the command prompt or terminal.

3. Once Python is successfully installed on the system, it will appear in all programs installed on the system, as illustrated in *Figure 3.3*:

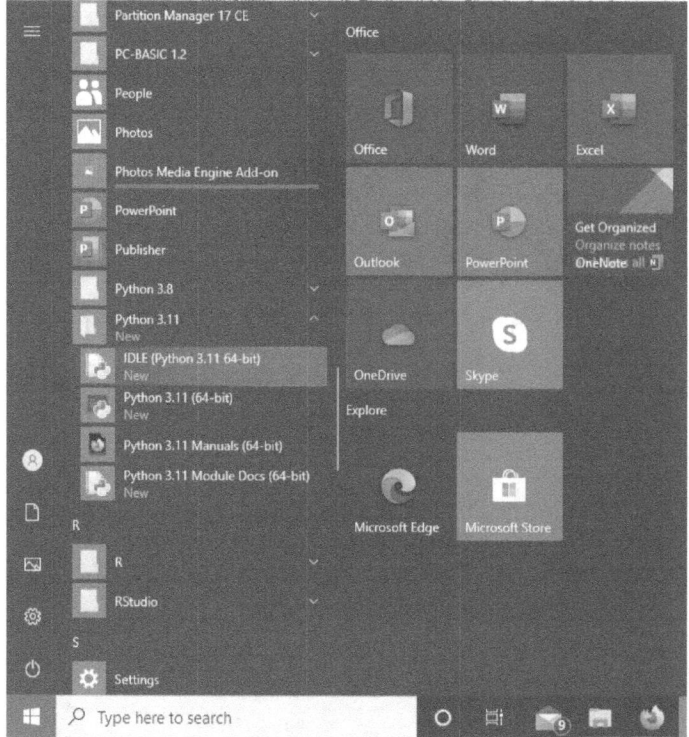

Figure 3.3: Listing of Python in the Program folder after successful installation

4. Now, click on **Python IDLE** and it will start the interactive mode of Python. Now, you may start typing your command at the prompt of **Python Idle**, as shown in *Figure 3.4*:

```
IDLE Shell 3.8.9                                              —    □    ×
File  Edit  Shell  Debug  Options  Window  Help
Python 3.8.9 (tags/v3.8.9:a743f81, Apr  6 2021, 14:02:34) [MSC v.1928 64 bit (AM
D64)] on win32
Type "help", "copyright", "credits" or "license()" for more information.
>>> |
```

Figure 3.4: Interactive mode of Python

How Python works

Python works in two modes, interactive mode and script mode.

The interactive mode of Python allows the execution of basic commands of Python at a command prompt. The interactive mode also allows the execution of code blocks along with a single command. The interactive mode of Python executes the code or command through the Python shell. Interactive mode is very helpful in running and testing various expressions and commands and the block of code as well. It also helps the new users to get acquainted with the working of basic commands.

The symbol >>> mentions that Python interactive mode is ready to execute commands. On successful execution of the command, the result is displayed at the command prompt itself. In order to run the command, you have to type it at the prompt and press *Enter* key. The successful execution of the command will display the result at the prompt itself.

For example, to print any DNA sequence you may type the command, as mentioned in *Figure 3.5*:

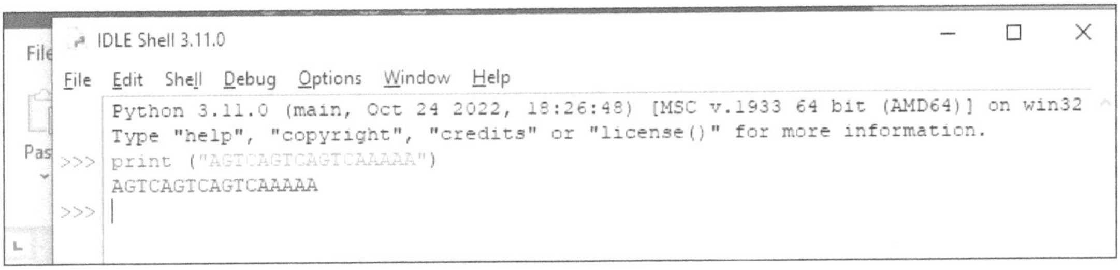

Figure 3.5: Interactive mode of Python

We can also perform mathematical operations as well on the command prompt of python, as shown in *Figure 3.6*:

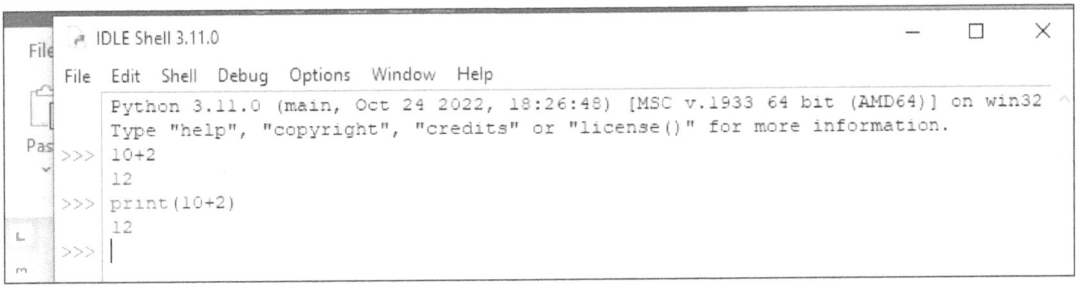

Figure 3.6: Performing mathematical operations in interactive mode

The interactive shell of Python not only computes single-line expressions, but it is also capable of computing multiple-line expressions as well, as shown in *Figure 3.7*:

```
IDLE Shell 3.11.0                                                    —    □    ×
File  Edit  Shell  Debug  Options  Window  Help
    Python 3.11.0 (main, Oct 24 2022, 18:26:48) [MSC v.1933 64 bit (AMD64)] on win32
    Type "help", "copyright", "credits" or "license()" for more information.
>>> 10+2
    12
>>> print(10+2)
    12
>>> if 5>10:
...     print ("Greater")
...
...
>>> if 10>5:
...     print ("Greater")
...
...
    Greater
>>>
```

Figure 3.7: Computing single-line expression on Python command prompt

Following are the merits and demerits of working in the interactive mode of Python:

- **Merits:**
    - For the small scripts, you may run the code and get the result there only.
    - Interactive mode is faster than shell mode as we only need to type commands and get the results.
    - Interactive mode is quite helpful for beginners to understand the commands.
- **Demerits:**
    - It is not good for executing long code.
    - Editing the code is hard in interactive mode.

Script mode

The user should use script mode in case one has to write programs based on multiple lines. The long programs should be saved in the form of script files and then executed. The user can open script mode through file menu in the menu bar and select **New File**, as shown in *Figure 3.8*:

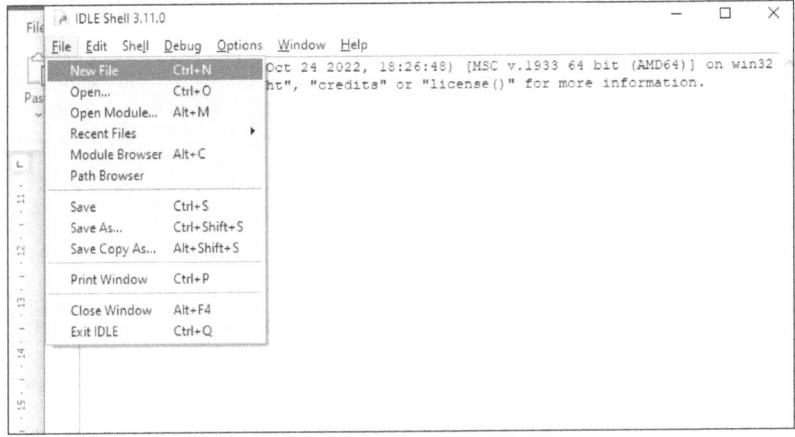

Figure 3.8: Creating a new script

This will open a script editor with **untitled** title bar, as shown in *Figure 3.9*:

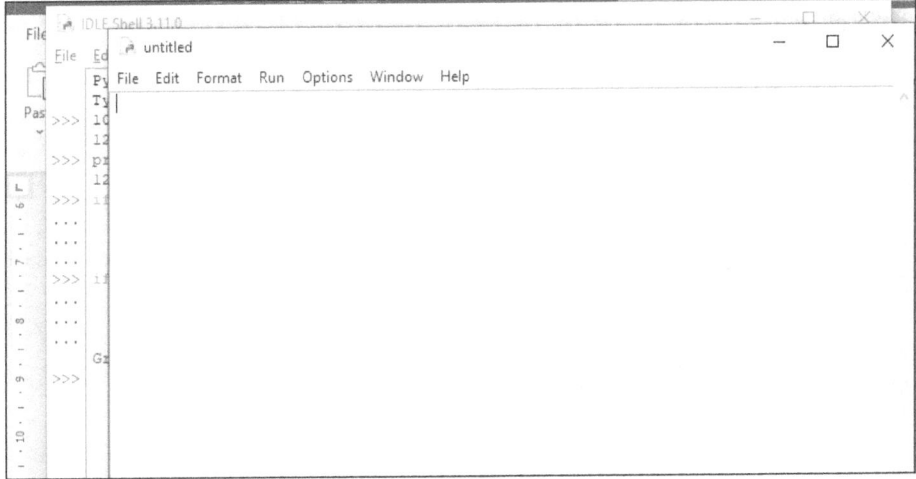

Figure 3.9: Script editor with untitled title bar

When the user will save the script file then the name will appear on the title bar (Extension of Python script file is **.py**), as shown in *Figure 3.10*:

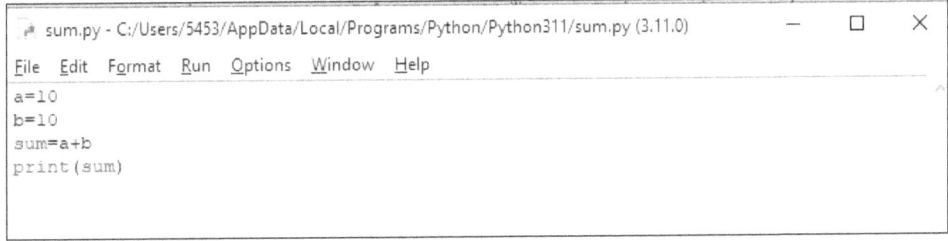

Figure 3.10: Saving a script file

In order to run this script, click **Run Module** from the **Run** option of menu bar, as shown below:

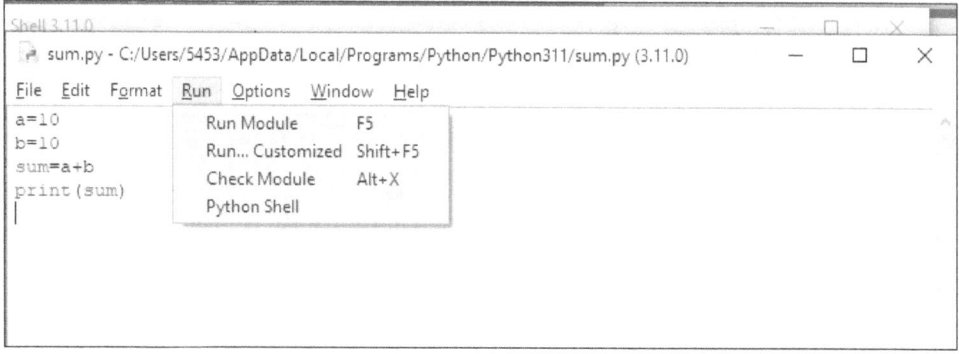

Figure 3.11: *Executing the script file*

Script mode also has its own merits and demerits, some are mentioned below:

- **Merits:**
    - It is easy to run large pieces of code.
    - Editing your script is easier in script mode.
    - Good for both beginners and experts.
- **Demerits:**
    - Can be tedious when you need to run only a single or a few lines of code.
    - You must create and save a file before executing your code.

Language fundamentals

Every programming language has some pre-defined rules and structures that help in writing a program in a structured manner. The basic language fundamentals are necessary to be understood by the end user to avoid the basic errors in the program. The section elaborates on the fundamentals of Python language.

Variables in Python

The variables are also called an **identifier**. The variables are used to store values required to perform the processing of data in various applications. The values assigned to the variables may be changed at the run-time of the program. There may be different types of values assigned to the variables, which can be the following:

- **Numeric:** 10,2,3,15
- **Float:** 10.3, 2.2, 3.3, 15.4

- **String:** "Hello", "Python", "Idle", "a"
- **Boolean:** "True", "False"

Python is a **dynamically typed language** which means the data type of the variables is decided according to the values assigned to the variables. The variables in Python can be created using simple assignment statements like:

`A=10 # integer variable`

`B=1.3 # float variable`

`Str1="Hello" #String variable`

`Flag="True" # Boolean variable`

There are some rules for variable names that the user must follow strictly to avoid any kind of abrupt conditions. Following are the key points to be followed for variable naming:

- The variable name may start with an underscore or a letter but cannot start with a digit. For example— **_counter1**, **counter_1**, **counter** are legal variables. However, **1_counter**, **counter_$**, **@counter** are not legal variables.

- The reserved words or keywords cannot be used as variable names. For example — if we take the variable name as **def**, Python will raise a syntax error. However, if we take the variables name as **defi** or **Defi** it will work fine.

- The Python language is case-sensitive in nature hence the variables **counter_1** and **COUNTER_1** will be treated as two different variables rather than one.

- The same variable may hold values of different data types at different times as shown in *Figure 3.12*:

```
IDLE Shell 3.11.0                                        —    □    ×
File  Edit  Shell  Debug  Options  Window  Help
    Python 3.11.0 (main, Oct 24 2022, 18:26:48) [MSC v.1933 64 bit (AMD64)] on win32
    Type "help", "copyright", "credits" or "license()" for more information.
>>> count=10
>>> count
    10
>>> count="Hello"
>>> count
    'Hello'
>>> count=2.3
>>> count
    2.3
>>>
```

Figure 3.12: *Variables in Python*

Data types in Python

There are different data type values that one may assign to the variables in Python. Python supports the following in-built data types:

- **str**: Text data type
- **int**, **float**, **complex**: Numeric data type
- **list**, **tuple**: Sequence types
- **dict**: Mapping type
- **set**, **frozenset**: Set types
- **bool**: Boolean data type
- **bytes**, **bytearray**, **memoryview**: Binary types

Text data type

Text data type handle strings. Strings are the set of characters that may consist of numbers, letters any special symbol like &, $, #, and the like. Strings enclosed with quotation marks may be double or single (**"ioPython"** or **'BioPython'**). To create any string type of variable we can assign a value, as mentioned in *Figure 3.13*:

```
IDLE Shell 3.11.0                                           —    □    ×
File  Edit  Shell  Debug  Options  Window  Help
    Python 3.11.0 (main, Oct 24 2022, 18:26:48) [MSC v.1933 64 bit (AMD64)] on win32
    Type "help", "copyright", "credits" or "license()" for more information.
>>> string1= "Bio-informatics"
>>> string1
    'Bio-informatics'
>>> string2="A101"
>>> string2
    'A101'
>>> string3="2400"
>>> string3
    '2400'
>>>
```

Figure 3.13: Text data type

Numeric data type

The numeric data type may include integer, float, or complex types. Integer values are whole numbers without any decimal part, as shown in *Figure 3.14*:

```
IDLE Shell 3.11.0                                    —   □   ×
File Edit Shell Debug Options Window Help
    Python 3.11.0 (main, Oct 24 2022, 18:26:48) [MSC v.1933 64 bit (AMD64)] on win32
    Type "help", "copyright", "credits" or "license()" for more information.
>>> a=9
>>> a
    9
>>> b=-240
>>> b
    -240
>>> c=223344
>>> c
    223344
>>>
```

Figure 3.14: *Integer data type*

Integer values can be positive or negative as well. There is no size limitation for Python integers. Python can handle large size integers automatically.

Floating point numbers do contain integer and decimal parts. The decimal point separates the decimal and integer parts. Python allows 53 bits of precision for floating point numbers, as shown in *Figure 3.15*:

```
IDLE Shell 3.11.0                                    —   □   ×
File Edit Shell Debug Options Window Help
    Python 3.11.0 (main, Oct 24 2022, 18:26:48) [MSC v.1933 64 bit (AMD64)] on win32
    Type "help", "copyright", "credits" or "license()" for more information.
>>> pi=3.14
>>> pi
    3.14
>>> x=234.567
>>> x
    234.567
>>> at_per=66.7
>>> at_per
    66.7
>>> y=-34.6789
>>> y
    -34.6789
>>>
```

Figure 3.15: *Float data type*

The complex data type in Python consists of two parts real part and imaginary part. Complex numbers are mostly used where we are using two real numbers. For instance, an electric circuit which is defined by **voltage (V)** and **current (C)** is used in geometry, scientific calculations, and calculus. The inbuilt function **complex()** of Python is used to create a complex number, as illustrated in *Figure 3.16*:

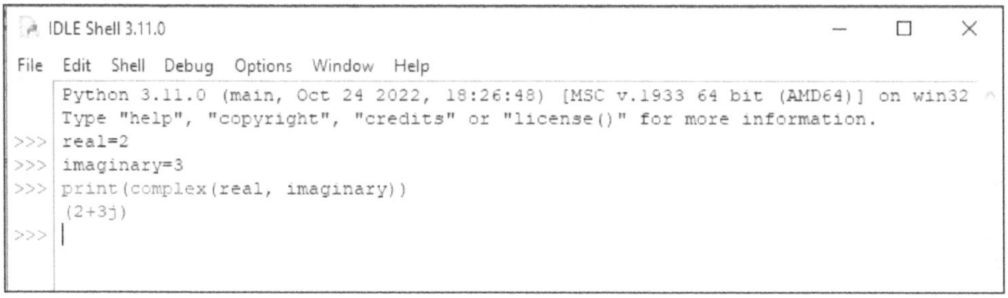

```
Python 3.11.0 (main, Oct 24 2022, 18:26:48) [MSC v.1933 64 bit (AMD64)] on win32
Type "help", "copyright", "credits" or "license()" for more information.
>>> real=2
>>> imaginary=3
>>> print(complex(real, imaginary))
(2+3j)
>>>
```

Figure 3.16: Complex data type

Sequence data type

Under sequence data type we can use list, tuple, and range to store a set of values in it. The sequence data types are used to store a set of data items as per the requirement of the application. The list is a mutable set of elements whereas tuple is an immutable set of elements. List is created using [] brackets and tuples are created using () brackets, as depicted in *Figure 3.17*:

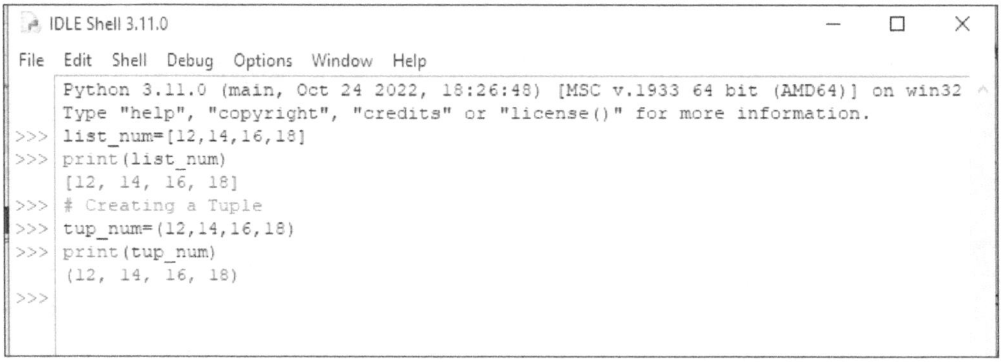

```
Python 3.11.0 (main, Oct 24 2022, 18:26:48) [MSC v.1933 64 bit (AMD64)] on win32
Type "help", "copyright", "credits" or "license()" for more information.
>>> list_num=[12,14,16,18]
>>> print(list_num)
[12, 14, 16, 18]
>>> # Creating a Tuple
>>> tup_num=(12,14,16,18)
>>> print(tup_num)
(12, 14, 16, 18)
>>>
```

Figure 3.17: Sequence data type

Mapping type

Under this data type dictionary is an un-ordered set of keys and values. It is an optimized data type for fast look-up of values. It stores the data in key-value pairs. The data from the dictionary can be accessed using keys that are immutable in nature. The dictionary is created using {} brackets. The data-item values and keys are segregated using the (:) symbol, as shown below:

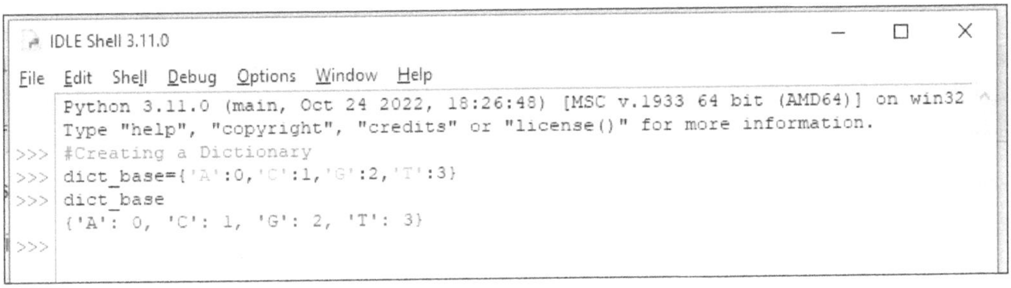

Figure 3.18: Mapping data type

Set type

This is another data type used to create sets in Python. There are two types of sets supported by Python, set and frozenset. The two inbuilt functions in Python are used to create these two types - **set()** and **frozenset()**.

The Set is an unordered and unindexed collection of unique elements. Sets are immutable which means we can make changes in the existing values of sets. Sets are created directly by defining the values of the set inside {}. However, we cannot create an empty set, as it will create a dictionary. We can add or remove any element from the set by using **add()** and **remove()** functions respectively. Refer to *Figure 3.19* for clarity:

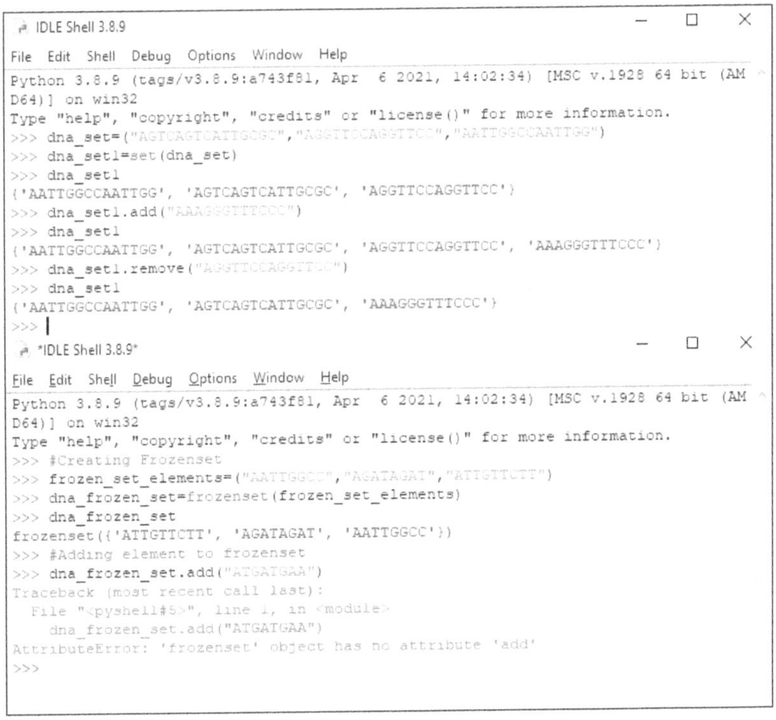

Figure 3.19: Set data type (Frozen-Set)

The frozenset is also an unordered and unindexed set of values. It is immutable in nature. One cannot make changes in the values of the frozenset, hence there is no add or remove functions for the frozenset. Frozensets are basically hashtable and they can also be used as a dictionary key. Frozenset is created by using the built-in function **frozenset()**.

Frozenset is immutable in nature. In *Figure 3.19,* we can see if we try to add a value to a frozenset, it will display an error as **AttributeError**.

Boolean data type

The Python Boolèan is a data type used to store Boolean values. It is mostly used to store results of Boolean expressions like **6>=5** which will result in **True** or **8==9** will result in **False**. The Boolean values in Python are numeric type, one can perform mathematical operations on it, and can also be compared by numbers. Refer to the following *Figure 3.20* for a better understanding:

```
Python 3.11.0 (main, Oct 24 2022, 18:26:48) [MSC v.1933 64 bit (AMD64)] on win32
Type "help", "copyright", "credits" or "license()" for more information.
>>> #Creating Boolean Variable
>>> flag=True
>>> flag
True
>>> flag=False
>>> flag
False
>>> #Boolean Vairable as Integer
>>> True==1
True
>>> False==0
True
>>> True + (False/True)
1.0
>>>
```

Figure 3.20: Boolean data type

Binary type

The byte and **bytearrays** in Python are used to handle binary data. The byte and bytearrays are supported by buffer protocol which is named **memoryview**. The memoryview can access the memory of another object without making a copy of the actual data. Bytes objects are immutable sequences of bytes. The usage of byte and bytearrays is done only when we are dealing with ASCII data. The byte literals are created the same way as string literals, the only difference is that **'b'** is added before byte literals. Bytearray objects are created by using **bytearray()** function, which creates a mutable object. The following *Figure 3.21* illustrates binary data type:

```
IDLE Shell 3.11.0                                      —    □    ×
File  Edit  Shell  Debug  Options  Window  Help
    Python 3.11.0 (main, Oct 24 2022, 18:26:48) [MSC v.1933 64 bit (AMD64)] on win32
    Type "help", "copyright", "credits" or "license()" for more information.
>>> a=b'character_data'
>>> a=b"character_data"
>>> print(a)
    b'character_data'
>>> b=bytearray(5)
>>> print(b)
    bytearray(b'\x00\x00\x00\x00\x00')
>>> c=memoryview(bytes(5))
>>> print(c)
    <memory at 0x000002179614CDC0>
>>>
```

Figure 3.21: Binary data type

Expressions

An expression is a combination of varied values, variables, operators, operands and function calls as well. An expression is evaluated by a Python interpreter and if everything is correct it will display the desired result. Expressions can be formulated using different statements. The expression is evaluated, and it produces a single value, this is the reason expressions are kept at the right-hand side of the assignment operator. For example:

>>a=10

In this expression, the variable is evaluated and assigned a value at the right side of the assignment operator.

>>a=10

>>b=a+5

The expressions are used in different ways in computer languages due to various types of operators used. Expressions may be simple or complex. A few examples of complex expressions are as follows:

```
# Complex mathematical expression with nested operations
root1 = (-b + math.sqrt(b**2 - 4*a*c)) / (2*a)
root2 = (-b - math.sqrt(b**2 - 4*a*c)) / (2*a)
# Complex logical expression
can_rent_car = (age >= 21 and has_driver_license) or (age >= 18 and has_driver_license and not no_criminal_record)
```

Type conversion

Type conversion simply means converting data of one data type to another data type. Let us take a simple example:

```
number = input("Enter a number::")
number = number *3
print(number)
```

Result:

```
Enter a number::5
555
```

The output you will get is **555**. The reason behind this is that the input statement takes input in a string format, and using ***3** will repeat the string value 03 times. However, if we want to perform a mathematical operation on the **number** variable, we need to typecast it to an integer like this:

```
number = input("Enter a number::")
number = int(number) *3
print(number)
```

Result:

```
Enter a number::5
15
```

In the same program, we performed minor changes by casting the **number** variable from string to integer, and then the result we got was **15**.

Such conversion of data from string to integer is called **type casting**. Python can perform typecasting in two ways. Implicit and explicit type casting.

Implicit type casting

When Python automatically converts the data type of a value then it is implicit type casting. It is also known as coercion, where the interpreter converts one data type to another without requiring explicit instructions from the programmer. It usually happens when operands of different types are used together in an expression, and Python converts them to a common type to prevent data loss or unexpected behavior:

```
Python 3.11.0 (main, Oct 24 2022, 18:26:48) [MSC v.1933 64 bit (AMD64)] on win32
Type "help", "copyright", "credits" or "license()" for more information.
>>> #Implicit Type Casting
>>> n1 = 10
>>> n2=23.0
>>> prod=n1*n2
>>> print(prod)
230.0
>>> print(type(prod))
<class 'float'>
>>>
```

Figure 3.22: Implicit type casting

In implicit type casting the data type of **prod** variable is automatically converted to float when the product of integer **n1** and float **n2** is computed, as shown in *Figure 3.22*.

Explicit type casting

In explicit type conversion, the data type of a variable is changed deliberately by the programmer. It is also known as **type casting** and is done manually by the programmer using built-in functions like **int()**, **float()**, **str()**, **bool()**, etc. Refer to the following example for a better understanding:

```
IDLE Shell 3.11.0
File Edit Shell Debug Options Window Help
    Python 3.11.0 (main, Oct 24 2022, 18:26:48) [MSC v.1933 64 bit (AMD64)] on win32
    Type "help", "copyright", "credits" or "license()" for more information.
>>> #Explicit Type Casting
>>> str="10"
>>> print(type(str))
    <class 'str'>
>>> str_num=int(str)
>>> print(type(str_num))
    <class 'int'>
>>>
```

Figure 3.23: Explicit type casting

This type of casting is required when Python cannot implicitly convert data types or when precision and control over the conversion are needed. *Figure 3.23* shows the explicit type conversion of variable **str** from string to int by using **int()** function.

Keywords in Python

Keywords are the pre-defined words in any language. Python also has a set of pre-defined words that we cannot use as a variable name. All these keywords have a specified meaning that is used as a language construct and recognized by a Python interpreter. One can check the list of Python keywords by importing the keyword library. Refer to *Figure 3.24* for clarity:

```
IDLE Shell 3.11.0
File Edit Shell Debug Options Window Help
    Python 3.11.0 (main, Oct 24 2022, 18:26:48) [MSC v.1933 64 bit (AMD64)] on win32
    Type "help", "copyright", "credits" or "license()" for more information.
>>> # Printing the Keywords of Python Language
>>> import keyword
>>> print(keyword.kwlist)
    ['False', 'None', 'True', 'and', 'as', 'assert', 'async', 'await', 'break', 'cla
    ss', 'continue', 'def', 'del', 'elif', 'else', 'except', 'finally', 'for', 'from
    ', 'global', 'if', 'import', 'in', 'is', 'lambda', 'nonlocal', 'not', 'or', 'pas
    s', 'raise', 'return', 'try', 'while', 'with', 'yield']
>>>
```

Figure 3.24: Keywords in Python

Operators in Python

There are different types of operators in Python. Every operator performs different roles with different types of operands. Operators and operands together form an expression. Operators can be classified as follows:

Arithmetic operators	+ (Addition)
	>> 2+2 (Output will be 4)
These are used to form mathematical expressions.	-(Subtraction)
	>> 5-2 (Output will be 3)
	* (Multiplication)
	>> 6*3 (Output will be 18)
	/ (Division)
	>> 10/2 (Output will be 5)
	% (Modulus)
	>> 13%5 (Output will be 3, modulus operator returns remainder)
	** (Exponentiation)
	>> 2**2 (Output will be 4)
	// (Floor division)
	>> 7.0//2 (Output will be 3.0 whereas 7.0/2 will give 3.5)
Relational operators	< (less than)
	>> 10<2 (Output will be 'False')
These operators are used to compare two expressions and result in a Boolean value of either 'True' or 'False'.	>> "hello"<"Hello" (Output will be 'False' as ASCII value of small 'h' is 97 and capital 'H' is 65
	>(greater than)
	>> 10>2 (Output will be 'True')
	>> "hello">"Hello" (Output will be 'True' as ASCII value of small 'h' is 97 and capital 'H' is 65
	<= (less than equal to)
	>> 2<=5 (Output will be 'True')
	>= (greater than equal to)
	>> 5>=2 (Output will be 'True')
	!=,<> (not equal to)
	>>5!=2 (Output will be 'True')
	== (equal to)
	>>10==10 (Output will be 'True')
	>> "Python"=="Python" (Output will be 'True')

Logical operators These are used to combine relational expressions and return results in the Boolean form either 'True' or 'False'.	It returns 'True' only when both the relational expressions are 'True', else returns 'False'. >> 10 >2 and 7>2 (Output will be 'True') >> 1>2 and 7>2 (Output will be 'False') >> 2>1 and 3>4 (Output will be 'False') >> 5>8 and 8>10 (Output will be 'False') or (It returns 'False' only when both the expressions are 'False', else returns 'True') >> 10 >2 or 7>2 (Output will be 'True') >> 1>2 or 7>2 (Output will be 'True') >> 2>1 or 3>4 (Output will be 'True') >> 5>8 and 8>10 (Output will be 'False') not (It reverses the state of operand) >> not (10>2) (Output will be 'False') >> not (10<2) (Output will be 'True')
Assignment operator / Shorthand assignment operator The assignment operator is used to set some value to the variable. The shorthand assignment operator is a combination of binary operation and assignment.	= (Assignment operator) >> x=8 += (added and assign back the result to left operand) >> x+=2 (Output will be 10) -= (subtracted and assigned back the result to left operand) >> x-=2 (Output will be 6) *= (multiplied and assigned back the result to left operand >> x*=2 (Output will be 16) /= (divided and assigned back the result to left operand) >> x/=2 (Output will be 4.0) %= (modulus is calculated using two operands and assign the result to left operand) >> x%=2 (Output will be 0) **= (exponentiation is performed on operators and assigned value to left operand) >>x**=2 (Output will be 64) //= (floor division is performed and assigned value to the left operand) >>x//=2 (Output will be 4)

Special operators	Identity operator (is, is not)
	It is used to compare objects if both of them are the same and share the same memory location. The operator 'is' and 'is not' are called identity operators and after comparing two objects they return 'True' or 'False'.
	'is' will return 'True' if both the objects are the same and from the same memory location and 'is not' will return 'True' if both the objects are not the same and not from the same memory location.
	>>X=10
	>>Y=X
	>>X is Y
	(Output will be 'True')
	>> X is not Y
	(Output will be 'False')
	Membership operator (in, not in)
	The operator is used to check the occurrence of any character in a string, any value in a list or tuple, or any key in the dictionary.
	The 'in' operator will return 'True' if the occurrence of a character or any value is there in a string or list, tuple, or dictionary. The 'not in' operator will return 'True' if the occurrence of a character or any value in List or Tuple or key in the dictionary is not there.
	>> 'h' in 'house' (Output will be 'True')
	>> 'h' not in 'house' (Output will be 'False')
	>> 'use' in 'house' (Output will be 'True')

Table 3.1: Operators in Python

Comments in Python

Comments are used to make your program more understandable. The purpose of comments is to provide information to the programmer. It helps the programmer to make changes in the program in the future if required. Comments are not interpreted by the Python interpreter; hence they do not affect the output of the program.

The comment starts with the # symbol. We can have single-line, inline, or multiline comments, as shown below:

`>> # This is single line comment`

`>> print("Comment")`

`>> print ("Comment") # This is inline comment`

In Python, **docstrings** (documentation strings) are used to describe the purpose and behavior of modules, classes, methods, and functions. Unlike regular comments, docstrings are stored as part of the object they document, making them accessible at runtime via the **__doc__** attribute.

Docstrings are mainly used for the following tasks:

- Documenting functions and methods.
- Documenting classes and modules.
- Providing details about the parameters, return values, and exceptions.

Syntax of docstrings

Docstrings are written using triple quotes (""" or ''') and can span multiple lines. The convention is to use triple double quotes (""") for consistency. An example of a Docstring is mentioned in *Figure 3.25*:

```
def calculate_area(radius):
    """
    Calculate the area of a circle given its radius.

    Args:
        radius (float): The radius of the circle.

    Returns:
        float: The area of the circle.

    Raises:
        ValueError: If the radius is negative.
    """
    if radius < 0:
        raise ValueError("The radius cannot be negative.")
    return 3.14159 * radius * radius
```

Figure 3.25: Docstrings example

Docstrings are multi-line comments designed to provide descriptive information about code components. It is an excellent way to document your code effectively and improve its maintainability.

Input statement in Python

We can get end user input using **input()** function. The **input()** function inputs value in String format only. However, if we wish to take an integer or some other data type value we need to perform explicit type casting for the input data:

```
>> gene_family = input ("Enter gene_family::")
>> print (gene_family)
>> dna_length = int(input ("Enter DNA length::"))
>> print (dna_length)
```

Handling invalid input in Python is essential to ensure that your program behaves correctly and does not crash when users provide unexpected or incorrect input. There are several techniques to handle invalid input, including:

- **Using conditional checks**: Validating input before processing it.
- **Using try and except blocks**: Handling exceptions that occur during the execution.
- **Using loops to prompt for valid input**: Continuously asking for input until valid data is provided.

Language constructs in Python

The program control flow of any programming language can be varied. There are many varied statements used in a program. The statement can be sequential, selection/conditional statement, or iterative statement.

Sequential statements execute in a linear fashion where one statement will execute just after another. The flow of a program where conditional statements are used is dependent on the various conditions. Depending upon whether the condition is true or false the flow of the program is going to be diverted.

Iterative statements are used in programs when we wish to execute a set of statements multiple times.

Indentation in Python

Indentation means adding a whitespace before a statement. In Python indentation is used to mention blocks of code. The indentation in Python is very important. Improper indentation in Python may lead to **IndentationError** and the program will not be compiled.

In other programming languages, the statements are blocked using curly braces. Python uses indentation to block the statements. In the nested structure also the concept of indentation is used.

Here are some of the most common indentation errors and how to avoid them:

IndentationError: unexpected indent

This error occurs when you introduce an indentation where it is not expected or necessary.

Example:
```
x = 10
    print(x)  # IndentationError: unexpected indent
```

The **print(x)** statement is indented unnecessarily. In Python, statements at the same level should not have an indentation unless they are inside a block (such as inside a function, loop, or conditional).

How to fix:
```
x = 10
print(x)  # Correct indentation
```

IndentationError: Expected an indented block

This error occurs when Python expects an indented block (usually after a statement that introduces a new block, like **if**, **for**, **while**, **def**, or **class**), but no indentation is provided.

Example:
```
if x > 5:
print("x is greater than 5")  # IndentationError: expected an indented block
```

The print statement should be indented to indicate it is part of the if block.

How to fix:
```
if x > 5:
    print("x is greater than 5")  # Correct indentation
```

The best practices to avoid indentation errors are mentioned below:

- **Use a consistent indentation style**:
  - Follow PEP 8 (Style guide for Python code) recommendations: Use four spaces per indentation level.
  - Avoid mixing tabs and spaces. Configure your code editor to insert spaces when you press the *Tab* key.
- **Use a linter or code formatter**:
  - Use tools like **flake8**, **pylint**, or **black** to automatically check or format your code for consistent indentation.

- **Configure your IDE/text editor**:
  - Most modern IDEs (like VS Code, PyCharm) or text editors have settings to highlight or fix indentation issues automatically.
- **Read and review your code regularly**:
  - Regularly reviewing your code can help you spot indentation issues early, especially if you are modifying existing code.

By following these best practices, you can reduce the likelihood of encountering indentation errors in your Python programs.

Conditional statements

Decision making statements are used to control the flow of instructions. The decision-making statements in Python help you to write programs based on different conditions and actions as well. The following are the conditional statements provided by Python:

- if statement
- if … else statement
- if…elif statement
- Nested if statements

if statement

It is the basic conditional statement in any programming language. **if** statement always mentions a condition, **if** condition stands true then the statements associated with the if are executed else nothing will happen if condition stands false.

Syntax of if:

```
if <condition>:
    statements
```

The colon : is a must after the condition. All statements inside if are indented at the same level. The statements after **if** should be aligned to the if statement. For example:

Example 3.1:

```
a=12
if a>10:
    print(a)                    -------------------→Statement1
    print ("a is greater")      ---------------------→Statement2
print ("After if")              ----------------→Statement3
```

In this example, **Statement1** and **2** are part of **if**. However, **Statement3** is not part of **if**. It will be executed after if block. If the condition stands **True**, then **Statement1** and **2** will be executed and after that **Statement3** will be executed. If the condition stands **False** then only **Statement3** will be executed after the if block.

The output when the condition is **True** and when it is **False** is shown in *Figure 3.26*:

```
Python 3.8.6 Shell                                                — □ ×
File Edit Shell Debug Options Window Help
Python 3.8.6 (tags/v3.8.6:db45529, Sep 23 2020, 15:52:53) [MSC v.1927 64 bit (AM
D64)] on win32
Type "help", "copyright", "credits" or "license()" for more information.
>>>
==== RESTART: C:/Users/5453/AppData/Local/Programs/Python/Python38/check.py ====
12
a is greater
After if
>>>
==== RESTART: C:/Users/5453/AppData/Local/Programs/Python/Python38/check.py ====
After if
>>>
```

Figure 3.26: if statement example

Finding AT content in a DNA sequence and printing the statement **"AT content is high"** if AT content is greater than 50 percent else program should print **"AT content is low"**. *Example 3.27* demonstrates it Output of the example program is shown in *Figure 3.27*:

Example 3.2:

```
seq="ATGCTGATATGGGGGGCCCCATAT"
ca=seq.count("A")
ct=seq.count("T")
cat = ca+ct
at_per= (cat/len(seq))*100
if at_per>=50:
    print("AT content is high")
else:
    print("AT content is low")
```

Refer to the following example for clarity:

```
==== RESTART: C:\Users\5453\AppData\Local\Programs\Python\Python38\at_per.py ===
AT content is low
>>>
```

Figure 3.27: if statement example

if...else statement

if statement evaluates the condition and if the condition stands **True** and executes the statements in the if block. But if the condition stands **False**, in that case, we wish to execute certain statements, then we may use another statement. This means the **else** statement is used to follow the **False** condition.

Syntax:

```
if condition:
    statements
else:
    statements
```

Example 3.3:

```
a=12
if a>10:
    print(a)                  --------------------→Statement1
    print ("a is greater")    ---------------------→Statement2
else:
    print("a is smaller")     ---------------→Statement3
print ("After if/else")       ---------------→Statement4
```

In this example, if the condition is true then **Statement1** and **Statement2** will be executed followed by **Statement4**. But if the condition is false, then **Statement3** will be executed and followed by **Statement4**.

If-elif-else statement

When the user has more than two conditions to consider, an if-elif-else block may be used. When any one of the elif statements is True, the associated set of statements will be executed. If none of the conditions is True, then the statements associated with the else block will be executed.

Syntax:

```
if condition:
    Statements
elif condition:
    Statements
elif condition:
    Statements
else:
    Statements
```

Example 3.4:
```
seq="ATGCTGATATGGGGGGCCCCATAT"
ca=seq.count("A")
ct=seq.count("T")
cat = ca+ct
at_per= (cat/len(seq))*100
if at_per>80:
    print("AT content is veryhigh")
elif at_per>=70 and at_per<=79:
    print("AT content is high")
elif at_per>=60 and at_per<=69:
   print("AT content is medium")
else:
    print("AT content is low")
```

The above example demonstrates the usage of if..elif..else block. The code will calculate the percentage of **"AT"** in a given sequence and print the appropriate messages as per the percentage of **"AT"** content in the sequence.

Nested if-elif-else statement

When we use if-elif-else statement inside another if…else statement. This is called a **nested if-elif-else** statement. It allows you to check for multiple test expressions and execute different codes for more than two conditions.

Syntax:
```
If condition:
      Statements
      If condition:
           Statements
elif condition:
      Statements
else:
     Statements
```

Example 3.5:
```
If (x==y):
   print(' x and y are equal')
else:
  if (x<y):
```

```
        print('x is less than y')
    else:
        print('x is greater than y')
```

The above example demonstrates the usage of nested if. The example will compare the values of two variables **x** and **y** if they are equal the message will be printed **'x and y are equal'**. Otherwise, in the else part, another if is executed for further checks.

Loops in Python

When you need to repeat the execution of a few sets of statements then we use iteration or loops. Iteration just means to repeat the set of statements until some condition stands **True** or **False** or the number of times we wish to iterate is over.

Let us take a very simple example if you wish to print a sequence five times then in that case either you write **print("AAATTTGCGC")** five times or you can use an iterative statement. The better option is to use an iterative statement. There are two types of iterative statements used in Python.

Definite loop

for loop in Python is a definite iterative statement. It is called a **definite loop** because it iterates for a range of values or a sequence. The iteration statement is executed for each value of the range. The range value can be numeric, or it may be some successive elements of a string, list, or tuple. In for loop, we know how many times the loop will be executed.

Syntax:

```
for <variable> in <sequence/items in range>:
        statements in body of loop
else:
        statements
```

Here variable will take a new value from the range or sequence in every iteration. **else** statement is not mandatory however, if mentioned, if will be executed after all the iterations of the for loop.

Example 3.6:

```
for i in range(5):
        print(i)
```

The value of **i** in *Example 3.6* will start from **0** and will go to 5-1. The output of the example program mentioned in *Figure 3.28*:

```
Python 3.8.6 Shell                                          —    □    ×
File  Edit  Shell  Debug  Options  Window  Help
Python 3.8.6 (tags/v3.8.6:db45529, Sep 23 2020, 15:52:53) [MSC v.1927 64 bit (AM
D64)] on win32
Type "help", "copyright", "credits" or "license()" for more information.
>>>
===== RESTART: C:/Users/5453/AppData/Local/Programs/Python/Python38/tt2.py =====
0
1
2
3
4
>>>
```

Figure 3.28: *for loop in Python*

Example 3.7:

```
for i in range(2,5):
    print(i)
```

In *Example 3.7, the* value of **i** will start from **2** and will go to 5-1. The output of the example program mentioned in *Figure 3.29*:

```
===== RESTART: C:/Users/5453/AppData/Local/Programs/Python/Python38/tt2.py =====
2
3
4
>>>
```

Figure 3.29: *for loop in Python*

Example 3.8:

```
for x in [2,3,4,5]:
    print(x)
```

In *Example 3.8, the* value of **x** will be picked from the list **[2,3,4,5]**. Every time the loop will iterate, it will pick one value from the list starting from the first element. The output of the example program is mentioned in *Figure 3.30*:

```
===== RESTART: C:/Users/5453/AppData/Local/Programs/Python/Python38/tt2.py =====
2
3
4
5
>>>
```

Figure 3.30: *for loop in Python*

Indefinite loop in Python

Another type of loop in Python is a **while** loop. It is also an indefinite loop. In this loop the test condition is evaluated first and if the condition stands **True** then only the loop will start its execution. The loop will terminate when the test condition stands **False**. This is the reason why a while loop is called an **indefinite loop** because the number of times a loop will execute depends upon the condition only.

Syntax:
```
while <test_condition>:
        statements
else:
        statements
```

The **test_condition** is evaluated first and if it stands **True** statement or set of statements will execute. If the **test_condition** is evaluated as **False**, it will execute the statements under the else section. However, the else statement is optional.

Example 3.9:
```
i=0
while i<5:
        print(i)
        i=i+1
```

In *Example 3.9*, the value of **i** is initialized. The loop will iterate till the value of **i** is less than **5**. The increment statement **i=i+1** increments the value of **i** in every iteration. The output of the example program is mentioned in *Figure 3.31*:

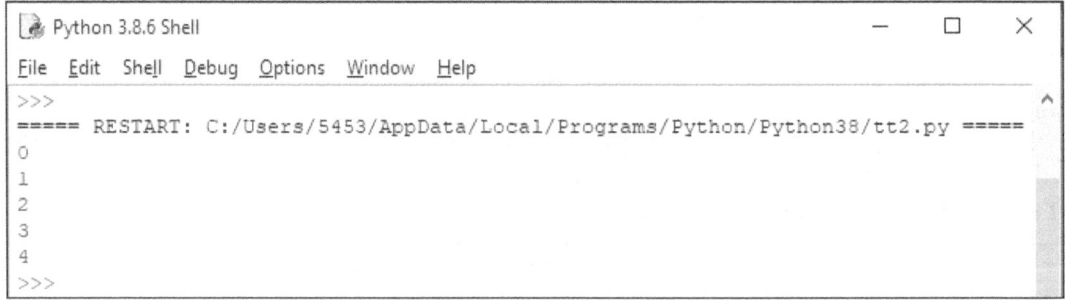

Figure 3.31: while loop in Python

Nested loops

When we use one loop inside another loop then it is called **nested loops**. When the condition for the outer loop is **True** control is transferred to the inner loop. The outer loop cannot terminate until the inner loop terminates.

Syntax for nested while:
```
while <test_condition>:
      while <test_condition>:
            Statements (Inner Loop)
      Statements (Outer Loop)
Statements (Outside the outer loop)
```

Syntax for nested for:
```
for var in sequence:
      for var1 in sequence:
            statements
      statements
statements
```

Example 3.10:
```
i=1
while i<=5:
    j=1
    while j<=i:
        print(j,end=" ")
        j=j+1
    print()
    i=i+1
```

The following figure shows nested while loop:

```
=== RESTART: D:\pvdata\book1\P4Bio\Review_done\Code\Chapter3_code\Ex_3.11.py ===
1
1 2
1 2 3
1 2 3 4
1 2 3 4 5
>>>
```

Figure 3.32: Nested while loop in Python

In the given *Example 3.10* nested while loop is used to print the pattern. The outer while loop will execute **for** five times and the counter variable for the same is **i**. The inner loop is executed every time from 1 to the value of **i**. **j** is a counter for the inner loop and it will execute every time starting from 1 to the value of **i**. That is why we need to re-initialize the value of **j**, every time to 1 after the inner loop completes its execution. The statement **print(j, end=" ")** here is used to print the value of j every time on the same line, and the **print()** statement after the inner loop will start printing the next row from the new line.

Example 3.11:

```
for i in range (1,6):
    for j in range(1,i+1):
        print(j,end=" ")
    print()
```

The output of the program is shown in *Figure 3.32*:

```
=== RESTART: D:\pvdata\book1\P4Bio\Review_done\Code\Chapter3_code\Ex_3.11.py ===
1
1 2
1 2 3
1 2 3 4
1 2 3 4 5
>>>
```

Figure 3.33: *Nested for loop in Python*

The same example of pattern printing is explained using nested for loop. In *Example 3.11*, **for** loop, we take a range from 1 to 6 as we know that the range function takes the counter value 1 less than the upper value mentioned in the range function. The same is the condition for the inner loop also where the upper range is mentioned as **i+1**. The output is shown in *Figure 3.33*.

Jump statements in Python

Loop statements do repeat the set of statements. In some conditions when we want to terminate the loop conditionally or we want to skip some statements of the loop and continue its execution, we may use jump statements **break** and **continue** statements. These jump statements give the programmer better control of the logic of the program.

Break statement

The **break** statement can be used to terminate the execution of the loop and the control will switch to the next statement just after that loop. If the **break** statement is used in the nested loop in that case **break** statement will terminate the innermost loop.

Syntax:

```
for control_var in range(n):
    statements inside loop
    if condition:
        break
statements outside loop
```

When the condition mentioned with if stands **true** the control will switch to the statements outside the loop block.

while test_condition:

    statements inside loop

    if test_condition1:

        break

statements outside loop

When the **test_condition1** stands **true**, the control will switch to the statements outside the while loop.

Example 3.12:

```
for val in [2,3,2,4,5,2]:
    if val==4:
        break
    print(val)
print("Outside the for loop")
```

The following figure shows the break statement:

```
Python 3.8.9 (tags/v3.8.9:a743f81, Apr  6 2021, 14:02:34) [MSC v.1928 64 bit (AM
D64)] on win32
Type "help", "copyright", "credits" or "license()" for more information.
>>>
=== RESTART: D:\pvdata\book1\P4Bio\Review_done\Code\Chapter3_code\EX_3.12.py ===
2
3
2
Outside the for loop
>>>
```

Figure 3.34: break statement in Python

In *Example 3.12*, the execution of the loop when the value of **val** variable is **4**, it will terminate the execution of the for loop and control will reach to last statement of the program.

Example 3.13:

```
sum=0
while True:
    x=int(input("Enter an integer value"))
    if (x<0):
        break
    sum=sum+x
print("Sum of values entered is:", sum)
```

The break statement in Python is shown below:

```
Python 3.8.9 (tags/v3.8.9:a743f81, Apr  6 2021, 14:02:34) [MSC v.1928 64 bit (AM
D64)] on win32
Type "help", "copyright", "credits" or "license()" for more information.
>>>
=== RESTART: D:\pvdata\book1\P4Bio\Review_done\Code\Chapter3_code\Ex_3.13.py ===
Enter an integer value1
Enter an integer value2
Enter an integer value3
Enter an integer value-4
Sum of values entered is: 6
>>>
```

Figure 3.35: break statement in Python

In *Example 3.13*, the while loop is infinite and will keep getting input from the user until the user enters a value less than zero. Once the user inputs a value less than zero the **break** statement will terminate the loop and the sum of values input by the end user will be printed.

continue statement

The **continue** statement takes control to the beginning of the loop for its next execution. When the **continue** statement is encountered, it skips the execution of the rest of the statements inside the loop. If the loop condition is checked and if condition is tested true then the loop will continue its execution.

Syntax for loop:

```
for control_var in range(n):
        statements inside loop
        if condition:
              continue
        statements inside loop
statements outside loop
```

Syntax while loop:

```
while test_condition:
        statements inside loop
        if condition:
              continue
        statements1 inside loop
statements outside loop
```

The loop will execute and all the statements inside the loop. When the if condition stands **True** the control will switch to the beginning of the loop for the next execution and it will skip **statements1** inside the loop.

Example 3.14:

```
for val in [2,3,4,5,6,7,8]:
    if val%2 !=0:
        continue
    print(val)
```

Refer to the following figure for a better understanding:

```
=== RESTART: D:\pvdata\book1\P4Bio\Review_done\Code\Chapter3_code\Ex_3.14.py ===
2
4
6
8
>>>
```

Figure 3.36: continue statement in Python

In *Example 3.14*, the code will print all even numbers. The loop will pick one value at a time from the set of values and if the value is odd and the remainder is not equal to 0 then the loop will execute for the next value.

pass statement

This statement is used when a particular statement is required but you do not want to execute that command. It is like a null statement. Nothing will happen when it executes.

Syntax:

Pass

Sometimes we plan for a function or loop but the implementation part we wish to write in the future. In that case, we can place pass statements so that the interpreter will not raise any issue at runtime. Refer to *Figure 3.37* for a better understanding:

```
nest.py - D:/pvdata/Python/nest.py (3.11.0)              —   □   ×
File  Edit  Format  Run  Options  Window  Help
for val in [2,3,4,5,6,7,8]:
    pass
```

Figure 3.37: pass statement in Python

Conclusion

Python is easy to learn language with simple syntax. Being an open source in nature, it is the most popular language in present scenario. The portable nature of Python makes its execution capable on various platforms. The basic language construct provides all the features that the programming language should support. Although Python belongs to the category of scripting language it supports all the features that the programming language will provide. The chapter discussed in detail variables, data types, keywords, operators, decision making constructs and looping constructs that will be the base of further learning of Python concepts.

Join our book's Discord space

Join the book's Discord Workspace for Latest updates, Offers, Tech happenings around the world, New Release and Sessions with the Authors:

https://discord.bpbonline.com

CHAPTER 4
String Handling, Modular Programming, and Data Structures

Introduction

In Biopython, a widely used library for bioinformatics, string manipulation is an essential aspect of working with biological sequences such as DNA, RNA, and proteins. Biopython provides various tools and functions specifically designed for manipulating and analyzing biological sequences. The objective of the chapter is to provide detailed knowledge about string basics, data structure, and modular programming with the help of example programs.

Structure

- String basics in Python
- Data structures
- Modular programming

Objectives

The objective of this chapter is to build a strong foundation of string manipulation, modular design principles, and essentials of data structures. Through this chapter, readers will understand the principles of string operations, learn the importance of modularity in programming for code reusability, readability and maintenance. Readers will also explore fundamentals of data structures.

String basic in Python

In Python, strings are **immutable**, meaning once they are created, their contents cannot be changed. If you attempt to modify a string, a new string is created instead. You can create a string by assigning a value to a variable using quotes or setting the variable type explicitly by using **str**, as shown below:

```
my_string = "Hello, World!"
my_location = str("India")
print(my_string)
print(my_location)
```

Take a look at the following figure illustrating the output:

```
= RESTART: C:\Users\3665\AppData\Local\Programs\Python\Python38\str_creation.py
Hello, World!
India
>>>
```

Figure 4.1: Creation of string

Accessing characters

You can access individual characters of a string using indexing. Indexing starts from 0 for the first character, for example:

```
my_string = "Hello, World!"
print(my_string[0])    # Output: 'H'
print(my_string[7])    # Output: 'W'
```

Take a look at the following figure illustrating the output:

```
== RESTART: C:/Users/3665/AppData/Local/Programs/Python/Python38/str_access.py =
H
W
>>>
```

Figure 4.2: Accessing characters from string

String length

You can find the length of a string using the **len()** function, for example:

```
my_string = "Hello, World!"
print(len(my_string))    # Output: 13
```

Take a look at the following figure illustrating the output:

```
== RESTART: C:\Users\3665\AppData\Local\Programs\Python\Python38\str_length.py =
13
>>>
```

Figure 4.3: String length

String concatenation

You can concatenate (combine) two or more strings using the **+** operator. For example:

```
string1 = "Hello"
string2 = "World!"
result = string1 + " " + string2
print(result)   # Output: "Hello World!"
```

Take a look at the following figure illustrating the output:

```
== RESTART: C:\Users\3665\AppData\Local\Programs\Python\Python38\str_conct.py ==
Hello World!
>>>
```

Figure 4.4: String concatenation

String slicing

You can extract a portion of a string using slicing. Slicing allows you to specify a range of indices to extract. For example, it provides a flexible way to work with substrings.

The basic syntax for string slicing is **string[start:end:step]**, where:

- **start** is the index of the first character you want to include in the slice (inclusive). If omitted, it defaults to the beginning of the string (index 0).

- **end** is the index of the character you want to stop just before (exclusive). If omitted, it defaults to the end of the **string (index len(string))**.

- **step** is an optional parameter that specifies the stride or the increment between characters. If omitted, it defaults to 1.

Let us explore various scenarios and examples to understand string slicing in detail:

Slicing with start and end indices:

```
my_string = "Hello, World!"
print(my_string[0:5])     # Output: "Hello"
print(my_string[7:12])    # Output: "World"
print(my_string[0:5:2])   # Output: "Hlo"
```

The explanation is given below:

- In the first example, **my_string[0:5]** extracts characters from index 0 to index 4 (5 is exclusive), resulting in **"Hello"**.

- In the second example, **my_string[7:12]** extracts characters from index 7 to index 11, resulting in **"World"**.

- In the third example, **my_string[0:5:2]** extracts characters with a step of 2, resulting in **"Hlo"** (characters at indices 0, 2, and 4).

Take a look at the following figure illustrating the output:

```
=== RESTART: C:\Users\3665\AppData\Local\Programs\Python\Python38\str_slic.py ==
Hello
World
Hlo
>>>
```

Figure 4.5: String slicing

Slicing from the start:

```
my_string = "Hello, World!"
print(my_string[:5])      # Output: "Hello"
print(my_string[:7:2])    # Output: "Hlo"
```

The explanation is given below:

- When you omit the start index, it defaults to the beginning of the string. In the first example, **my_string[:5]** extracts characters from index 0 to index 4, resulting in **"Hello"**.

- In the second example, **my_string[:7:2]** extracts characters with a step of 2 from the start, resulting in **"Hlo"**.

Take a look at the following figure illustrating the output:

```
== RESTART: C:\Users\3665\AppData\Local\Programs\Python\Python38\str_slic_2.py =
Hello
Hlo
>>>
```

Figure 4.6: String slicing from the start

Slicing to the end:

```
my_string = "Hello, World!"
print(my_string[7:])      # Output: "World!"
print(my_string[::2])     # Output: "Hlo ol!"
```

The explanation is given below:

- When you omit the end index, it defaults to the end of the string. In the first example, **my_string[7:]** extracts characters from index 7 to the end, resulting in **"World!"**.

- In the second example, **my_string[::2]** extracts characters with a step of 2 until the end, resulting in **"Hlo ol!"**.

Take a look at the following figure illustrating the output:

```
=== RESTART: C:\Users\3665\AppData\Local\Programs\Python\Python38\slic_end.py ==
World!
Hlo ol!
>>>
```

Figure 4.7: String slicing from end

Slicing with negative indices:

```
my_string = "Hello, World!"
print(my_string[-6:-1])    # Output: "World"
print(my_string[-1::-1])   # Output: "!dlroW ,olleH"
```

The explanation is given below:

- Negative indices allow you to count from the end of the string. In the first example, **my_string[-6:-1]** extracts characters from the 6th last index to the second last index, resulting in **"World"**.

- In the second example, **my_string[-1::-1]** extracts characters with a step of -1 (reverse order) from the last index to the beginning, resulting.

Take a look at the following figure illustrating the output:

```
= RESTART: C:\Users\3665\AppData\Local\Programs\Python\Python38\slic_negative.py
World
!dlroW ,olleH
>>>
```

Figure 4.8: String slicing with negative indices

String methods

Strings have various built-in methods that allow you to manipulate and perform operations on them. Some commonly used methods include **upper()**, **lower()**, **strip()**, **split()**, **replace()**, and **find()**. Let us explore this in detail.

upper()

This method converts all characters in a string to uppercase. The following factors can be considered:

- **Highlighting or emphasizing**: Converting text to uppercase can make certain parts of your output stand out.

- **Standardizing input**: Similar to **lower()**, you might want to convert input to uppercase for consistency.

- **Case insensitive comparisons**: Just like with **lower()**, you can use **upper()** for case insensitive comparisons.

  ```
  my_string = "Hello, World!"
  print(my_string.upper())   # Output: "HELLO, WORLD!"
  ```

Take a look at the following figure illustrating the output:

```
== RESTART: C:\Users\3665\AppData\Local\Programs\Python\Python38\str_upper.py ==
HELLO, WORLD!
>>>
```

Figure 4.9: String slicing with negative indices

lower()

This method converts all characters in a string to lowercase. The following factors can be considered:

- **Case insensitive comparisons**: When you want to compare strings without worrying about their case.

- **Standardizing input**: When processing user input, converting to lowercase can help ensure consistency.

- **Searching or filtering**: When searching for keywords in a text, converting both the text and the keyword to lowercase can help avoid case-related issues.

  ```
  my_string = "Hello, World!"
  print(my_string.lower())   # Output: "hello, world!"
  ```

Take a look at the following figure illustrating the output:

```
== RESTART: C:\Users\3665\AppData\Local\Programs\Python\Python38\str_lower.py ==
hello, world!
>>>
```

Figure 4.10: String slicing with negative indices

strip()

This method removes leading and trailing whitespace from a string, as shown below:

```
my_string = "   Hello, World!   "
print(my_string.strip())   # Output: "Hello, World!"
```

Take a look at the following figure illustrating output:

```
== RESTART: C:\Users\3665\AppData\Local\Programs\Python\Python38\str_strip.py ==
Hello, World!
>>>
```

Figure 4.11: Strip method

split()

This method splits a string into a list of substrings based on a specified delimiter, as shown below:

```
my_string = "Hello, World!"
print(my_string.split(","))   # Output: ["Hello", " World!"]
```

Take a look at the following figure illustrating the output:

```
== RESTART: C:/Users/3665/AppData/Local/Programs/Python/Python38/str_spilit.py =
['Hello', ' World!']
>>>
```

Figure 4.12: Split method

replace()

This method replaces all occurrences of a specified substring with another substring within a string, as shown below:

```
my_string = "Hello, World!"
new_string = my_string.replace("World", "Python")
print(new_string)    # Output: "Hello, Python!"
```

Take a look at the following figure illustrating the output:

```
= RESTART: C:/Users/3665/AppData/Local/Programs/Python/Python38/str_replace.py =
Hello, Python!
>>>
```

Figure 4.13: Replace method

find()

This method searches for a specified substring within a string and returns the index of the first occurrence (or **-1** if not found), as shown below:

```
my_string = "Hello, World!"
print(my_string.find("World"))   # Output: 7
print(my_string.find("Python"))  # Output: -1
```

Take a look at the following figure illustrating the output:

```
=== RESTART: C:/Users/3665/AppData/Local/Programs/Python/Python38/str_find.py ==
7
-1
>>>
```

Figure 4.14: Find method

These methods allow you to perform various operations and manipulations on strings in Python. Remember that strings in Python are immutable, meaning that these methods return a new modified string rather than modifying the original one.

Data structures

Python provides several built-in data structures that are widely used to store, organize, and manipulate data. Here are some commonly used data structures in Python:

Lists

Lists are ordered, mutable collections of elements. They can contain elements of different data types and allow duplicates. Lists are defined using square brackets [] and elements are separated by commas. You can access elements using indexing, modify elements, add or remove elements, and perform various operations like slicing and concatenation.

Creating a list

Lists can be created by enclosing elements within square brackets, separated by commas, as shown below:

```
my_list = [1, 2, 3, "apple", "banana"]
```

Accessing elements

You can access individual elements of a list using indexing. Indexing starts from 0 for the first element, as shown below:

```
my_list = [1, 2, 3, "apple", "banana"]
print(my_list[0])      # Output: 1
print(my_list[3])      # Output: "apple"
print(my_list[-1])     # Output: "banana" (negative indexing)
```

Take a look at the following figure illustrating the output:

```
= RESTART: C:/Users/3665/AppData/Local/Programs/Python/Python38/list_creation.py
1
apple
banana
>>>
```

Figure 4.15: List creation

Modifying element

Lists are mutable, so you can modify elements by assigning new values to specific indices, as shown below:

```
my_list = [1, 2, 3, "apple", "banana"]
my_list[2] = 4           # Modifying the third element
my_list.append(5)        # Adding a new element at the end
my_list.remove("apple")  # Removing an element by value
print(my_list)
```

Take a look at the following figure illustrating the output:

```
= RESTART: C:/Users/3665/AppData/Local/Programs/Python/Python38/list_modify.py
[1, 2, 4, 'banana', 5]
>>>
```

Figure 4.16: Modifying element of list

List length

You can find the length of a list using the **len()** function, as shown below:

```
my_list = [1, 2, 3, "apple", "banana"]
print(len(my_list))    # Output: 5
```

Take a look at the following figure illustrating the output:

```
= RESTART: C:/Users/3665/AppData/Local/Programs/Python/Python38/list_length.py
5
>>>
```

Figure 4.17: Length of list

List concatenation and repetition

You can concatenate two lists using the + operator. Additionally, you can repeat a list using the * operator.

List slicing

List slicing allows you to extract a portion of a list using a specified range of indices, as shown below:

```
my_list = [1, 2, 3, 4, 5]
print(my_list[1:4])    # Output: [2, 3, 4]
print(my_list[2:])     # Output: [3, 4, 5]
print(my_list[:3])     # Output: [1, 2, 3]
print(my_list[::-1])   # Output: [5, 4, 3, 2, 1] (reversed list)
```

Take a look at the following figure illustrating the output:

```
= RESTART: C:/Users/3665/AppData/Local/Programs/Python/Python38/list_slicing.py
[2, 3, 4]
[3, 4, 5]
[1, 2, 3]
[5, 4, 3, 2, 1]
>>>
```

Figure 4.18: List slicing

List methods

Lists provide several built-in methods for manipulating and working with lists. Some commonly used methods include **append()**, **remove()**, **pop()**, **sort()**, and **reverse()**:

```
my_list = [4, 2, 1, 3, 5]
my_list.append(6)          # Adding an element at the end
my_list.remove(2)          # Removing an element by value
popped_element = my_list
print(popped_element)
```

Take a look at the following figure illustrating the output:

```
= RESTART: C:/Users/3665/AppData/Local/Programs/Python/Python38/list_method.py =
[4, 1, 3, 5, 6]
>>>
```

Figure 4.19: List methods

One more example of modifying elements, add or remove elements is mentioned below:

```
# To-Do List
todo_list = ["Buy groceries", "Read a book", "Exercise"]
# Adding a task
todo_list.append("Finish homework")
# Removing a task
todo_list.remove("Read a book")
print(todo_list)
# Output: ['Buy groceries', 'Exercise', 'Finish homework']
```

Tuples

Tuples are ordered, immutable collections of elements. Like lists, tuples can contain elements of different data types and allow duplicates. Tuples are defined using parentheses

() or simply by separating elements with commas. You can access elements using indexing but cannot modify them. Tuples are often used for grouping related data.

Creating a tuple

Tuples can be created by enclosing elements within parentheses or by separating them with commas, as demonstrate below:

```
my_tuple = (1, 2, 3, "apple", "banana")
print(my_tuple[0])   # Output: 1
```

Take a look at the following figure illustrating the output:

```
= RESTART: C:/Users/3665/AppData/Local/Programs/Python/Python38/tuple_creation.py
1
>>>
```

Figure 4.20: Tuple creation

Accessing elements

You can access individual elements of a tuple using indexing, similar to lists, as shown below:

```
my_tuple = (1, 2, 3, "apple", "banana")
print(my_tuple[0])     # Output: 1
print(my_tuple[3])     # Output: "apple"
print(my_tuple[-1])    # Output: "banana" (negative indexing)
```

Take a look at the following figure illustrating the output:

```
= RESTART: C:/Users/3665/AppData/Local/Programs/Python/Python38/tuple_accessing_element.py
1
apple
banana
>>>
```

Figure 4.21: Accessing elements of tuple

Tuple length

You can find the length of a tuple using the `len()` function, just like with lists, as shown below:

```
my_tuple = (1, 2, 3, "apple", "banana")
print(len(my_tuple))    # Output: 5
```

Take a look at the following figure illustrating the output:

```
= RESTART: C:/Users/3665/AppData/Local/Programs/Python/Python38/tuple_length.py
5
>>>
```

Figure 4.22: Tuple length

Tuple packing and unpacking

Tuple packing is the process of combining multiple values into a single tuple. Tuple unpacking allows you to assign values from a tuple to multiple variables simultaneously, as shown below:

```
# Tuple packing
my_tuple = 1, 2, 3
print(my_tuple)         # Output: (1, 2, 3)
# Tuple unpacking
a, b, c = my_tuple
print(a, b, c)          # Output: 1 2 3
```

Take a look at the following figure illustrating the output:

```
= RESTART: C:/Users/3665/AppData/Local/Programs/Python/Python38/tuple_packing_un
packing.py
(1, 2, 3)
1 2 3
>>>
```

Figure 4.23: Tuple packing and unpacking

Immutable nature

Tuples are immutable, so you cannot modify their elements or reassign values to indices.

The advantages of tuples are mentioned below:

- Tuples are often used to represent collections of related values.
- Tuples can be used as keys in dictionaries, while lists cannot.
- Tuples are commonly used in functions to return multiple values.

Tuples are useful when you want to store a collection of values that should not be modified. They are frequently used in scenarios where immutability and integrity of data are desired, such as representing coordinates, dates, or configuration settings.

Sets

Sets are unordered collections of unique elements. Sets do not allow duplicates and do not maintain the order of elements. Sets are defined using curly braces **{}** or by using the **set()** function. Sets support mathematical set operations like union, intersection, and difference. Refer to the following example for a better understanding:

```
my_set = {1, 2, 3, 4, 4}
print(my_set)   # Output: {1, 2, 3, 4}
my_set.add(5)
my_set.remove(2)
print(my_set)
```

Take a look at the following figure illustrating the output:

```
= RESTART: C:/Users/3665/AppData/Local/Programs/Python/Python38/set_creation.py
{1, 2, 3, 4}
{1, 3, 4, 5}
>>>
```

Figure 4.24: Sets creation

Dictionaries

Dictionaries are key-value pairs, where each key is unique and associated with a value. Dictionaries are mutable and unordered. They are defined using curly braces **{}** with key-value pairs separated by colons **:**. You can access values by using keys, modify values, add or remove key-value pairs, and perform various dictionary operations. A nested dictionary in Python is a dictionary that contains other dictionaries as values. This structure is useful for representing complex data models, like JSON objects or hierarchical data, as demonstrated below:

```
my_dict = {"name": "Alice", "age": 30, "city": "London"}
print(my_dict["name"])   # Output: "Alice"
my_dict["age"] = 31
my_dict["country"] = "UK"
print(my_dict)
```

Take a look at the following figure illustrating the output:

```
= RESTART: C:/Users/3665/AppData/Local/Programs/Python/Python38/dictionay_creati
on.py
Alice
{'name': 'Alice', 'age': 31, 'city': 'London', 'country': 'UK'}
>>>
```

Figure 4.25: Dictionary creation

Strings

Though not a data structure in the traditional sense, strings are sequences of characters and are commonly used to store and manipulate textual data. Strings are immutable, meaning they cannot be modified once created. They support various string operations like concatenation, slicing, and formatting, as demonstrated below:

```
my_string = "Hello, World!"
print(my_string[0])        # Output: "H"
print(my_string[7:12])     # Output: "World"
new_string = my_string.upper()
print(new_string)
```

Take a look at the following figure illustrating the output:

```
== RESTART: C:/Users/3665/AppData/Local/Programs/Python/Python38/string_eg.py ==
H
World
HELLO, WORLD!
>>>
```

Figure 4.26: *String creation*

These are some of the fundamental data structures available in Python. They provide flexibility and efficiency in handling different types of data and performing operations on them. Python also provides additional data structures through built-in modules and libraries, such as arrays, deque, and heaps, which offer more specialized functionalities.

Modular programming

Modular programming in Python refers to the practice of breaking down a program into smaller, self-contained modules or functions that perform specific tasks. These modules can be developed and tested independently, making the code more organized, reusable, and easier to understand and maintain.

Here are some key concepts and techniques related to modular programming in Python:

- **Functions**: Functions are a fundamental unit of modularity in Python. They allow you to encapsulate a specific set of instructions into a named block of code that can be called and reused whenever needed. Functions promote code reusability and help in dividing the program logic into manageable parts.
- **Modules**: A module is a Python file that contains a collection of functions, classes, and variables. It serves as a container for related code. By organizing code into modules, you can group related functionality together and access it from other parts of your program using import statements.

- **Packages**: Packages are a way to organize related modules into a directory hierarchy. They provide a hierarchical structure to the modules in your project, making it easier to manage and reuse code across multiple files and directories.
- **Encapsulation**: Encapsulation is a concept that allows you to hide the internal details of a module or function and expose only the necessary interfaces or public functions. This helps in abstracting the complexity and providing a clean and concise interface for other parts of the program to interact with.
- **Separation of concerns**: Modular programming promotes the separation of concerns, where different aspects of the program's functionality are handled by separate modules. Each module focuses on a specific task, making the codebase easier to understand, test, and maintain.
- **Code reusability**: By dividing your program into smaller modules, you create reusable components that can be utilized in different parts of your application or even in other projects. This saves development time and effort, as you can leverage existing modules instead of rewriting code from scratch.
- **Testing and debugging**: Modular programming facilitates easier testing and debugging since modules can be isolated and tested individually. This makes it simpler to identify and fix issues within specific components of the program.

In order to practice modular programming in Python, start by identifying different logical components or tasks within your program. Then, create separate functions or modules for each task, ensuring they have well-defined inputs, outputs, and interfaces. Finally, organize your modules into packages and use import statements to access and utilize the functionality across your program.

By following modular programming principles, you can improve code structure, readability, reusability, and maintainability, making your Python projects more efficient and scalable.

Examples of modular programming in Python

Let us say you want to create a program that calculates the area and circumference of a circle. You can break down the functionality into separate modules, as shown below:

- **circle.py**: This module contains functions related to circle calculations. Refer to the following example for a better understanding:

```
import math
def calculate_area(radius):
    return math.pi * radius ** 2
def calculate_circumference(radius):
    return 2 * math.pi * radius
```

- **main.py**: This is the main program module where you use the functions from the **circle.py** module, as depicted below:

```python
import circle
def main():
    radius = float(input("Enter the radius of the circle: "))
    area = circle.calculate_area(radius)
    circumference = circle.calculate_circumference(radius)
    print(f"The area of the circle is: {area}")
    print(f"The circumference of the circle is: {circumference}")
if __name__ == '__main__':
    main()
```

Take a look at the following figure illustrating the output:

```
===== RESTART: C:\Users\3665\AppData\Local\Programs\Python\Python38\main.py ====
Enter the radius of the circle: 2
The area of the circle is: 12.566370614359172
The circumference of the circle is: 12.566370614359172
>>>
```

Figure 4.27: Modular programming

Functions

In the example above, the **circle.py** module contains the functions **calculate_area()** and **calculate_circumference()** which handle the calculations for the area and circumference of a circle, respectively.

The **main.py** module imports the circle module and uses its functions to perform the calculations. The **main()** function prompts the user for the radius, calls the appropriate functions from the circle module, and displays the results.

By separating the circle calculations into a separate module, you can reuse the **circle.py** module in other programs or expand it with additional functionality without modifying the main program logic.

This is a basic example, but modular programming becomes even more powerful as programs grow larger and more complex. It allows for better code organization, reusability, and easier maintenance and debugging.

Let us create a module called math_operations.py that contains some basic mathematical operations:

```python
def add(a, b):
    return a + b
```

```
def subtract(a, b):
    return a - b

def multiply(a, b):
    return a * b

def divide(a, b):
    if b != 0:
        return a / b
    else:
        print("Error: Division by zero")
```

In the example above, the **math_operations.py** module defines four functions: **add()**, **subtract()**, **multiply()**, and **divide()**. Each function performs a specific mathematical operation on the given input values.

Now, let us create a separate Python script called **main.py** that uses the functions from the **math_operations** module:

```
import math_operations

a = 10
b = 5
sum_result = math_operations.add(a, b)
difference_result = math_operations.subtract(a, b)
product_result = math_operations.multiply(a, b)
quotient_result = math_operations.divide(a, b)

print(f"Sum: {sum_result}")
print(f"Difference: {difference_result}")
print(f"Product: {product_result}")
print(f"Quotient: {quotient_result}")
```

Take a look at the following figure illustrating the output:

```
==== RESTART: C:\Users\3665\AppData\Local\Programs\Python\Python38\main1.py ====
Sum: 15
Difference: 5
Product: 50
Quotient: 2.0
>>>
```

Figure 4.28: Functions

In the `main.py` script, we import the `math_operations` module. Then, we use the functions from the module to perform various mathematical operations on the variables **a** and **b**. The results are stored in separate variables and then printed to the console.

By creating a separate module for mathematical operations, we can easily reuse the functions in other scripts or projects without rewriting the code. This modular approach promotes code reusability, organization, and separation of concerns.

To run this example, you would save the `math_operations.py` module and `main.py` script in the same directory and execute `main.py`. You will see the results of the mathematical operations displayed in the console.

> Note: It is a good practice to include error handling in your functions, as demonstrated in the divide() function to handle potential exceptions and provide appropriate feedback or actions when necessary.

MODULES

Let us say you want to create a program that generates a random number and calculates its square root. You can utilize two built-in modules: **random** and **math**. Refer to the following example for a better understanding:

```
import random
import math
def generate_random_number():
    return random.randint(1, 100)
def calculate_square_root(number):
    return math.sqrt(number)
def main():
    random_number = generate_random_number()
    square_root = calculate_square_root(random_number)
    print(f"The random number is: {random_number}")
    print(f"The square root of the random number is: {square_root}")
if __name__ == '__main__':
    main()
```

PACKAGES

In the example above, the random module is imported to generate a random number using the `randint()` function. The math module is imported to calculate the square root using the `sqrt()` function.

The `generate_random_number()` function utilizes the `random.randint()` function to generate a random number between 1 and 100.

The **calculate_square_root()** function uses the **math.sqrt()** function to calculate the square root of a given number.

The **main()** function calls the **generate_random_number()** function to obtain a random number and then calls the **calculate_square_root()** function to calculate its square root. The results are then printed to the console.

By importing and utilizing modules, you can access various functionalities and libraries provided by Python or third-party developers. Modules allow you to organize and encapsulate related code, making your program more modular, reusable, and easier to maintain.

Here is an example of using packages in Python.

Imagine you want to create a program for basic mathematical operations and organize it into multiple modules within a package called **math_operations**. The package will contain two modules: basic and advanced. The basic module will handle simple arithmetic operations, while the advanced module will include more complex mathematical functions.

First, create a directory called math_operations, and within it, create two Python files, as shown below:

- **basic.py**: This module will handle basic arithmetic operations, as shown below:

    ```
    def add(a, b):
        return a + b

    def subtract(a, b):
        return a - b

    def multiply(a, b):
        return a * b

    def divide(a, b):
        if b != 0:
            return a / b
        else:
            print("Error: Division by zero")
    ```

- **advanced.py**: This module will handle advanced mathematical functions, as shown below:

    ```
    import math

    def power(base, exponent):
    ```

```
            return math.pow(base, exponent)

        def square_root(number):
            return math.sqrt(number)
```

Now, let us create a separate Python script called **main.py** to utilize the package and its modules, as shown below:

```
from math_operations import basic, advanced

a = 10
b = 5

sum_result = basic.add(a, b)
difference_result = basic.subtract(a, b)
product_result = basic.multiply(a, b)
quotient_result = basic.divide(a, b)

power_result = advanced.power(a, b)
square_root_result = advanced.square_root(a)

print(f"Sum: {sum_result}")
print(f"Difference: {difference_result}")
print(f"Product: {product_result}")
print(f"Quotient: {quotient_result}")
print(f"Power: {power_result}")
print(f"Square Root: {square_root_result}")
```

Take a look at the following figure illustrating the output:

```
= RESTART: C:\Users\3665\AppData\Local\Programs\Python\Python38\math_operation\m
ain2.py
Sum: 15
Difference: 5
Product: 50
Quotient: 2.0
Power: 100000.0
Square Root: 3.1622776601683795
>>>
```

Figure 4.29: Package

In the `main.py` script, we import the modules basic and advanced from the `math_operations` package. We use the functions from these modules to perform various mathematical operations.

By organizing the modules within a package, we can easily access and use their functions in other scripts or projects. This modular approach promotes code reusability, separation of concerns, and a clean project structure.

To run this example, save the `math_operations` package (directory) and the `main.py` script in the same directory. Execute `main.py`, and you will see the results of the mathematical operations displayed in the console.

> Note: Make sure to have an empty __init__.py file inside the math_operations directory. This file is necessary to mark the directory as a Python package.

Conclusion

It is important to recognize that string manipulation and modular programming are not isolated skills; they are essential threads woven into the fabric of programming proficiency. Data structures form the backbone of effective and efficient programming in Python. They provide the tools to organize, manage, and manipulate data, enabling us to tackle a wide range of problems with clarity and precision.

Join our book's Discord space

Join the book's Discord Workspace for Latest updates, Offers, Tech happenings around the world, New Release and Sessions with the Authors:

https://discord.bpbonline.com

CHAPTER 5
File Handling and Object Oriented Concepts

Introduction

File handling in Python refers to the ability to work with files, both for reading from and writing to them. Files are a fundamental part of data processing and storage in programming. Python provides a straightforward and powerful way to interact with files, making it easy to manipulate data stored in various formats.

Here is an introduction to file handling in Python.

Structure

- Opening files
- Introduction to working with directories
- Object-oriented programming concepts
- Classes in Python
- Inheritance
- Polymorphism

Objectives

Files and **object-oriented programming** (**OOP**) are two fundamental aspects of Python programming that play distinct but complementary roles in software development. Let us explore the roles of files and OOP in Python:

Opening files

In order to work with a file, you need to open it first using the **open()** function. This function takes two arguments: the file path and the mode (read, write, append, etc.). For example:

```
file = open("example.txt", "r")   # Opens the file for reading
```

Common file modes include:

- **"r"**: Read (default mode).
- **"w"**: Write (creates a new file or truncates an existing file).
- **"a"**: Append (appends to an existing file).
- **"b"**: Binary mode (e.g., **"rb"** for reading a binary file).

Reading from files:

You can read data from files using methods like **read()**, **readline()**, or **readlines()**, as shown below:

```
content = file.read()       # Reads the entire file
line = file.readline()      # Reads one line at a time
lines = file.readlines()    # Reads all lines into a list
```

Writing to files:

To write data to a file, open it in write mode and use methods like **write()** or **writelines()**, as shown below:

```
with open("example.txt", "w") as file:
    file.write("Hello, World!\n")
    file.writelines(["Line 1\n", "Line 2\n"])
```

The with statement ensures that the file is properly closed after writing.

Appending to files:

In order to append data to an existing file, open it in append mode and use the **write()** method, as shown below:

```
with open("example.txt", "a") as file:
    file.write("New data\n")
```

Closing files:

It is essential to close files properly using the **close()** method when you are done with them. However, using a with statement (context manager) is recommended because it automatically closes the file when you exit the block.

Checking file existence:

You can use the os.path module to check if a file exists before trying to open it, as shown below:

```
import os
if os.path.exists("example.txt"):
    # File exists, do something
```

File iteration:

You can iterate through a file line by line using a for loop, as shown below:

```
with open("example.txt", "r") as file:
    for line in file:
        print(line)
```

Working with binary files:

In order to work with binary files (e.g., images), use binary file modes and read/write bytes instead of text, as shown below:

```
with open("image.jpg", "rb") as binary_file:
    image_data = binary_file.read()
```

File handling in Python is a crucial skill for tasks such as data processing, log file analysis, configuration file management, and more. Properly handling files includes closing them when done, handling exceptions, and following best practices for reading and writing data to and from files.

Here are examples of reading from and writing to a text file in Python:

```
with open("example.txt", "r") as file:
    Content=file.read()
print(Content)
```

Reading from a text file:

Hello, World!

This is a sample text file.

Python is awesome!

Suppose you have a text file named **"example.txt"** with the following content:

Take a look at the following figure illustrating the output:

```
= RESTART: C:/Users/3665/AppData/Local/Programs/Python/Python38/example_file.py
Hello, World!
This is a sample text file.
Python is awesome!

>>> |
```

Figure 5.1: Reading from text file

Handling different types of files in Python

Python provides a versatile set of libraries and modules to handle different types of files, including text, binary, CSV, JSON, XML, and more. Here is an overview of how to handle various file types in Python:

Python can handle various types of files based on their content and format. Here is a list of common file types that Python can work with:

- **Text files**: These files contain plain text data and are typically encoded in formats like ASCII or UTF-8. Python can easily read and write text files using built-in methods.

- **Binary files**: Binary files contain data in a format that is not human-readable, such as images, audio files, or executables. Python can read and write binary files using binary read and write modes.

- **CSV files**: **Comma-separated values** (CSV) files store tabular data with rows and columns. Python's `csv` module is used to read and write CSV files.

- **JSON files**: JavaScript Object Notation (JSON) files store structured data in a human-readable format. Python's `json` module is used to work with JSON files.

- **XML files**: eXtensible Markup Language (XML) files store structured data using tags. Python can parse and create XML files using libraries like `xml.etree.ElementTree` or third-party libraries like `lxml`.

- **Excel files**: Excel files store tabular data with formatting and formulas. Python can work with Excel files using libraries like `openpyxl` or `pandas`.

- **HTML files**: Hypertext Markup Language (HTML) files are used for web page content. Python can parse and manipulate HTML using libraries like `BeautifulSoup` or `lxml`.

- **YAML files**: YAML Ain't Markup Language (YAML) files are used for configuration and data serialization. Python can work with YAML files using the PyYAML library.

- **PDF files**: **Portable Document Format (PDF)** files contain documents that can include text, images, and formatting. Python can read and manipulate PDF files using libraries like `PyPDF2` or `pdfplumber`.
- **Image files**: Python can work with various image formats (e.g., JPG, PNG, GIF) using libraries like PIL (Pillow) for image manipulation.
- **SQLite databases**: SQLite is a self-contained, serverless, and zero-configuration SQL database engine. Python includes the `sqlite3` module for working with SQLite databases.
- **Log files**: Log files store records of events or messages generated by software applications. Python can parse and analyze log files to extract useful information.
- **Configuration files**: Configuration files (e.g., INI files, YAML files) store settings and configurations for applications. Python can read and modify these files to manage application settings.
- **Compressed files**: Python can work with compressed files such as ZIP or GZIP files using libraries like `zipfile` or `gzip`.
- **Binary data files**: These files store binary data in custom or proprietary formats. Python can read and write such files based on their specifications.
- **Shapefiles**: Shapefiles are a geospatial vector data format used in **geographic information system (GIS)** applications. Python can work with shapefiles using libraries like `geopandas`.
- **Audio files**: Python can work with audio files in various formats (e.g., MP3, WAV) using libraries like `pydub` or `librosa` for audio processing.

These are just some of the many file types that Python can handle. Python's versatility and the availability of numerous libraries make it a powerful language for working with a wide range of data and file formats.

Binary files

Binary files contain non-textual data, such as images, videos, audio, and other binary formats. Python provides several ways to work with binary files, allowing you to read, write, and manipulate their contents. Here are the basic operations for working with binary files in Python:

Opening binary files

You can open a binary file using Python's built-in `open()` function by specifying the file mode as `'rb'` for reading or `'wb'` for writing in binary mode. Use `'rb+'` for both reading and writing.

Reading from a binary file, an example is shown below:
:
```
# Opening a binary file for reading
with open('binary_file.bin', 'rb') as file:
    binary_data = file.read()
# Process binary_data as needed
```

Writing to a binary file, an example is shown below:
```
# Opening a binary file for writing
with open('binary_file.bin', 'wb') as file:
    binary_data = b'\x01\x02\x03\x04\x05'  # Example binary data
    file.write(binary_data)
```

Reading binary data

When reading from a binary file, you can use the **read()** method to read a specified number of bytes from the file. If you omit the argument, it reads the entire file, an example is shown below:

```
with open('binary_file.bin', 'rb') as file:
    binary_data = file.read(4)  # Read the first 4 bytes
    # Process binary_data
```

You can also read the file line by line, as you would with text files, using a for loop.

Writing binary data

When writing to a binary file, you can use the **write()** method to write binary data to the file.

```
with open('binary_file.bin', 'wb') as file:
    binary_data = b'\x01\x02\x03\x04\x05'  # Example binary data
    file.write(binary_data)
```

Seeking and position

You can use the **seek()** method to change the file position within a binary file. This is useful when you need to read or write data at specific positions within the file.

```
with open('binary_file.bin', 'rb') as file:
    file.seek(2)  # Set the file position to the third byte
    binary_data = file.read(4)  # Read 4 bytes starting from the third byte
```

Closing files

It is essential to close binary files properly using the with statement or explicitly calling the **close()** method to free up system resources when you are done with them.

```
with open('binary_file.bin', 'rb') as file:
    # Process binary_data
# File is automatically closed when exiting the 'with' block
```

Working with binary files in Python is crucial for tasks like reading and writing images, videos, audio, and other non-textual data. Make sure to handle exceptions and errors appropriately when working with binary files to ensure the integrity of your data and the reliability of your code.

Comma-separated values files

CSV files are a common and straightforward way to store structured data, such as tables, in a plain text format. Python provides built-in libraries for reading and writing CSV files, making it easy to work with tabular data. Here is how to work with CSV files in Python:

Reading CSV files

You can use the CSV module in Python to read data from CSV files. Here is a basic example:

```
import csv
# Open the CSV file for reading
with open('data.csv', mode='r') as file:
    # Create a CSV reader object
    csv_reader = csv.reader(file)
    # Iterate through each row in the CSV file
    for row in csv_reader:
        # Each row is a list of values
        print(row)
```

This code will read the contents of the **`data.csv`** file and print each row as a list of values.

Reading CSV files with headers:

If your CSV file has headers (column names), you can use the **csv.DictReader** class to read the data into dictionaries, where the keys are the header names:

```
import csv
# Open the CSV file for reading
with open('data_with_headers.csv', mode='r') as file:
    # Create a CSV reader object
    csv_reader = csv.DictReader(file)
    # Iterate through each row in the CSV file
    for row in csv_reader:
```

```
    # Each row is a dictionary
    print(row['Name'], row['Age'])
```

Writing CSV files:

To write data to a CSV file, you can use the **csv.writer** class. Here is an example of writing data to a CSV file:

```
import csv
# Data to be written to the CSV file
data = [
    ['Name', 'Age'],
    ['Alice', 30],
    ['Bob', 25],
    ['Charlie', 35]
]


# Open the CSV file for writing
with open('output.csv', mode='w', newline='') as file:
    # Create a CSV writer object
    csv_writer = csv.writer(file)

    # Write the data to the CSV file
    csv_writer.writerows(data)
```

This code will create a CSV file named **'output.csv'** and write the data from the data list to it.

Writing CSV files with headers:

To write data to a CSV file with headers, you can use the **csv.DictWriter** class:

```
import csv

# Data to be written to the CSV file
data = [
    {'Name': 'Alice', 'Age': 30},
    {'Name': 'Bob', 'Age': 25},
    {'Name': 'Charlie', 'Age': 35}
]
# Open the CSV file for writing
with open('output_with_headers.csv', mode='w', newline='') as file:
```

```
    # Specify the fieldnames (headers)
    fieldnames = ['Name', 'Age']
    # Create a CSV writer object with headers
    csv_writer = csv.DictWriter(file, fieldnames=fieldnames)
    # Write the headers to the CSV file
    csv_writer.writeheader()
    # Write the data to the CSV file
    csv_writer.writerows(data)
```

This code will create a CSV file named **'output_with_headers.csv'** with headers and write the data to it.

The CSV module provides various options for handling different CSV formats and delimiters, making it a versatile tool for working with CSV files in Python.

FASTA File

FASTA (pronounced "fast-ay") is a common file format used to represent nucleotide and amino acid sequences in bioinformatics. Python provides libraries and tools to read, parse, and manipulate FASTA files. Here is how you can work with FASTA files in Python:

Reading FASTA files:

In order to read sequences from a FASTA file, you can use a simple custom parser or the Biopython library, which provides extensive functionality for bioinformatics tasks. Here is an example using the Biopython library:

Using Biopython:

First, you will need to install the Biopython library if you have not already, refer to the following example:

pip install biopython

Then, you can use Biopython to read FASTA files, as shown below:

```
from Bio import SeqIO

# Open the FASTA file for reading
with open('sequences.fasta', 'r') as file:
    # Parse the FASTA file
    sequences = SeqIO.parse(file, 'fasta')

    # Iterate through the sequences
    for record in sequences:
        # Access sequence information
```

```
        print("Sequence ID:", record.id)
        print("Sequence description:", record.description)
        print("Sequence length:", len(record))
        print("Sequence:", record.seq)
```

Custom parser:

If you prefer not to use external libraries, you can create a simple custom parser for FASTA files, as shown below:

```
# Open the FASTA file for reading
with open('sequences.fasta', 'r') as file:
    sequence = ''
    for line in file:
        if line.startswith('>'):
            if sequence:
                # Process the previous sequence
                print("Sequence:", sequence)
                sequence = ''
            header = line.strip()
            print("Sequence ID:", header)
        else:
            sequence += line.strip()

    # Process the last sequence in the file
    if sequence:
        print("Sequence:", sequence)
```

Writing FASTA files:

In order to write sequences to a FASTA file, you can use the Biopython library or create a custom writer. Here is an example using Biopython:

```
from Bio import SeqIO
# Sample sequence data
sequences = [
    {'id': 'seq1', 'description': 'First sequence', 'sequence': 'ATGCATGC'},
    {'id': 'seq2', 'description': 'Second sequence', 'sequence': 'GCTAGCTA'}
]
```

```
# Open the FASTA file for writing
with open('output.fasta', 'w') as file:
    # Create a list of SeqRecord objects
    records = [
        SeqIO.SeqRecord(seq, id=data['id'], description=data['description'])
        for data, seq in zip(sequences, ['ATGCATGC', 'GCTAGCTA'])
    ]

    # Write the records to the FASTA file
    SeqIO.write(records, file, 'fasta')
```

This code will create a FASTA file named **'output.fasta'** and write the sequences to it using Biopython.

Working with FASTA files is a fundamental part of many bioinformatics and genomics tasks, and Python libraries like Biopython make it easier to handle sequence data in these files.

Introduction to working with directories

Working with directories in Python is essential for managing files and organizing your data. Python provides built-in modules like **os** and **shutil** that make it easy to interact with directories. Here is an introduction to working with directories in Python:

- **Checking directory existence**: Refer to the following code for a better understanding:

    ```
    import os
    directory_name="my_directory"
    if os.path.exists(directory_name):
        print("The directory '(driect_name)' exists")
    else:
        print("The directory '(driect_name)' does not exists")
    ```

    You can check if a directory exists using the **os.path.exists()** function. For example:

Take a look at the following figure illustrating output:

```
=============================== RESTART: C:/Users/3665/AppData/Local/Programs/Python/Python38/example_file3.py
The directory '(driect_name)' does not exists
>>>
```

Figure 5.2: Reading from text file

- **Creating directories**: You can create directories using **os.makedirs()**. This function can create multiple nested directories at once:

    import os

    directory_name="my_new_directory"

    os.makedirs(directory_name)

    Output:

    Directory will be created with my_new_drectory name

- **Listing directory contents**: To list the files and subdirectories within a directory, you can use **os.listdir()**, for example:

    import os

    directory_name="my_new_directory"

    if os.path.exists(directory_name):

        contents=os.listdir(directory_name)

        for item in contents:

            print(item)

The following figure is illustrating the output:

```
= RESTART: C:/Users/3665/AppData/Local/Programs/Python/Python38/example_file4.py
dictionary_creation.png
functions.png
list_creation.png
list_length.png
list_method.png
list_modify.png
list_slicing.png
modulary_prog.png
package.png
sets_creation.png
slicing_start.png
slicing_with_negative.png
string_example.png
str_concat.png
str_creation.png
str_length.png
str_lower.png
str_slicing.png
str_slic_end.png
str_strip.png
str_upper.png
tuple_accessing_element.png
tuple_creation.png
tuple_length.png
tuple_pack_unpack.png
>>>
```

Figure 5.3: Listing directory contents

- **Changing the current directory**: You can change the current working directory using **os.chdir()**. This is useful when you want to work within a specific directory, the code is shown below:

    import os

    new_directory="my_new_directory"

    os.chdir(new_directory)

- **Renaming and moving directories**: You can rename directories using **os.rename()** and move them using **shutil.move()**, the code is shown below:

    import os

    import shutil

    old_directory="old_name"

    new_directory="new_name"

    if os.path.exists(old_directory):

    os.rename(old_directory,new_directory)

- **Removing directories**: To remove directories, you can use **os.rmdir()** to remove an empty directory or **shutil.rmtree()** to remove a directory and its contents, the code is shown below:

    import os

    import shutil

    directory_to_remove="directory_to_remove"

    if os.path.exists(directory_to_remove):

       os.rmdir(directory_to_remove)

    Output:

    Remove a directory and its contents

Working with directories in Python is crucial for various file management tasks, including data processing, file organization, and project management. These directory-related functions allow you to efficiently navigate, create, rename, and remove directories as needed within your Python scripts and applications.

Object-oriented programming concepts

OOP is a programming paradigm that is widely used in Python. OOP is based on the concept of objects, which are instances of classes, and it allows you to structure your code in a way that models real-world entities and their interactions. Python supports all the fundamental OOP concepts, which include:

- **Class**: A class is a blueprint or template for creating objects. It defines the attributes (data) and methods (functions) that the objects of the class will have. Classes are defined using the class keyword.

- **Object**: An object is an instance of a class. It represents a real-world entity with data (attributes) and behaviors (methods). You create objects from classes.

- **Attributes**: They are data members or properties of a class. They represent the characteristics or state of objects. Attributes are defined in the class constructor (__init__ method).

- **Methods**: They are functions defined within a class. They represent the behaviors or actions that objects can perform. Methods take the self-parameter, which refers to the instance of the class.

- **Inheritance**: It is a mechanism that allows you to create a new class (subclass or derived class) based on an existing class (base class or superclass). The subclass inherits attributes and methods from the superclass and can also override or extend them.

- **Encapsulation**: It is the concept of bundling data (attributes) and methods that operate on that data within a class. It restricts direct access to an object's internal data and provides methods for interaction.

- **Polymorphism**: This allows objects of different classes to be treated as objects of a common base class. This simplifies code by enabling you to work with objects at a higher level of abstraction.

- **Abstraction**: It is the process of simplifying complex systems by breaking them into smaller, more manageable parts. It focuses on exposing the essential features of an object while hiding the unnecessary details.

These OOP concepts in Python help you organize code, create reusable and maintainable software, and model real-world systems in a structured manner. Python's support for OOP makes it a versatile and powerful language for a wide range of applications.

Classes in Python

In Python, a class is a blueprint or template for creating objects. A class defines the attributes (data) and methods (functions) that objects created from the class will have. Classes are a fundamental concept in OOP, and they allow you to model real-world entities and their behaviors in your code.

Here is a basic overview of how to define and use classes in Python:

Defining a class

To define a class in Python, you use the **class** keyword followed by the class name. Class names conventionally use CamelCase (e.g., **MyClass**, **Person**, **Car**). Inside the class, you define attributes and methods.

```python
class MyClass:
    # Class attributes (shared among all instances)
    class_attribute = "I am a class attribute"
    # Constructor (initializer) method
    def __init__(self, attribute1, attribute2):
        # Instance attributes (unique to each instance)
        self.attribute1 = attribute1
        self.attribute2 = attribute2
    # Instance method
    def instance_method(self):
        return f"Instance method called with {self.attribute1} and {self.attribute2}"
    # Class method (works with class-level data)
    @classmethod
    def class_method(cls):
        return f"Class method called with {cls.class_attribute}"
    # Static method (independent of instance or class)
    @staticmethod
    def static_method():
        return "Static method called"
```

Creating objects (Instances):

Once a class is defined, you can create objects (instances) of that class using the class name followed by parentheses.

```python
# Creating instances of MyClass
obj1 = MyClass("value1", "value2")
obj2 = MyClass("value3", "value4")
```

Accessing attributes and methods:

You can access the attributes and methods of an object using dot notation.

```python
# Accessing attributes
print(obj1.attribute1)  # Output: "value1"
print(obj2.attribute2)  # Output: "value4"
```

```python
# Calling instance methods
result = obj1.instance_method()
print(result)  # Output: "Instance method called with value1 and value2"
# Calling class methods
class_result = MyClass.class_method()
print(class_result)  # Output: "Class method called with I am a class attribute"
# Calling static methods
static_result = MyClass.static_method()
print(static_result)  # Output: "Static method called"
```

This example demonstrates the fundamental concepts of defining a class, creating instances, and working with attributes and methods in Python classes.

In this example:

- We define a class named **Person** with a constructor (**__init__**) that initializes instance attributes **name** and **age**.
- The introduced method is an instance method that returns a string introducing the person.
- We create two instances (**person1** and **person2**) of the **Person** class with different attributes.
- We access the instance attributes (name and age) and call the introduce method on each instance to retrieve personalized introductions. The code is shown below:

```python
class Person:
    # Constructor method (initializer)
    def __init__(self, name, age):
        # Instance attributes
        self.name = name
        self.age = age
    # Instance method
    def introduce(self):
        return f"My name is {self.name} and I am {self.age} years old."
# Creating instances of the Person class
person1 = Person("Alice", 30)
person2 = Person("Bob", 25)
# Accessing instance attributes
```

```
    print(person1.name)    # Output: "Alice"
    print(person2.age)     # Output: 25

    # Calling instance method
    introduction1 = person1.introduce()
    introduction2 = person2.introduce()
    print(introduction1)   # Output: "My name is Alice and I am 30 years old."
    print(introduction2)   # Output: "My name is Bob and I am 25 years old."
```

Output:

Take a look at the following figure illustrating output:

```
=========== RESTART: C:\Users\3665\AppData\Local\Programs\Python\Python38\class_example.py ===========
Alice
25
My name is Alice and I am 30 years old.
My name is Bob and I am 25 years old.
>>>
```

Figure 5.4: Creation of class and objects

Inheritance

Inheritance is a fundamental concept in OOP that allows you to create a new class (called a **subclass** or **derived class**) by inheriting properties and behaviors from an existing class (called a superclass or base class). In Python, inheritance is supported, and it allows you to build new classes based on the characteristics of existing ones. Here's an overview of inheritance in Python:

Syntax of inheritance:

To create a subclass that inherits from a superclass, you define the subclass with the superclass name in parentheses. The subclass can then inherit attributes and methods from the superclass. Here is the syntax:

`class Superclass: # Attributes and methods of the superclass class Subclass(Superclass): # Attributes and methods specific to the subclass`

Example of inheritance:

Let us illustrate inheritance with an example using an `Animal` superclass and `Dog` and `Cat` subclasses:

In this example:

- **Animal** is the superclass, defining attributes and methods common to all animals.

- **Dog** and **Cat** are subclasses of **Animal**, inheriting the name and species attributes from the superclass.

- Both **Dog** and **Cat** override the **speak** method inherited from **Animal** to provide their own implementations. The code is shown below:

```
class Animal:
    def __init__(self, name, species):
        self.name = name
        self.species = species
    def speak(self):
        pass  # This method is overridden in subclasses
class Dog(Animal):
    def speak(self):
        return f"{self.name} says Woof!"
class Cat(Animal):
    def speak(self):
        return f"{self.name} says Meow!"
# Creating instances of subclasses
dog = Dog("Buddy", "Dog")
cat = Cat("Whiskers", "Cat")
# Calling the overridden method
print(dog.speak())  # Output: "Buddy says Woof!"
print(cat.speak())  # Output: "Whiskers says Meow!"
```

Output:

Take a look at the following figure, it illustrates the output:

```
=========== RESTART: C:\Users\3665\AppData\Local\Programs\Python\Python38\inheritance.py ============
Buddy says Woof!
Whiskers says Meow!
>>>
```

Figure 5.5: Inheritance

The benefits of inheritance are mentioned below:

- **Code reusability**: Inheritance allows you to reuse code from existing classes, reducing duplication and promoting a more efficient codebase.

- **Polymorphism**: Inheritance enables polymorphism, where objects of different subclasses can be treated as objects of the superclass. This simplifies code and promotes flexibility.

- **Hierarchy**: You can create class hierarchies that represent real-world relationships, making code more intuitive and easier to understand.

- **Modification**: You can modify and extend the behavior of existing classes without altering their original code. This promotes maintainability.

- **Specialization**: Subclasses can specialize in specific behaviors while inheriting general characteristics from the superclass.

In Python, multiple inheritance is also supported, allowing a subclass to inherit from multiple superclasses. However, it should be used with caution, as it can lead to complex class hierarchies and potential issues.

Inheritance is a powerful concept that helps structure code in a way that models relationships between objects and promotes code reuse and flexibility.

Polymorphism

Polymorphism is a fundamental concept in OOP that allows objects of different classes to be treated as objects of a common base class. It enables you to write code that can work with objects of different types in a uniform way. In Python, polymorphism is achieved through method overriding and duck typing. Here is how polymorphism works in Python:

Method overriding:

Method overriding is a way to provide a specific implementation of a method in a subclass that is already defined in the superclass. When a method is called on an object, Python looks for the method in the object's class. If it is not found, Python searches for it in the superclass, and so on, up the class hierarchy.

Here is an example of method overriding:

```
class Animal:
    def speak(self):
        pass
class Dog(Animal):
    def speak(self):
        return "Woof!"
class Cat(Animal):
    def speak(self):
        return "Meow!"
# Using polymorphism
def make_animal_speak(animal):
    return animal.speak()
dog = Dog()
```

```
cat = Cat()
print(make_animal_speak(dog))   # Output: "Woof!"
print(make_animal_speak(cat))   # Output: "Meow!"
```

Output:

Take a look at the following figure, which illustrates the output:

```
============= RESTART: C:\Users\3665\AppData\Local\Programs\Python\Python38\polymorph.py =============
Woof!
Meow!
>>>
```

Figure 5.6: Polymorphism

In this example, both **Dog** and **Cat** classes have a **speak** method that overrides the method defined in the **Animal** superclass. The **make_animal_speak** function takes an object of type **Animal** and calls it **speak** method. When we pass a **Dog** or **Cat** object to the function, it invokes the appropriate **speak** method based on the object's actual type, demonstrating polymorphism.

Duck typing:

Python follows the principle of duck typing, which means that the type or class of an object is determined by its behavior rather than its explicit type. If an object behaves like a particular type, it is treated as an instance of that type. This allows for flexible and dynamic polymorphism without the need for explicit type declarations.

Here is a simple example illustrating duck typing:

```
class Duck:
    def sound(self):
        return "Quack!"
class Dog:
    def sound(self):
        return "Woof!"
# Using duck typing and polymorphism
def make_sound(animal):
    return animal.sound()
duck = Duck()
dog = Dog()
print(make_sound(duck))   # Output: "Quack!"
print(make_sound(dog))    # Output: "Woof!"
```

Output:

Take a look at the following figure, which illustrates the output:

```
============ RESTART: C:\Users\3665\AppData\Local\Programs\Python\Python38\duck_poly.py ============
Quack!
Woof!
>>> 
```

Figure 5.7: Duck_Typing

In this example, both **Duck** and **Dog** classes have a **sound** method, and the **make_sound** function works with objects of any class that provides a **sound** method.

Polymorphism in Python allows you to write more generic and reusable code, as you can work with objects based on their behaviors rather than their specific types. It promotes flexibility and ease of extension in your programs.

Conclusion

Files and OOP are two essential aspects of Python programming. While they may seem unrelated, you can effectively combine them to create OOPs that involve reading from and writing to files. Combining file handling and OOP in Python can result in clean and structured code that is easier to maintain and extend, especially in applications that involve working with various types of files and data.

Join our book's Discord space

Join the book's Discord Workspace for Latest updates, Offers, Tech happenings around the world, New Release and Sessions with the Authors:

https://discord.bpbonline.com

CHAPTER 6
Basic Concept of Biopython Module

Introduction

Biopython is one of the most popular modules of Python. The module further has many sub-modules that are used for various bioinformatics applications. Biopython is developed by *Chapman* and *Chang*. It also consists of C code which is used for the optimization of complex software problems. It is platform-independent and runs on the following platforms Windows, Linux, Mac OS, etc. It provides standard ways of accessing bioinformatics resources. It provides reusable modules and faster manipulation of arrays which can be used in clustering and other similar applications. It requires less code for complex computations and can read/write complex types of data from the files. It supports the processing of structured data like PDB files and supports the BioSQL database used popularly for many Bioinformatics applications. Biopython also facilitates genomic analysis.

The Biopython module provides various functions that are used for processing DNA, RNA, and protein sequences, like finding a complement, translation, and transcription as well. Biopython also provides parsers that may be used for parsing genetic databases like – SwissProt, GenBank, FASTA, etc.

Structure

The chapter covers the following topics:
- How to install Biopython

- Sequence object in Biopython
- Sequence working as a string
- Sequence object operations
- Mutable sequence
- SequenceRecord object
- Sequence input-output module
- Accessing sequences from FASTA and GenBank

Objectives

The objective of the chapter is to introduce the reader to the working of the Biopython module. Detailed knowledge of the objects of the Biopython module is covered in the chapter. Sequences play an important role in Bioinformatics. The Biopython module provides all the basic functionalities required to handle protein or nucleotide sequences.

How to install Biopython

You must follow the following steps to download and install Biopython:

The first step is to download the latest version of Biopython from the following URL:

https://biopython.org/wiki/Download

Do check the presence of a Python package management tool named **pip** in your system. This tool helps you to install any package by simple commands from the command prompt itself. You may install Biopython by using this command at the command prompt:

`pip install biopython`

In case you have an old version of Biopython, and you wish to upgrade it, then you may use the following command. It will remove older versions of **biopython** and **numpy** and install the latest version:

`pip install biopython -upgrade`

How Biopython works

To start working with Biopython we need to import the **Bio** module:

`>> import Bio`

If the statement does not give any error, it means that Biopython is installed successfully. When we use Biopython, we majorly focus on sequences like DNA, RNA, or protein sequence. To handle these Sequences, we can create them normally as string variables. However, the better option is to make use of the sequence object of the Biopython module.

Sequence object in Biopython

The sequence is the core of any Bioinformatics application. Various types of sequences are created using the Bioinformatics module. The sequence is a set of letters that is used to represent an organism's DNA, RNA, or protein sequence.

Sequence object allows you to perform any operation of string handling on it. Sequence objects may perform various functions like finding a complement, **reverse_complement**, translation, and transcription using built-in functions. Handling sequence objects with reading/writing in files is quite easier as compared with normal strings. Hence, it is always advisable to use biological sequences in bioinformatics applications by making use of a sequence object rather than a normal string.

We can create a simple sequence object by importing the **Bio.Seq** object. Here is the example to demonstrate the same in *Figure 6.1*:

```
Python 3.8.6 (tags/v3.8.6:db45529, Sep 23 2020, 15:52:53) [MSC v.1927 64 bit (AMD64)] on win32
Type "help", "copyright", "credits" or "license()" for more information.
>>> from Bio.Seq import Seq
>>> dna_seq=Seq("AAGGTTCC")
>>> dna_seq
Seq('AAGGTTCC')
>>> print(dna_seq)
AAGGTTCC
>>>
```

Figure 6.1: Creating simple sequence object

Sequence working as a string

Sequences represent a biological sequence object but they do perform all functions similar to string, as mentioned below:

- **Finding the length of the sequence**: The length of the sequence can be calculated using the **len()** function, as demonstrated in *Figure 6.2*:

```
Python 3.8.6 (tags/v3.8.6:db45529, Sep 23 2020, 15:52:53) [MSC v.1927 64 bit (AMD64)] on win32
Type "help", "copyright", "credits" or "license()" for more information.
>>> from Bio.Seq import Seq
>>> dna_seq=Seq("AAGGTTCC")
>>> dna_seq
Seq('AAGGTTCC')
>>> print(dna_seq)
AAGGTTCC
>>> print(len(dna_seq))
8
>>>
```

Figure 6.2: Finding length of a sequence

- **Counting occurrence of a character in a sequence**: We can count the occurrence of a character in any sequence using the **count()** function, as demonstrated in *Figure 6.3*:

```
Python 3.8.6 Shell                                              — □ ×
File Edit Shell Debug Options Window Help
Python 3.8.6 (tags/v3.8.6:db45529, Sep 23 2020, 15:52:53) [MSC v.1927 64 bit (AM
D64)] on win32
Type "help", "copyright", "credits" or "license()" for more information.
>>> from Bio.Seq import Seq
>>> dna_seq=Seq("ATGCATGCATGC")
>>> print(dna_seq)
ATGCATGCATGC
>>> dna_seq.count("A")
3
>>>
```

Figure 6.3: *Counting occurrence of a character in a sequence*

- **Concatenating sequences**: We can concatenate two sequences very easily by using the **+** operator, as demonstrated in *Figure 6.4*:

```
Python 3.8.6 Shell                                              — □ ×
File Edit Shell Debug Options Window Help
Python 3.8.6 (tags/v3.8.6:db45529, Sep 23 2020, 15:52:53) [MSC v.1927 64 bit (AM
D64)] on win32
Type "help", "copyright", "credits" or "license()" for more information.
>>> from Bio.Seq import Seq
>>> dna_seq1=Seq("AATTGGCC")
>>> dna_seq2=Seq("CCGGTTAA")
>>> dna_concat=dna_seq1+dna_seq2
>>> dna_concat
Seq('AATTGGCCCCGGTTAA')
>>>
```

Figure 6.4: *Concatenating sequences*

- **Slicing a sequence**: Slicing means extracting a portion of a string. Slicing can be performed using the "**:**" operator, as demonstrated in *Figure 6.5*:

```
Python 3.8.6 Shell                                              — □ ×
File Edit Shell Debug Options Window Help
Python 3.8.6 (tags/v3.8.6:db45529, Sep 23 2020, 15:52:53) [MSC v.1927 64 bit (AM
D64)] on win32
Type "help", "copyright", "credits" or "license()" for more information.
>>> from Bio.Seq import Seq
>>> dna_seq = Seq("AATTGGCCCCGGTTAA")
>>> #printing third codon positions of the sequence
>>> print(dna_seq[2::3])
TGCGA
>>> #printing codon position from 1 to 4
>>> print(dna_seq[1:5])
ATTG
>>>
```

Figure 6.5: *Slicing sequence*

Sequence object operations

Biological sequences can be represented in various applications. These sequences can be represented using string variables as well. However, handling sequences using string variables restricts you from performing many biological functions on the sequence, like – finding **complement**, **reverse_complement**, **translation**, **transcription**, etc. Therefore, it is advisable to create such sequences using a sequence object rather than a normal string variable.

Complement of a sequence

The complementary sequence is a **nucleic acid** sequence that can create a double-stranded structure of Nucleic Acid by matching base pairs. For example, the complementary sequence for – GATC will be CTAG. In any bioinformatics application finding the complementary strand allows the comparison of the sequences of different species.

Complement and reverse complement function

Biopython provides an inbuilt function to find out the complementary sequence of any nucleotide sequence. The example is demonstrated in *Figure 6.6*:

Syntax: Nucleotide_Sequence. complement()

```
Python 3.8.6 (tags/v3.8.6:db45529, Sep 23 2020, 15:52:53) [MSC v.1927 64 bit (AMD64)] on win32
Type "help", "copyright", "credits" or "license()" for more information.
>>> from Bio.Seq import Seq
>>> dna_seq = Seq("AATTTGGCCC")
>>> print(dna_seq.complement())
TTAAACCGGG
>>>
```

Figure 6.6: Complement of a sequence

The reverse complement function will return the complementary sequence after reversing it. The example is demonstrated in *Figure 6.7*:

Syntax: Nucleotide_Sequence. reverse_complement()

```
Python 3.8.6 (tags/v3.8.6:db45529, Sep 23 2020, 15:52:53) [MSC v.1927 64 bit (AMD64)] on win32
Type "help", "copyright", "credits" or "license()" for more information.
>>> from Bio.Seq import Seq
>>> dna_seq = Seq("AATTTGGCCC")
>>> print(dna_seq.complement())
TTAAACCGGG
>>> #Finding Reverse Complement
>>> print(dna_seq.reverse_complement())
GGGCCAAATT
>>>
```

Figure 6.7: Reverse complement of a sequence

Transcription of a sequence

Transcription involves making a copy of a gene DNA sequence to make an RNA sequence. The process of transcription is performed by an enzyme called **RNA polymerase** that links nucleotides to make an RNA strand. The basic motive of transcription is to generate RNA molecules through a gene DNA sequence. The actual biological process is performed to get a reverse complement (ATCG->TAGC) to get messenger RNA (mRNA) that considers the DNA as a template strand. In Biopython, we directly use a coding strand to get mRNA by changing the base T to U.

Transcribe function

The basic role of the transcribe function is to convert DNA sequence into RNA sequence. The inbuild transcribes function of the sequence object can do so. The example demonstrated in *Figure 6.8*:

Syntax: **DNA_Sequence.transcribe()**

```
Python 3.8.6 Shell                                          —    □   ×
File Edit Shell Debug Options Window Help
Python 3.8.6 (tags/v3.8.6:db45529, Sep 23 2020, 15:52:53) [MSC v.1927 64 bit (AM
D64)] on win32
Type "help", "copyright", "credits" or "license()" for more information.
>>> from Bio.Seq import Seq
>>> dna_seq = Seq("AATTTGGCC")
>>> dna_seq
Seq('AATTTGGCC')
>>> # Transcribing the Sequence
>>> dna_seq.transcribe()
Seq('AAUUUGGCC')
>>>
```

Figure 6.8: Transcribing a sequence

Back transcription

If you wish to transcribe the mRNA back into the DNA sequence, you can use the **back_transcribe()** function. This function translates the mRNA back into the DNA sequence. Refer to *Figure 6.9* for clarity:

Syntax: **mRNA.back_transcribe()**

```
Python 3.8.6 Shell                                    —   □   ×
File Edit Shell Debug Options Window Help
Python 3.8.6 (tags/v3.8.6:db45529, Sep 23 2020, 15:52:53) [MSC v.1927 64 bit (AM
D64)] on win32
Type "help", "copyright", "credits" or "license()" for more information.
>>> from Bio.Seq import Seq
>>> dna_seq = Seq("AATTTGGCC")
>>> dna_seq
Seq('AATTTGGCC')
>>> # Transcribing the Sequence
>>> dna_seq.transcribe()
Seq('AAUUUGGCC')
>>> # Generating an mRNA
>>> mRNA= dna_seq.transcribe()
>>> # Translating Messenger RNA
>>> mRNA.translate()
Seq('NLA')
>>> # Back Transcribing the mRNA sequence
>>> mRNA.back_transcribe()
Seq('AATTTGGCC')
>>>
```

Figure 6.9: Back transcribing a sequence

Translation of a sequence

Sequence translation is used to translate nucleic acid sequences to corresponding peptide sequences. Back-translation is used to predict the possible nucleic acid sequence that a specified peptide sequence has originated from. The four steps of translation are shown in *Figure 6.10*:

```
Python 3.8.9 (tags/v3.8.9:a743f81, Apr  6 2021, 14:02:34) [MSC v.1928 64 bit (AM
D64)] on win32
Type "help", "copyright", "credits" or "license()" for more information.
>>> from Bio.Seq import Seq
>>> dna_seq = Seq("AATTTGGCC")
>>> dna_seq
Seq('AATTTGGCC')
>>> # Transcribing the Sequence
>>> dna_seq.transcribe()
Seq('AAUUUGGCC')
>>> # Generating a mRNA
>>> mRNA = dna_seq.transcribe()
>>> # Translating Messenger RNA
>>> mRNA.translate()
Seq('NLA')
>>>
```

Figure 6.10: Translating a sequence

The process of forming a polypeptide chain from mRNA codons is known as translation. It takes place in four steps, namely, tRNA charging, Initiation, Elongation, and Termination.

Syntax:
coding_DNA.translate(table="Standard", stop_symbol="*", to_stop=False, cds=False, gap=None)

The arguments used in the syntax are as follows:

- **Table**: This argument specifies the name of the codon table to be used. The default value of this argument is **Standard**. However, the value may be the specific name of the codon table (String). It may be an integer that represents an NCBI identifier or an object of **CodonTable**.

- **stop_symbol**: This specifies a single character of a string that specifies the terminators. The default value is "*".

- **to_stop**: It is a Boolean value. The default value is **False**, which means to perform a full translation as per the specified stop symbol. If True, translation is terminated at the first in-frame stop codon.

- **Cds**: It is a Boolean value that indicates **True/False**. If True, it checks whether the sequence starts with a valid codon or not. The length of the sequence is in multiples of three, and there is a single in-frame codon at the end of the sequence. In case these parameters do not match, then an exception will be raised. CDS is a sequence of nucleotides that corresponds with the sequence of amino acids in a protein. A typical CDS starts with ATG and ends with a stop codon. Refer to the following figure for a better understanding:

```
Python 3.8.9 (tags/v3.8.9:a743f81, Apr  6 2021, 14:02:34) [MSC v.1928 64 bit (AM
D64)] on win32
Type "help", "copyright", "credits" or "license()" for more information.
>>> from Bio.Seq import Seq
>>> coding_dna = Seq("ATGGGCCATTGTAATGGGCCGCTGAAAGGGTGTTTGATAG")
>>> print(coding_dna.translate())

Warning (from warnings module):
  File "C:\Users\5453\AppData\Local\Programs\Python\Python38\lib\site-packages\B
io\Seq.py", line 2804
    warnings.warn(
BiopythonWarning: Partial codon, len(sequence) not a multiple of three. Explicit
ly trim the sequence or add trailing N before translation. This may become an er
ror in future.
MGHCNGPLKGCLI
>>> coding_dna=Seq("GTGGCATTGTAATGGGCCGCTAAAGGGTGCCCGATAGT")
>>> coding_dna.translate()
Seq('VAL*WAAKGCPI')
>>>
```

Figure 6.11: Translating a sequence

As discussed earlier, the **codon_dna** is initialized, and later it is translated using the **translate()** function of the Biopython module. In the first instance, it is raising an exception because the **codon_dna** is not a multiple of three. However, re-initializing it with the correct value translates the **codon_dna** and returns the peptide sequence successfully.

The **translate()** function takes many parameters. The first one is the *codon table*. If we do not mention any name, then by default, it will use the *standard codon table*. However, another option is to mention the specific name of the table. Using the standard table, as shown in *Figure 6.12*:

```
>>> coding_dna=Seq("GTGGCATTGTAATGGGCCGCTAAAGGGTGCCCGATAGT")
>>> coding_dna.translate()
Seq('VAL*WAAKGCPI')
>>>
```

Figure 6.12: Translating a sequence using standard table

Using NCBI table 2, where TGA is not a stop codon. Refer to *Figure 6.13* for a better understanding. Stop codons are trinucleotides in mRNA that mark the end of protein coding sequences.

```
>>> # Performing Translation
>>> coding_dna.translate(table=2)
Seq('VAL*WAAKGCPM')
>>>
```

Figure 6.13: Translating a sequence using NCBI table 2

Mutable sequence

The sequences created using string or sequence objects are immutable in nature. However, we can create editable sequences using mutable sequence object that belongs to **Bio.Seq.MutableSeq** class. **MutableSeq** object cannot be used as a dictionary key, as shown below:

```
Python 3.8.6 Shell                                           —   □   ×
File  Edit  Shell  Debug  Options  Window  Help
Python 3.8.6 (tags/v3.8.6:db45529, Sep 23 2020, 15:52:53) [MSC v.1927 64 bit (AM
D64)] on win32
Type "help", "copyright", "credits" or "license()" for more information.
>>> from Bio.Seq import MutableSeq
>>> dna_seq = MutableSeq("ATCATCGTCGTCG")
>>> dna_seq
MutableSeq('ATCATCGTCGTCG')
>>> dna_seq[4]
'T'
>>> dna_seq[4]="G"
>>> dna_seq
MutableSeq('ATCAGCGTCGTCG')
>>> dna_seq[4:6]="MM"
>>> dna_seq
MutableSeq('ATCAMMGTCGTCG')
>>>
```

Figure 6.14: Mutable sequence

In *Figure 6.14*, we created an object of **MutableSeq** class, and then we modified the sequence by editing the base at index 4. We can also edit the sequence by making changes in multiple bases as well by specifying the range as mentioned in the statement **Dna_seq[4:6]="MM"**. It will replace the base at index positions 4 and 5 with **"MM"**.

The class **MutableSeq** will provide various other functions that may be used for its modification, as mentioned below:

- **append()**: The function will allow you to add any other subsequent character at the end of the sequence, as demonstrated in the following code:

```
Python 3.8.6 (tags/v3.8.6:db45529, Sep 23 2020, 15:52:53) [MSC v.1927 64 bit (AMD64)] on win32
Type "help", "copyright", "credits" or "license()" for more information.
>>> from Bio.Seq import MutableSeq
>>> dna_seq = MutableSeq("ATCATCGTCGTCG")
>>> dna_seq
MutableSeq('ATCATCGTCGTCG')
>>> dna_seq[4]
'T'
>>> dna_seq[4]="G"
>>> dna_seq
MutableSeq('ATCAGCGTCGTCG')
>>> dna_seq[4:6]="MM"
>>> dna_seq
MutableSeq('ATCAMMGTCGTCG')
>>> #Appending at the end of the Sequence
>>> dna_seq.append("T")
>>> dna_seq
MutableSeq('ATCAMMGTCGTCGT')
```

Figure 6.15: Append function in mutable sequence

- **insert()**: The insert function of **MutableSequence** class helps in inserting any subsequent character in the sequence, as shown in *Figure 6.16*:

```
Python 3.8.6 (tags/v3.8.6:db45529, Sep 23 2020, 15:52:53) [MSC v.1927 64 bit (AMD64)] on win32
Type "help", "copyright", "credits" or "license()" for more information.
>>> from Bio.Seq import MutableSeq
>>> dna_seq = MutableSeq("ATCATCGGGCC")
>>> dna_seq
MutableSeq('ATCATCGGGCC')
>>> #Inserting at any index position in Sequence
>>> dna_seq.insert(0,"T")
>>> dna_seq
MutableSeq('TATCATCGGGCC')
>>>
```

Figure 6.16: Insert function in mutable sequence

- **del ()**: This function may be used to delete any character from the sequence. Refer to *Figure 6.17* for clarity:

```
Python 3.8.6 (tags/v3.8.6:db45529, Sep 23 2020, 15:52:53) [MSC v.1927 64 bit (AMD64)] on win32
Type "help", "copyright", "credits" or "license()" for more information.
>>> from Bio.Seq import MutableSeq
>>> dna_seq = MutableSeq("ATCATCGGGCC")
>>> dna_seq
MutableSeq('ATCATCGGGCC')
>>> #Inserting at any index position in Sequence
>>> dna_seq.insert(0,"T")
>>> dna_seq
MutableSeq('TATCATCGGGCC')
>>> #Deleting any character at a index position
>>> del dna_seq[2]
>>> dna_seq
MutableSeq('TACATCGGGCC')
>>> del(dna_seq[2])
>>> dna_seq
MutableSeq('TAATCGGGCC')
>>>
```

Figure 6.17: Delete function in mutable sequence

- **pop()**: This function removes and returns the last character of the mutable sequence, as shown below:

```
>>>
>>> # Popping a character from a Sequence
>>> x = dna_seq.pop()
>>> x
'C'
>>> dna_seq.pop()
'C'
>>>
```

Figure 6.18: Pop function in mutable sequence

- **remove()**: It removes the first occurrence of any specific character. It will not return any value, as shown below:

```
>>>
>>> # Removing a character from a Sequence
>>> dna_seq = MutableSeq("TAATCGGGCC")
>>> dna_seq.remove("A")
>>> dna_seq
MutableSeq('TATCGGGCC')
>>>
```

Figure 6.19: Remove function in mutable sequence

Multiplying mutable sequence

We can multiply a mutable sequence by any integer number and get multiples of the sequence, as shown below:

```
>>> dna_seq*2
MutableSeq('TATCGGGCCTATCGGGCC')
>>>
```

Figure 6.20: Multiplying mutable sequence

SequenceRecord object

The **SeqRecord** object is defined in the **Bio.SeqRecord** module. The object associates various features of the sequence object with it. The **SeqRecord** object is treated as the basic data type for the **Bio.SeqIO** object. The sequence record object provides the following information about the sequence:

- **.seq**: This attribute represents the sequence itself in the form of a **Seq** object.
- **.id**: This attribute is an identification value for the sequence. It may be a string that somehow resembles the accession number.
- **.name**: It is also a kind of id, but it is treated as an alias.
- **.description**: It gives detailed information about the sequence.
- **.annotations**: It will provide additional information about the sequence. It allows to store the unstructured information about the sequence.
- **.features**: It stores more structured information about the various features of a sequence, like the domain of protein sequence and the position of genes on the genome.

Creating a sequence record object

We can create a sequence record object and store the information related to the sequence in that object. Though sequences can be handled easily using the **SeqIO** object while handling files, the sequence record object can be created manually to store related information of sequence. Refer to *Figure 6.21* for a better understanding:

```
>>> from Bio.Seq import Seq
>>> from Bio.SeqRecord import SeqRecord
>>> record = SeqRecord(Seq(" mpkpvanqededptpylfvsleqrridqsk"), id="NP_001303327"
,description="sequence of the Drosophila melanogaster genome")

>>> print(record)
ID: NP_001303327
Name: <unknown name>
Description: sequence of the Drosophila melanogaster genome
Number of features: 0
Seq(' mpkpvanqededptpylfvsleqrridqsk')
>>>
```

Figure 6.21: Creating SequenceRecord object

In the example, we created a sequence record object manually and stored its detail like **id**, **sequence**, and **description**. By using the **print** command, we are printing the record, and it is printing.

This **format()** function converts the **SequenceRecord** object into a string format using any output format, as shown below:

```
>>> from Bio.Seq import Seq
>>> from Bio.SeqRecord import SeqRecord
>>> record = SeqRecord(Seq(" mpkpvanqededptpylfvsleqrridqsk"), id="NP_001303327" ,description="sequence of the Drosophila melanogaster genome")

>>> print(record)
ID: NP_001303327
Name: <unknown name>
Description: sequence of the Drosophila melanogaster genome
Number of features: 0
Seq(' mpkpvanqededptpylfvsleqrridqsk')
>>> print (record.format("fasta"))
>NP_001303327 sequence of the Drosophila melanogaster genome
 mpkpvanqededptpylfvsleqrridqsk

>>>
```

Figure 6.22: Format function in SequenceRecord object

Sequence input-output module

The sequence input-output module is meant to work with miscellaneous file formats in a uniform way. The basic purpose of **Bio.SeqIO** module is to parse the **SequenceRecord** object while dealing with large FASTA or FASTQ files. There are two basic functions of **SeqIO** module. The **parse()** function returns an iterator giving **SeqRecord** objects. The **parse()** function will activate the relevant parser. Some of the parsers work as wrappers that work around low-level parsers that generate **SeqRecord** objects for the consistent **SeqIO** interface. For the large FASTA and FASTQ files, using underlying parsers will make the execution faster. Refer to *Example 6.23* and for its output, refer to *Figure 6.23*.

Example 6.23:

from Bio import SeqIO
for record in SeqIO.parse("example.fastq", "fastq"):
    print("%s %i" % (record.id, len(record)))

```
=== RESTART: D:\pvdata\book1\P4Bio\Review_done\Code\Chapter6_code\Ex_6.23.py ===
EAS54_6_R1_2_1_413_324 25
EAS54_6_R1_2_1_540_792 25
EAS54_6_R1_2_1_443_348 25
>>>
```

Figure 6.23: Using SequenceInputOutput module

The **read()** function is used when a file contains a single record; the function will read the record and return a **SeqRecord** object. Refer to *Example 6.24* and for its output refer *Figure 6.24*.

Example 6.24:

```
from Bio import SeqIO
record = SeqIO.read("NC_005816.fna", "fasta")
print("%s %i" % (record.id, len(record)))
```

```
== RESTART: C:/Users/5453/AppData/Local/Programs/Python/Python38/seqio_read.py =
gi|45478711|ref|NC_005816.1| 9609
>>>
```

Figure 6.24: Using the read function of SequenceInputOutput module

To access only the first record of the file containing multiple records, we can use the **next()** function. Refer to *Example 6.25* and for its output, refer to *Figure 6.25*.

Example 6.25:

```
from Bio import SeqIO
record = next(SeqIO.parse("example.fastq", "fastq"))
print("%s %i" % (record.id, len(record)))
```

```
>>>
>>>
== RESTART: C:/Users/5453/AppData/Local/Programs/Python/Python38/seqio_next.py =
EAS54_6_R1_2_1_413_324 25
>>>
```

Figure 6.25: Reading the first record of a file using the SequenceInputOutput module

The above code will work if the file contains at least one record. Note that if there is more than one record, the remaining records will be silently ignored.

Accessing sequences from FASTA and GenBank

The sequence iterators are quite handy if we are accessing records from interlaced files like FASTA and GenBank, as they save a lot of memory. However, the limitation of the iterator is that it may access the records sequentially one by one. To access the record randomly, we may use a list.

Sequence iterator for FASTA file

In bioinformatics applications, protein or nucleotide sequences are stored in different format files. FASTA file format is the most common format used. Initially, in the older versions of Biopython, there was an application called **FASTA** for fast search of sequences in a huge volume of sequences. In the present scenario, FASTA files are used to store protein and nucleotide sequences in a specific format. *Figure 6.26* shows the structure of a FASTA file:

```
>gi|2765658|emb|Z78533.1|CIZ78533 C.irapeanum 5.8S rRNA gene and ITS1 and ITS2 DNA
CGTAACAAGGTTTCCGTAGGTGAACCTGCGGAAGGATCATTGATGAGACCGTGGAATAAACGATCGAGTG
AATCCGGAGGACCGGTGTACTCAGCTCACCGGGGGCATTGCTCCCGTGGTGACCCTGATTTGTTGTTGGG
CCGCCTCGGGAGCGTCCATGGCGGGTTTGAACCTCTAGCCCGGCGCAGTTTGGGCGCCAAGCCATATGAA
AGCATCACCGGCGAATGGCATTGTCTTCCCCAAAACCCGGAGCGGCGGCGTGCTGTCGCGTGCCCAATGA
ATTTTGATGACTCTCGCAAACGGGAATCTTGGCTCTTTGCATCGGATGGAAGGACGCAGCGAAATGCGAT
AAGTGGTGTGAATTGCAAGATCCCGTGAACCATCGAGTCTTTTGAACGCAAGTTGCGCCCGAGGCCATCA
GGCTAAGGGCACGCCTGCTTGGGCGTCGCGCTTCGTCTCTCCTGCCAATGCTTGCCCGGCATACAGCC
AGGCCGGCGTGGTGCGGATGTGAAAGATTGGCCCCTTGTGCCTAGGTGCGGCGGGTCCAAGAGCTGGTGT
TTTGATGGCCCGGAACCCGGCAAGAGGTGGACGGATGCTGGCAGCAGCTGCCGTGCGAATCCCCCATGTT
GTCGTGCTTGTCGGACAGGCAGGAGAACCCTTCCGAACCCCAATGGAGGGCGGTTGACCGCCATTCGGAT
GTGACCCCAGGTCAGGCGGGGGCACCCGCTGAGTTTACGC

>gi|2765657|emb|Z78532.1|CCZ78532 C.californicum 5.8S rRNA gene and ITS1 and ITS2 DNA
CGTAACAAGGTTTCCGTAGGTGAACCTGCGGAAGGATCATTGTTGAGACAACAGAATATATGATCGAGTG
AATCTGGAGGACCTGTGGTAACTCAGCTCGTCGTGGCACTGCTTTTGTCGTGACCCTGCTTTGTTGTTGG
GCCTCCTCAAGAGCTTTCATGGCAGGTTTGAACTTTAGTACGGTGCAGTTTGCGCCAAGTCATATAAAGC
ATCACTGATGAATGACATTATTGTCAGAAAAAATCAGAGGGGCAGTATGCTACTGAGCATGCCAGTGAAT
TTTTATGACTCTCGCAACGGATATCTTGGCTCTAACATCGATGAAGAACGCAGCTAAATGCGATAAGTGG
TGTGAATTGCAGAATCCCGTGAACCATCGAGTCTTTGAACGCAAGTTGCGCTCGAGGCCATCAGGCTAAG
GGCACGCCTGCCTGGGCGTCGTGTGTTGCGTCTCTCCTACCAATGCTTGCTTGGCATATCGCTAAGCTGG
CATTATACGGATGTGAATGATTGGCCCCTTGTGCCTAGGTGCGGTGGGTCTAAGGATTGTTGCTTTGATG
GGTAGGAATGTGGCACGAGGTGGAGAATGCTAACAGTCATAAGGCTGCTATTTGAATCCCCCATGTTGTT
GTATTTTTTCGAACCTACACAAGAACCTAATTGAACCCCAATGGAGCTAAAATAACCATTGGGCAGTTGA
TTTCCATTCAGATGCGACCCCAGGTCAGGCGGGGCACCCGCTGAGTTGAGGC
```

Figure 6.26: Structure of a FASTA file

We can clearly observe that each sequence has a header section greater than the sign > and mentions the unique ID of the sequence, followed by the sequence and other details of the sequence.

Bio.SeqIO module of Biopython provides an inbuilt function **parse()** that returns an iterable object. Example *6.27* demonstrates how it works. Here in this example **open()** function returns the file handle and the **parse()** function returns an iterable object named a **record** which iterates through all sequences and returns the id of each sequence as visible in the output. Please refer to the *Figure 6.27*:

Example 6.27:

```
from Bio import SeqIO
from Bio.SeqIO import parse
file = open('orchid.fasta')
for record in parse(file, "fasta"):
    print(record.id)
```

```
Python 3.8.6 Shell
Python 3.8.6 (tags/v3.8.6:db45529, Sep 23 2020, 15:52:53) [MSC v.1927 64 bit (AM
D64)] on win32
Type "help", "copyright", "credits" or "license()" for more information.
>>>
=== RESTART: C:\Users\5453\AppData\Local\Programs\Python\Python38\SEq_iter.py ==
gi|2765658|emb|Z78533.1|CIZ78533
gi|2765657|emb|Z78532.1|CCZ78532
gi|2765656|emb|Z78531.1|CFZ78531
gi|2765655|emb|Z78530.1|CMZ78530
gi|2765654|emb|Z78529.1|CLZ78529
gi|2765652|emb|Z78527.1|CYZ78527
gi|2765651|emb|Z78526.1|CGZ78526
gi|2765650|emb|Z78525.1|CAZ78525
gi|2765649|emb|Z78524.1|CFZ78524
gi|2765648|emb|Z78523.1|CHZ78523
gi|2765647|emb|Z78522.1|CMZ78522
gi|2765646|emb|Z78521.1|CCZ78521
```

Figure 6.27: Parsing FASTA file

Another function, **next()**, returns the next sequence in the iterable object. It can be used to get the first sequence also as demonstrated in *Example 6.28*. For the output, refer to *Figure 6.28*:

Example 6.28:

from Bio import SeqIO

from Bio.SeqIO import parse

first_record = next(SeqIO.parse(open('orchid.fasta'),'fasta'))

print(first_record.id)

print(first_record.name)

print(first_record.seq)

print(first_record.description)

print(first_record.annotations)

```
>>>
=== RESTART: C:\Users\5453\AppData\Local\Programs\Python\Python38\SEq_iter.py ==
gi|2765658|emb|Z78533.1|CIZ78533
gi|2765658|emb|Z78533.1|CIZ78533
CGTAACAAGGTTTCCGTAGGTGAACCTGCGGAAGGATCATTGATGAGACCGTGGAATAAACGATCGAGTGAATCCGGAGG
ACCGGTGTACTCAGCTCACCGGGGGCATTGCTCCCGTGGTGACCCTGATTTGTTGTTGGGCCGCCTCGGGAGCGTCCATG
GCGGGTTTGAACCTCTAGCCCGGCGCAGTTTGGGCGCCAAGCCATATGAAAGCATCACCGGCGAATGGCATTGTCTTCCC
CAAAACCCGGAGCGGCGGCGTGCTGTCGCGTGCCCAATGAATTTTGATGACTCTCGCAAACGGGAATCTTGGCTCTTTGC
ATCGGATGGAAGGACGCAGCGAAATGCGATAAGTGGTGTGAATTGCAAGATCCCGTGAACCATCGAGTCTTTTGAACGCA
AGTTGCGCCCGAGGCCATCAGGCTAAGGGCACGCCTGCTTGGGCGTCGCGCTTCGTCTCTCTCCTGCCAATGCTTGCCCG
GCATACAGCCAGGCCGGCGTGGTGCGGATGTGAAAGATTGGCCCCTTGTGCCTAGGTGCGGCGGGTCCAAGAGCTGGTGT
TTTGATGGCCCGGAACCCGGCAAGAGGTGGACGGATGCTGGCAGCAGCTGCCGTGCGAATCCCCCATGTTGTCGTGCTTG
TCGGACAGGCAGGAGAACCCTTCCGAACCCCAATGGAGGGCGGTTGACCGCCATTCGGATGTGACCCCAGGTCAGGCGGG
GGCACCCGCTGAGTTTACGC
gi|2765658|emb|Z78533.1|CIZ78533 C.irapeanum 5.8S rRNA gene and ITS1 and ITS2 DN
A
{}
>>>
```

Figure 6.28: Next function to access the FASTA file

In the end, we can see empty annotations as FASTA files do not support annotations. The sequence iterator allows us to explore all sequences one by one in an order. However, if we need to explore any specific sequence, we can convert the FASTA file into a list of sequences to access any sequence randomly, as demonstrated in *Example 6.29* the output of the program is shown in *Figure 6.29* In the example we can observe after converting **fasta** file into a list of sequences we are accessing sequence id of index position 2 in the list.

Example 6.29:
```
from Bio import SeqIO
from Bio.SeqIO import parse

iterator = SeqIO.parse(open('orchid.fasta'),'fasta')
sequences = [seq_record for seq_record in iterator]
print(sequences[2].id)
```

```
>>>
=== RESTART: C:/Users/5453/AppData/Local/Programs/Python/Python38/iter_seq.py ==
94
gi|2765656|emb|Z78531.1|CFZ78531
>>>
```

Figure 6.29: Converting the FASTA file into a list of sequences

Filtering sequences from the FASTA file

While reading the sequences from the FASTA file, you may select specific sequences, which means you may filter the sequences as per the filter criteria. *Example 6.30* demonstrates the working of a filter in FASTA file data. The output for the same is mentioned in *Figure 6.30*, the parsing of a file is done that returns **sequence_iter** (iterator). The iterator will iterate one **seq_rec** at a time and, while processing it, checks the length of the sequence as well; if it is **< 700**, then only it will be appended in the sequence list **seq_700**.

Example 6.30:
```
from Bio import SeqIO
from Bio.SeqIO import parse
sequence_iter = SeqIO.parse(open('orchid.fasta'),'fasta')
# Filtering sequence from orchid.fasta having length < 700
seq_700 = [seq_rec for seq_rec in sequence_iter if len(seq_rec.seq) < 700]
for seq_1 in seq_700:
    print(seq_1.id)
    print(seq_1.seq)
```

```
=== RESTART: D:/pvdata/book1/P4Bio/Review_done/Code/Chapter6_code/Ex_6.30.py ===
gi|2765644|emb|Z78519.1|CPZ78519
ATATGATCGAGTGAATCTGGTGGACTTGTGGTTACTCAGCTCGCCATAGGCTTTGCTTTTGCGGTGACCCTAATTTGTCATTGGGCCTCCTCCCAA
GCTTTCCTTGTGGGTTTGAACCTCTAGCACGGTGCAGTATGCACCAAGTCATATGAAGCATTGCCGATGAATGACATTATTGTCCAAAAGTTGGAG
TGGAAGCGTGCTACTGCATGCATGCAAATGAATTTTTTTATGACTCTCGACAACGGATATCTTGGCTCTTGCATCGATGAAGAACGCAGCGAAATG
CGATAAGTGGTGTGAATTGCAGAATCCCGTGAACCATCGAGTCTTTGAACGCAAGTTGCGCCCGATGCCATCAGGCTAAGGGCACGCCTGCCTGGG
CGTCGTGTGCTGCGTCTCTCCTGTCAATGCTTTCCCATCATATAGATAGGTTTGCATTGTGTGGATGTGAAAGATTGGCCCCTTGTGCCTAGGTGC
GGTGGGTCTAAGAACTTAATGTTTTGATGGTTCGAAACCTGGCAGGAGGTGGAGGATGTTGGCAGCTATATAAGGCTATCATTTGAATCCCCCATA
TTGTCGCGTTTGTTGGACCTAGAGAAGAACATGTTTGAATCCCAATGGAGGCAAACAACCCTCGGGCGGTTGATTGCCATTCATATGCGACCCCAG
GTCAGGCGGGGCCACCCGCTGAGTTTA
gi|2765643|emb|Z78518.1|CRZ78518
CGTAACAAGGTTTCCGTAGGTGAACCTGCGGGAGGATCATTGTTGAGATAGTAGAATATTCGATCGAGTGAATCCGGAGGACTTGTGGTTACTCGG
CTCGTCGAAGGCTTAACTTTTGTGGTGACCCTGATTTGTAGTTGGGCATCCTCGAGAGCTTTTATGGCGGGTTTGAGCCTCTATCACGGCGCAGTT
TGCGCCAAGTCATATGAAGCATCGCCGACGAATTACATTATTGTCCCCCAAACTCGGATGGACGGTGTGTGTTACGCATACCCGTGAACCATCGAG
TCTTTGAACGCAAGTTGCGCCCAAGGCCATCAGGCTAAGGGCACGCCTGCCTGGGCGTCGTGTGCTGCATCTCTTTTGCCAATGCTTGCTCGACAT
ACAATTAGGCCAGTATTGCATAGATATGAAAGATTGACCCCTTGTGCTTAGGTGCGGTGGGTCTAAGGATTGGTGTTTTGATGGCCAAACCCCGG
CAGGAGGTGGAGCATGTTGATAGTCGCAAGGCTGTCGTTCAAATCCCACATGTTGTCGTATTTGCCGGACCCACAGAAGAACCTATTTGAACCCCT
ATGGAGGCAAAACAACCCTTGAGCGATTGATTGCCATTCAGATACGACCCCAGGTCAGGCGGGGCCACCCGCTGAGTTTTCC
gi|2765619|emb|Z78494.1|PNZ78494
CGTAACAAGGTTTCCGTAGGTGAACCTGCGGAAGGATCATTGTTGAGGTCGCATAATAATTGATCGAGTTAATCTGGAGGATCAGTTTACTTTGGT
CACCCATGGACATTTACTGTTGCAGTGACCTAGATTTACCATCGGGCCTCCTTGGGAACTTTCCTGCTGGCGATCTATACCCTTGCCCGGCGCAGT
AATGCGCCAAATCAAATGACCCATAATTAATGAAGGGGGACGGCATACTGCCTTGACCAACTCCCCATTATTGAGGTAACACTCTCAACTTCGGAT
ATCTCAGGTGTGAATTGCAGAATCCCGTTAACATCGAGTCTTTGAACGCAAGTTGGGCCCGAGGCCAACAGGCCAAGGGAACGCCTGTCTGGGCAT
TGCGAGTCATATCTCTCCCTTAATGAGGCTGTCCATACGTACTGTTCAGCCGGTGCGGATGTGAGTTTGGCCCCTTGTTCTTCGGTACGGGGGGTC
TAAGAGCTGCATGGGCTTTTGATGGTCCTAAATACGGCAAGAGGTGGACGAACTATGCTACAACAAAACTGTTGTGCGAATGCCCCGGGTTGTTGT
GTTTAATCAGAAGACCCTTTTGAACCCCATTGGAGGCCCATCGACCCATGATCAGTTGAATGGCCATTTGGTTGCGATCCCAGGTCAGGTGAGGCA
ACCCGCTGAGTTTAAG
gi|2765613|emb|Z78488.1|PTZ78488
CTGTAGGTGAACCTGCGGAAGGATCATTGTTGAGATCACGCAATAATTGATCGAGTTAATCTGGAGGATCAGTTTACTTTGGTCACCCATGGGCAT
TTGTTATTGCAGTGACCGAGATTTGCCATCGAGCCTCCTTGGGAGCTTTCTTGCTGGCGATCTTAACCCTAGCCCGGCGCAGTTTTGCGCCAAGTC
ATACGACACATAATTGGTGAAGGGGGCGGCATGGTGCCTTGACCCTCCCCTAATTATTTTCTAACAACTCTCATCAACGGGATGGAGAACGCAGCG
AAATGCGATAAATGGTGTGAATTGCAGAATCCCGTGAACCATCGAGTCTTTGAACCCAAGTTGCGCCCGAGGCCATCAGGCCAAGGGCACGCCTGC
```

Figure 6.30: Filtering sequences into a list

Sequence iterator for GenBank file

GenBank is an elaborate database of nucleotide sequences. It is prepared by the **National Center for Biotechnology Information** (**NCBI**), which keeps GenBank open access. It is considered the best database for various bioinformatics research. It is quite comprehensive in nature and fulfills the demands of data with respect to various research work related to bioinformatics.

Biopython provides a single **parse()** function for the parsing of all file formats. Parsing contents from the GenBank file is like parsing of FASTA file. Example 6.31 demonstrates the same. For the output, refer to *Figure 6.31*:

Example 6.31:
```
from Bio import GenBank
with open("ls_orchid.gb") as handle:
    for rec in GenBank.parse(handle):
        print("Accession Number")
        print(rec.accession)
        print("Keywords")
        print(rec.keywords)
```

```
print("Sequence Line")
print(rec._sequence_line)
```

Figure 6.31: Iterating GenBank using SequenceRecord object

Conclusion

In this chapter, we learned that Biopython is one of the most popular modules of Python and is used quite extensively in various research related to bioinformatics applications. The sequence object is the backbone of this module, and it helps in managing various sequences and their variations. The supporting objects like SequenceRecord, MutableSequence, and sequence, input-output module, are added on facilities for the processing of different format files supported by bioinformatics applications.

CHAPTER 7
Pattern Matching with Regular Expression

Introduction

Pattern recognition is a field of study that focuses on identifying patterns or regularities in data. In bioinformatics, pattern recognition involves the analysis of biological data to identify underlying patterns that may be useful for understanding biological processes, disease mechanisms, and other phenomena.

One of the main applications of pattern recognition in bioinformatics is the analysis of DNA and protein sequences. By identifying patterns in these sequences, researchers can gain insights into the structure and function of genes and proteins, as well as their evolution over time. For example, pattern recognition techniques can be used to identify conserved regions of DNA or protein sequences that are critical for their function or to identify mutations associated with disease.

Pattern recognition is also used in other areas of bioinformatics, such as image analysis and classification of gene expression data. In image analysis, pattern recognition can identify features of biological structures, such as cells, tissues, or organs, in images produced by microscopes or other imaging technologies. In gene expression analysis, pattern recognition can be used to identify patterns of gene expression that are associated with particular diseases or other biological processes.

Overall, pattern recognition plays an important role in bioinformatics by enabling researchers to identify patterns and relationships in biological data that may be difficult or impossible to detect using traditional analytical methods. These insights can lead to new discoveries and improved understanding of biological systems, which can have important implications for human health and other fields.

Structure

In this chapter, we will cover the following topics:

- Importance of patterns in bioinformatics sequences
- String splitting using regular expression in bioinformatics

Objectives

The main goal of this chapter is to explain the importance of pattern matching in bioinformatics sequences. Python programming utilizes regular expressions for pattern matching, and the chapter provides a comprehensive understanding of how regular expressions are used in handling bioinformatics sequences.

Importance of patterns in bioinformatics sequences

Patterns in bioinformatics sequences are of critical importance as they can provide valuable information about the biological functions and evolution of genes, proteins, and other molecules. Here are a few examples of the importance of patterns in bioinformatics sequences:

- **Conserved domains**: One of the most important patterns in bioinformatics sequences is the presence of conserved domains. These are stretches of amino acid residues in protein sequences that are highly conserved across different species, suggesting that they have an important functional role. For example, the homeobox domain is a conserved DNA-binding domain found in many transcription factors that regulate development in animals.

- **Motifs**: Another important pattern in bioinformatics sequences is the presence of motifs, which are short, recurring patterns in DNA or protein sequences. Motifs can be indicative of particular structural or functional features of the molecule. For example, the leucine zipper motif is a recurring pattern of amino acids in proteins that can form a coiled-coil structure and is involved in protein-protein interactions.

- **Regulatory regions**: Patterns in DNA sequences can also provide information about regulatory regions, which are regions of DNA that control the expression of genes. These regions often contain specific patterns, such as transcription factor binding sites or CpG islands, which can indicate their regulatory function. For example, the presence of a TATA box sequence in the promoter region of a gene can indicate the location of the transcription start site and the initiation of gene expression.

Overall, the identification of patterns in bioinformatics sequences is critical for understanding the structure, function, and evolution of genes, proteins, and other biological molecules. These patterns can provide insights into the mechanisms of biological processes and the development of diseases, which can lead to the development of new therapies and treatments.

Regular expressions (regex) in Python are a powerful tool for pattern matching and manipulation of text. They allow you to search, extract, and replace specific patterns within strings.

To use regular expressions in Python, you need to import the **re** module, as shown below:

`import re`

Here are some fundamental concepts and functions for working with regular expressions in Python:

- **Matching patterns:**
    - **re.match(pattern, string)**: Attempts to match the pattern at the beginning of the string.
    - **re.search(pattern, string)**: Searches for the pattern anywhere in the string.
    - **re.findall(pattern, string)**: Returns all non-overlapping matches of the pattern in the string.

- **Creating patterns:**
    - **Metacharacters**: Special characters with a symbolic meaning in regex (for example, ., +, *, ?).
    - **Character classes**: Represent a group of characters (for example, [a-z] matches any lowercase letter).
    - **Quantifiers**: Specify the number of repetitions for a pattern (for example, + matches one or more occurrences).
    - **Anchors**: Define the position of a pattern within a string (for example, ^ matches the start, $ matches the end).

- **Modifying patterns:**
    - **re.sub(pattern, replacement, string)**: Replaces occurrences of the pattern in the string with the replacement.
    - **Flags**: Optional arguments that modify the behavior of regex functions (for example, `re.IGNORECASE` for case-insensitive matching).

- **Grouping and capturing:**
    - **Parentheses ( )**: Create groups to capture and extract specific parts of a pattern.
    - **match.group(n)**: Retrieve the matched groups by index n.

For more advanced regex operations, the **re** module offers additional functions and features, such as lookahead and look-behind assertions, backreferences, and more. Regular expressions can be complex and require practice to master. There are various online resources and tutorials available to learn and explore the intricacies of regular expressions in Python.

Regular expressions in Python are handled through the **re** module. It provides functions and methods to work with regular expressions. Here is a concise overview of using regular expressions in Python:

- For more advanced regex operations, the **re** module offers additional functions and features, such as lookahead and look behind assertions, backreferences, and more.

- Regular expressions can be complex and require practice to master. There are various online resources and tutorials available to learn and explore the intricacies of regular expressions in Python.

- Regular expressions in Python are handled through the **re** module. It provides functions and methods to work with regular expressions. Here is a concise overview of using regular expressions in Python:

    o Import the re module:

    `import re`

    o Use **re.match()** to check if a pattern matches at the beginning of a string:

    `pattern = r"abc"`
    `text = "abcdef"`
    `match = re.match(pattern, text)`

    o Use **re.search()** to search for a pattern anywhere in a string:

    `pattern = r"def"`
    `text = "abcdef"`
    `match = re.search(pattern, text)`

    o Use **re.findall()** to find all occurrences of a pattern in a string:

    `pattern = r"ab"`
    `text = "ababab"`
    `matches = re.findall(pattern, text)`

    o Use **re.sub()** to replace occurrences of a pattern in a string:

    `pattern = r"apple"`
    `replacement = "orange"`

```
text = "I have an apple"
new_text = re.sub(pattern, replacement, text)
```
- Use regular expression flags for case-insensitive and multiline matching:
```
pattern = r"abc"
text = "ABCDEF"
match = re.search(pattern, text, re.IGNORECASE)
```
- Use groups to extract specific parts of a matched pattern:
```
pattern = r"(\d+)-(\d+)-(\d+)"
text = "Date: 2023-05-19"
match = re.search(pattern, text)
year = match.group(1)
month = match.group(2)
day = match.group(3)
```

These are a few basic operations you can perform using regular expressions in Python. The **re** module offers many more functions and options for advanced pattern matching and manipulation.

Searching for a pattern using regular expression

Regular expressions can be useful for searching and extracting patterns in bioinformatics sequences, such as DNA or protein sequences. Here is an example of how you can use regular expressions in Python to search for a specific pattern in a bioinformatics sequence; use the following *Example 7.1*:

Example 7.1

```
import re
sequence = "ATCGATCGAAGTACG"
pattern = "AAG"
# The pattern will be searced in the sequence and will return the first occurence of the pattern match
matches = re.search(pattern, sequence)
print(matches
if matches:
    print("Pattern found in the sequence.")
```

```
else:
    print("Pattern not found in the sequence.")
```

Figure 7.1 shows the output of the program:

```
==== RESTART: D:\pvdata\book1\P4Bio\Review_done\Code\Chapter7_code\Ex_7.1.py ===
<re.Match object; span=(8, 11), match='AAG'>
Pattern found in the sequence.
>>>
```

Figure 7.1: *Searching pattern in bioinformatics sequence*

In this example, we define the pattern as AAG, which represents the start codon in DNA sequences. The **re.search()** function is used to search for this pattern in the given sequence. If a match is found, we can access the matched substring using **match.group()**. In this case, if the pattern AAG is found, the relevant message will be displayed.

You can customize the pattern using regular expression metacharacters and character classes to search for more complex motifs or patterns specific to your bioinformatics application.

Alternation feature of regular expression

The alternation feature in regular expressions allows you to specify multiple alternative patterns to search for in a bioinformatics sequence. It is useful to match different possibilities at a specific position. Here is an example of using alternation in Python to search for alternative patterns in a bioinformatics sequence. The following *Example 7.2* demonstrates the usage of alternation feature:

Example 7.2

```
import re
sequence = "ATCGATCGAAGTACG"
pattern = r"AAG|GTA|ACG"
# All the three pattern will be searced in the sequence
# Function will return boolean value "True" if any one of them is found
# Function will return boolean value "False" if none of them are found
matches = re.search(pattern, sequence)
if matches:
    print("Pattern found in the sequence.")
else:
    print("Pattern not found in the sequence.")
```

Figure 7.2 shows the output:

```
==== RESTART: D:\pvdata\book1\P4Bio\Review_done\Code\Chapter7_code\Ex_7.2.py ===
<re.Match object; span=(8, 11), match='AAG'>
Pattern found in the sequence.
>>>
```

Figure 7.2: Alternation feature of pattern matching in bioinformatics sequence

In this example, we define the pattern as **AAG|GTA|ACG**. It means we are looking for either AAG, GTA, or ACG in the sequence. The pipe symbol (**|**) acts as an OR operator, allowing multiple alternatives to be specified.

The `re.search()` function is used to search for the first occurrence of any alternative pattern in the given sequence. If a match is found, we can access the matched substring using `match.group()`, and it will be printed as the output. Refer to *Figure 7.2* for output.

You can extend the alternation pattern to include more alternatives or modify it as needed to match specific patterns or motifs in your bioinformatics sequences.

Character groups in regular expression

Character groups, also known as **character classes**, are a powerful feature of regular expressions that allow you to specify a set of characters to match in a bioinformatics sequence. They provide a convenient way to express patterns involving different possibilities for a specific position. *Example 7.3* demonstrates the use of character groups in Python to search for specific character patterns in a bioinformatics sequence:

Example 7.3

```
import re
sequence = "ATCGATCGAAGTACTG"
pattern = r"[AT]G"
# The findall function will search for Character Group formation as "AG" and "TG"
# The function will return the list of patterns found
matches = re.findall(pattern, sequence)
print(matches)
if matches:
    print("Pattern(s) found in the sequence.")
    for match in matches:
        print(match)
else:
```

```
    print("No patterns found in the sequence.")
```

The output is shown in the following Figure 7.3.

```
==== RESTART: D:\pvdata\book1\P4Bio\Review_done\Code\Chapter7_code\Ex_7.3.py ===
['AG', 'TG']
Pattern(s) found in the sequence.
AG
TG
>>>
```

Figure 7.3: Character groups in pattern matching

In this example, we define the pattern as **[AT]G**. The square brackets indicate a character group, and the characters inside it specify the options to match at that position. In this case, we are looking for **A** or **T** followed by **G** in the sequence.

The **re.findall()** function is used to find all occurrences of the character group in the given sequence. If matches are found, they will be returned as a list and printed as the output.

You can customize character groups by including additional characters or using character ranges to specify a range of characters to match. For example, **[A-Z]** matches any uppercase letter, and **[ACGT]** matches any of the DNA bases.

Character groups provide flexibility and expressiveness in defining patterns in bioinformatics sequences using regular expressions.

Quantifiers in regular expression

Quantifiers in regular expressions are powerful tools for specifying the number of occurrences of a pattern in a bioinformatics sequence. They allow for flexibility in searching and matching patterns of interest. Here are some commonly used quantifiers in regular expressions applied to bioinformatics sequences:

- **Asterisk (*)**: The asterisk quantifier matches zero or more occurrences of the preceding element. In *Example 7.4*, the pattern ATG* matches AT, ATG, ATGG, ATGGG, and so on. It is useful for finding repetitive patterns or variable-length motifs.

    Example 7.4

    ```
    import re
    sequence = "ATCGATGAAGTATGGCG"
    pattern = r"ATG*"
    # The findall function will search for pattern ATG*
    ```

```
# The function will return the list of patterns found
matches = re.findall(pattern, sequence)
print(matches)
if matches:
    print("Pattern(s) found in the sequence.")
    for match in matches:
        print(match)
else:
    print("No patterns found in the sequence.")
```

The output is shown in Figure 7.4.

```
==== RESTART: D:\pvdata\book1\P4Bio\Review_done\Code\Chapter7_code\Ex_7.4.py ===
['AT', 'ATG', 'ATGG']
Pattern(s) found in the sequence.
AT
ATG
ATGG
>>>
```

*Figure 7.4: * quantifier in regular expression*

- **Plus sign (+)**: The plus sign quantifier matches one or more occurrences of the preceding element. In *Example 7.5*, the pattern AGC+ matches AGC, AGCC, AGCCC, and so forth. It ensures that there is at least one occurrence of the specified element.

Example 7.5

```
import re
sequence = "ATCGAGCTGAAGTATGAGCCCGCG"
pattern = r"AGC+"
# The findall function will search for pattern AGC+
# The function will return the list of patterns found
matches = re.findall(pattern, sequence)
print(matches)
if matches:
    print("Pattern(s) found in the sequence.")
    for match in matches:
        print(match)
else:
    print("No patterns found in the sequence.")
```

The output is shown in *Figure 7.5*:

```
============================================ RESTART: D:/pvdata/book1/P4Bio/Review_
['AGC', 'AGCCC']
Pattern(s) found in the sequence.
AGC
AGCCC
>>>
```

Figure 7.5: + quantifier in regular expression

- **Question mark (?)**: The question mark quantifier matches zero or one occurrence of the preceding element. In example 7.6, the pattern GAT? matches GA and GAT. It is useful for identifying optional elements or variations in sequences.

Example 7.6

```python
import re
sequence = "ATCGATCGAAGTACG"
pattern = r"GAT?"
# The findall function will search for pattern GAT?
# The function will return the list of patterns found
matches = re.findall(pattern, sequence)
print(matches)
if matches:
    print("Pattern(s) found in the sequence.")
    for match in matches:
        print(match)
else:
    print("No patterns found in the sequence.")
```

The output is shown in *Figure 7.6*:

```
==== RESTART: D:\pvdata\book1\P4Bio\Review_done\Code\Chapter7_code\Ex_7.6.py ===
['GAT', 'GA']
Pattern(s) found in the sequence.
GAT
GA
>>>
```

Figure 7.6: (?) quantifier in regular expression

- **Curly braces ({m})**: The curly braces quantifier matches exactly the m occurrences of the preceding element. In *Example 7.7*, the pattern **AG{3}** matches AGGG but not AGG or AGGGG. It is useful for finding specific repetitive patterns with a fixed length.

Example 7.7

```
import re
sequence = "ATCGATCGAAGGGTAGG"
pattern = r"AG{3}"
# The findall function will search for pattern AG{3}
# The function will return the list of patterns found
matches = re.findall(pattern, sequence)
print(matches)
if matches:
    print("Pattern(s) found in the sequence.")
    for match in matches:
        print(match)
else:
    print("No patterns found in the sequence.")
```

The output is shown in *Figure 7.7*:

```
==== RESTART: D:\pvdata\book1\P4Bio\Review_done\Code\Chapter7_code\Ex_7.7.py ===
['AGGG']
Pattern(s) found in the sequence.
AGGG
>>>
```

Figure 7.7: ({}) quantifier in regular expression

- **Curly braces ({m, n})**: The curly braces quantifier matches a range of m to n occurrences of the preceding element. In *Example 7.8*, the pattern **AT{2,4}** matches ATT, ATTT, and ATTTT, but not AT or ATTTTT. It allows for specifying a variable range of occurrences.

Example 7.8

```
import re
sequence = "ATCGATTCGAAGTATTTCGATTTT"
pattern = r"AT{2,4}"
# The findall function will search for pattern GAT?
# The function will return the list of patterns found
matches = re.findall(pattern, sequence)
print(matches)
if matches:
    print("Pattern(s) found in the sequence.")
    for match in matches:
```

```
            print(match)
    else:
        print("No patterns found in the sequence.")
```

The output is shown in *Figure 7.8*:

```
==== RESTART: D:\pvdata\book1\P4Bio\Review_done\Code\Chapter7_code\Ex_7.8.py ===
['ATT', 'ATTT', 'ATTTT']
Pattern(s) found in the sequence.
ATT
ATTT
ATTTT
>>>
```

Figure 7.8: ({m,n}) quantifier in regular expression

- **Curly braces ({m,})**: The curly braces quantifier matches m or more occurrences of the preceding element. In Example 7.9, the pattern **CG{2,}** matches CGG, CGGG, CGGGG, and so on. It is useful for identifying repetitive patterns of a minimum length.

Example 7.9

```
import re
sequence = "ATCGGATCGGGGAAGTACGGG"
pattern = r"CG{2,}"
# The findall function will search for pattern CG{2,}
# The function will return the list of patterns found
matches = re.findall(pattern, sequence)
print(matches)
if matches:
    print("Pattern(s) found in the sequence.")
    for match in matches:
        print(match)
else:
    print("No patterns found in the sequence.")
```

The output is shown in *Figure 7.9*:

```
==== RESTART: D:\pvdata\book1\P4Bio\Review_done\Code\Chapter7_code\Ex_7.9.py ===
['CGG', 'CGGGG', 'CGGG']
Pattern(s) found in the sequence.
CGG
CGGGG
CGGG
>>>
```

Figure 7.9: ({m,}) quantifier in regular expression

These quantifiers provide flexibility in defining patterns in bioinformatics sequences and allow researchers to search for specific motifs or variations within sequences. They play a crucial role in various sequence analysis tasks such as pattern discovery, motif searching, sequence validation, and data extraction in bioinformatics research.

Positions in regular expression

In regular expressions for bioinformatics sequences in Python, you can use position anchors to match patterns at specific positions within a sequence. Here are some commonly used position anchors:

- **Start of line (^)**: The caret symbol (^) matches the beginning of a line or sequence.

    Example 7.10
    ```
    import re
    sequence = "ATGAGGGCTAGGCTGATCGATCGATCGTAGCTAGCTAGCTAGCTAG"
    pattern = r"^ATG"
    # The findall function will search for pattern ^ATG at the beginning of the sequence
    # The function will return the list of patterns found
    matches = re.findall(pattern, sequence)
    print(matches)
    if matches:
        print("Pattern found at the begining of the sequence.")
    else:
        print("No patterns found in the sequence.")
    ```

    The output is shown in *Figure 7.10*:

    ```
    ==================================================
    ['ATG']
    Pattern found at the begining of the sequence.
    >>>
    ```

    Figure 7.10: Positional character in regular expression

In *Example 7.10*, the pattern ^ATG matches ATG only when it appears at the beginning of the sequence:

- **End of line ($)**: The dollar sign ($) matches the end of a line or sequence. *Example 7.11:*

Example 7.11

```
import re
sequence = "ATGAGGGCTAGGCTGATCGATCGATCGTAGCTAGCTAGCTAGCTAG"
pattern = r"TAG$"
# The findall function will search for pattern $TAG at the end of the sequence
# The function will return the list of patterns found
matches = re.findall(pattern, sequence)
print(matches)
if matches:
    print("Pattern found at the end of the sequence.")
else:
    print("No patterns found in the sequence.")
```

The output is shown in *Figure 7.11*:

```
['TAG']
Pattern found at the end of the sequence.
>>>
```

Figure 7.11: Positional character in regular expression

In *Example 7.11*, the pattern **TAG$** matches **TAG** only when it appears at the end of the sequence.

These position anchors can be combined with other regular expression elements and quantifiers to create more complex patterns for matching specific positions within bioinformatics sequences.

Group function in regular expression

In regular expressions, the **group()** method allows you to access the specific parts of a matched pattern or capturing group. Here is *Example 7.12* of using **group()** function to extract parts of a string in a bioinformatics sequence:

Example 7.12

```
import re
sequence = "ATGAGGGCTAGGCTGATCGATCGATCGTAGCTAGCTAGCTAGCTAG"
pattern = r"(ATG)(.*?)(TAG)"
# The findall function will search for pattern $TAG at the end of the sequence
# The function will return the list of patterns found
```

```
matches = re.search(pattern, sequence)
print(matches)
if matches:
    full_match=matches.group(0) #The entire matched pattern
    start_codon=matches.group(1) # Contents of the first capturing group
    middle_part=matches.group(2) # Contents of the second capturing group
    stop_codon=matches.group(3)  # Contents of the third capturing group
    print("Full Match:", full_match)
    print("Start Codon:", start_codon)
    print("Middle Part:", middle_part)
    print("Stop Codon:", stop_codon)
```

The output is shown in *Figure 7.12*:

```
=== RESTART: D:\pvdata\book1\P4Bio\Review_done\Code\Chapter7_code\Ex_7.12.py ===
<re.Match object; span=(0, 11), match='ATGAGGGCTAG'>
Full Match: ATGAGGGCTAG
Start Codon: ATG
Middle Part: AGGGC
Stop Codon: TAG
>>>
```

Figure 7.12: Group function in regular expression

In this example, the regular expression **(ATG)(.*?)(TAG)** is used to match and capture three parts: the start codon, the middle part, and the stop codon. The **search()** function from the **re** module is used to find the first match in the sequence.

The **group()** method is then used to access the contents of each capturing group. **group(0)** returns the entire matched pattern, while **group(1)**, **group(2)**, and **group(3)** return the contents of the first, second, and third capturing groups, respectively.

By using **group()**, you can extract and access specific parts of the matched pattern or capture groups in bioinformatics sequences for further analysis or manipulation.

Getting a match position using regular expression

To obtain the position of a match in a regular expression for a bioinformatics sequence in Python, you can use the **search()** function from the **re** module and access the start and end positions of the match. Refer to *Example 7.13* for a better understanding:

Example 7.13
```
import re
sequence = "ATGAGGGCTAGGCTGATCGATCGATCGTAGCTAGCTAGCTAGCTAG"
pattern = r"ATG"   # Pattern to match
```

```python
match = re.search(pattern, sequence)
if match:
    start_position = match.start()  # Start position of the match
    end_position = match.end()  # End position of the match
    print("Start position:", start_position)
    print("End position:", end_position)
```

The output is shown in *Figure 7.13*:

```
=== RESTART: D:\pvdata\book1\P4Bio\Review_done\Code\Chapter7_code\Ex_7.13.py ===
Start position: 0
End position: 3
>>>
```

Figure 7.13: Retrieving match position

In this example, the regular expression **ATG** is used to search for a match in the sequence. The **search()** function finds the first occurrence of the pattern.

The **start()** method returns the starting position of the match, while the **end()** method returns the ending position (one character past the last character of the match). Note that the positions are 0-based indices.

By using **start()** and **end()**, you can obtain the positions of the matched pattern in a bioinformatics sequence. This information can be helpful for further analysis or manipulation of specific regions within the sequence.

Finding multiple matches in regular expression

To find multiple matches using regular expressions in a bioinformatics sequence, you can use the **finditer()** function from the **re** module in Python. It allows you to iterate over all matches in a sequence. Here is *Example 7.14*:

Example 7.14

```python
import re

sequence = "ATGAGGGCTAGGCTGATCGATCGATCGTAGCTAGCTAGCTAGCTAG"
pattern = r"GCT"   # Pattern to match
matches = re.finditer(pattern, sequence)
for match in matches:
    start_position = match.start()  # Start position of the match
    end_position = match.end()  # End position of the match
    print("Match found at position:", start_position, "-", end_position)
```

The output is shown in *Figure 7.14*:

```
=== RESTART: D:\pvdata\book1\P4Bio\Review_done\Code\Chapter7_code\EX_7.14.py ===
Match found at position: 6 - 9
Match found at position: 11 - 14
Match found at position: 29 - 32
Match found at position: 33 - 36
Match found at position: 37 - 40
Match found at position: 41 - 44
>>>
```

Figure 7.14: *Finding position of multiple matches*

In this example, the regular expression **GCT** is used to search for matches in the sequence. The **finditer()** function returns an iterator yielding match objects.

By iterating over the match objects, you can access the start and end positions of each match using the **start()** and **end()** methods, respectively. The example shows that the pattern **GCT** is found at multiple positions in the sequence. By using **finditer()**, you can identify and analyze all occurrences of a pattern in a bioinformatics sequence.

String splitting using regular expression

In bioinformatics, you can use regular expressions to split strings based on specific patterns or delimiters. This can be useful for separating and extracting relevant information from bioinformatics sequences or data. Here is *Example 7.15* of string splitting using regular expressions in Python:

Example 7.15

```
import re
sequence = "ATCGNNNATCGAAGTACG"
pattern = r"N+"
result = re.split(pattern, sequence)
print("Split sequence:")
for substring in result:
    print(substring)
```

The output is shown in *Figure 7.15*:

```
=== RESTART: D:\pvdata\book1\P4Bio\Review_done\Code\Chapter7_code\Ex_7.15.py ===
Split sequence:
ATCG
ATCGAAGTACG
>>>
```

Figure 7.15: *Split function of regular expression*

In this example, we define the **sequence** variable to store a bioinformatics sequence with **N** representing ambiguous bases, and the pattern variable to store the regular expression pattern. The pattern **N+** matches one or more occurrences of the character **N**. The `re.split()` function is used to split the sequence into a list of substrings based on the occurrence of the pattern. The function returns the list of substrings. The list of substrings can be iterated.

You can modify the regular expression pattern to split the string based on different criteria or patterns relevant to your specific bioinformatics task. By using regular expression-based string splitting, you can extract and separate relevant components from bioinformatics sequences or data for further analysis or processing.

Conclusion

Regular expressions are powerful tools in bioinformatics applications for pattern matching and sequence manipulation. It provides a flexible and efficient way to search, extract, and manipulate bioinformatics sequences based on specific patterns or motifs. Using metacharacters, character groups, quantifiers, and other features of regular expressions, you can build complex patterns to match specific sequences or patterns of interest in bioinformatics data. Overall, regular expressions are valuable tools for bioinformatics sequence analysis, enabling efficient and precise manipulation of sequence data for various research and application areas in the field.

CHAPTER 8
Data Handling and Visualization in Bioinformatics

Introduction

Data handling is a critical aspect of bioinformatics, as the field deals with large volumes of biological data generated from various sources, such as genomics, transcriptomics, proteomics, and metabolomics experiments. Effective data handling involves organizing, storing, processing, analyzing, and visualizing biological data to extract meaningful insights. Data handling is the culmination of various activities in bioinformatics like data storage and management, data preprocessing, data integration, data analysis and algorithm, and data visualization. Data handling in bioinformatics requires a combination of domain knowledge, computational skills, and expertise in data management and analysis. Effective data handling practices ensure the quality, integrity, and accessibility of biological data, enabling researchers to extract meaningful insights and improve our understanding of biological systems.

Data visualization refers to the graphical representation of biological data to aid in the exploration, analysis, and interpretation of complex biological phenomena. It involves using visual elements such as charts, graphs, maps, and diagrams to present and communicate biological information effectively. Data visualization is crucial in bioinformatics as it helps researchers understand patterns, trends, relationships, and structures within biological datasets, facilitating data-driven discoveries and hypothesis generation.

Structure

The chapter covers the following topics:

- Data handling
- Data visualization
- Working with NumPy
- Working with Pandas
- Working with Matplotlib
- Working with ggplot

Objectives

The chapter's objective is to provide readers with detailed knowledge of data handling and visualization. The reader will be able to understand the significance of data visualization with respect to bioinformatics applications. Various tools of Python programming language are used for the purpose of data visualization. The chapter will explore the various tools of Python used for data visualization and analysis.

Data handling

Data handling in bioinformatics requires domain knowledge, computational skills, and expertise in data management and analysis. Effective data handling practices ensure the quality, integrity, and accessibility of biological data, enabling researchers to extract meaningful insights and advance our understanding of biological systems.

Data handling in bioinformatics covers various aspects as follows:

- **Management of data storage**: Bioinformatics deals with huge amounts of data, which requires proper management. It uses various structured and unstructured databases like the **National Center for Biotechnology Information (NCBI)**, **European Bioinformatics Institute (EBI)**, and **Protein Data Bank (PDB)**. Besides these databases, specialized RDBMS and NoSQL databases may also be used for data storage.

- **Preprocessing of data**: The biological data collected from various sources must be pre-processed before processing it. Preprocessing involves quality control, filtering data, normalization, etc. Various in-built tools are used for this similar purpose, ensuring the reliability and accuracy of the data.

- **Data integration**: In bioinformatics applications, data is integrated from various sources to get wider insights into the application. Data integration involves merging datasets, reconciling different data types, and normalizing data formats.

The integration allows researchers to combine diverse data modalities and identify patterns, correlations, and relationships that may not be evident when analyzing individual datasets.

- **Analysis of data**: There are a variety of algorithms and statistical models used for the analysis of biological data. These include sequence alignment algorithms, clustering algorithms, classification algorithms, statistical tests, and ML approaches. The role of Bioinformatics tools is to provide implementation of the various algorithms and models.

- **Visualization of data**: The visualization of biological data is very important for interpreting the results of bioinformatics applications. BI uses a variety of visualization tools that include bar charts, scatter plots, and genome browsers, to name a few. Visualization tools and software enable researchers to explore and present data in an intuitive and visually appealing manner, facilitating data interpretation and hypothesis generation.

- **Sharing of data**: Researchers do share their data among themselves or make it public so that the scientific community can access it. Standards and protocols, such as the **Genomic Data Commons (GDC)**, the **Genomic Data Sharing (GDS)** policy, and the **Findable, Accessible, Interoperable, and Reusable (FAIR)** principles, promote data sharing, interoperability, and reproducibility.

Data visualization

Data visualization in bioinformatics refers to the graphical representation of biological data to aid in the exploration, analysis, and interpretation of complex biological phenomena. It involves using visual elements such as charts, graphs, maps, and diagrams to present and communicate biological information effectively. Effective data visualization in bioinformatics helps researchers gain insights, communicate findings, and make informed decisions. It enhances the understanding of complex biological phenomena, supports hypothesis generation, and enables the discovery of novel biological knowledge. By transforming raw data into visually appealing and intuitive representations, data visualization is crucial in accelerating scientific discoveries and advancements in bioinformatics. Data visualization in bioinformatics covers various aspects as follows:

- **Genome annotation**: Genomes are linear representations of annotated DNA sequences. Genome annotation is identifying and labeling the functional elements within a genome. It involves analyzing the DNA sequence to determine the locations and functions of genes, regulatory regions, and other genomic features. Genome annotation plays a crucial role in understanding the structure of the organization and function of genes and their associated elements.

- **Sequence analysis**: Information visualization techniques are widely used to analyze biological sequences. Sequence alignment and further analyzing it using various visualization techniques is a common practice.

- **Phylogeny and taxonomy**: Phylogeny and taxonomy are two closely related fields in biology that focus on understanding the evolutionary relationships and classification of organisms. While they are distinct concepts, they are often interconnected and used to study and categorize the diversity of life on Earth. These are commonly represented as trees where different items are arranged in a hierarchical manner, having one parent. Various information visualization tools are used for similar purposes.

- **Expression profile**: Information visualization techniques are commonly used as an assessment method for clustering of DNA microarray expression profiles and 2D gel electrophoresis. The high-level outcome of such clustering can be visualized dendrogram or colored mosaic, which is also one of the information visualization techniques.

- **Molecular pathway**: Molecular pathway, also known as biochemical pathway or metabolic pathway, refers to a series of interconnected chemical reactions that occur within a cell to accomplish a specific biological function. These pathways involve the conversion of one molecule into another through a series of enzymatic reactions, ultimately leading to the synthesis of the breakdown of complex molecules. Molecular pathways are critical for the normal functioning and regulation of cellular processes. They play key roles in various biological functions, including energy production, biosynthesis of macromolecules, signal transduction, and cell cycle control.

Tools for data handling and visualization in bioinformatics

Python programming language consists of various libraries for data handling and visualization. These libraries do support versatile activities as follows:

- **NumPy**: NumPy or Numerical Python is a powerful Python library that supports large, multi-dimensional arrays and matrices, along with a collection of mathematical functions to operate on these arrays efficiently. It is one of the fundamental libraries for scientific computing in Python and serves as a foundation for many other data analysis and scientific libraries.

- **Pandas**: It is a powerful open-source data manipulation and analysis library for Python. It provides high-performance, easy-to-use data structures, such as DataFrames and Series, and a wide range of data manipulation functions.

- **Matplotlib**: It is a popular plotting library for Python that provides various visualization tools. It is widely used for generating static, animated, and interactive plots in various formats. Matplotlib is designed to closely resemble MATLAB's plotting capabilities, making it a popular choice among scientists, engineers, and data analysts. Matplotlib is used in various bioinformatics applications to visualize genomic data, expression profiles, protein structures, and other biological data.

- **Scikit-Learn**: It is also known as `sklearn` and is a popular open-source machine-learning library for Python. It provides various tools and functionalities for machine learning tasks, including classification, regression, clustering, dimensionality reduction, model selection, and data pre-processing. Scikit-Learn is built on top of NumPy, SciPy, and Matplotlib, and it integrates well with the Python data science ecosystem. It is a simple and efficient tool for data mining and analysis. The library consists of various algorithms related to data analytics, like regression, classification, clustering, Support Vector Machine, and random forest, to name a few.

Working with NumPy

NumPy is a popular Python library used for big multidimensional arrays and matrices. NumPy arrays are homogenous in nature, and they perform various operations on array elements. These arrays may be single or multidimensional in nature. These arrays may be single or multidimensional in nature.

To work with NumPy, we need to install it. For installation of NumPy, we can start the command-line interface in Windows and use the `pip` utility to install NumPy, as shown in *Figure 8.1*:

Figure 8.1: Installation of NumPy

Arrays in NumPy

An array is the main object of NumPy. It consists of a set of elements that are indexed by some positive integer value. Array in NumPy can be single or multi-dimensional. Dimensions in NumPy are called axes. NumPy's array class is `ndarray`.

Working with arrays in NumPy involves creating arrays, accessing, and modifying their elements, performing mathematical operations, and utilizing various array manipulation techniques. Here is an overview of some commonly used operations with arrays in NumPy:

Creating a single and multidimensional array:

Single dimensional array

Execute the following code in Example 8.1 to create a single-dimensional array:

Example 8.1

```
import numpy as np
arr1 = np.array([10, 20, 30, 40, 50])
print(arr)
```

Output:

`[10 20 30 40 50]`

Multidimensional array

In order to create a multi-dimensional array, execute the following code *example 8.2*:

Example 8.2

```
import numpy as np
# Creating and printing numpy double dimensional array
arr = np.array([[10, 20, 30], [40, 50, 60]])
print(arr)
```

Output:

`[[10 20 30]`
` [40 50 60]]`

Accessing a single and multidimensional array

To access a single element from the single and multidimensional array, execute the following code:

Single dimensional array

Example 8.3

```
import numpy as np
# Accessing first elment of the single dimensional array
arr = np.array([10, 20, 30, 40])
print(arr[0])
```

Output:

`[10]`

Multidimensional array

Example 8.4
```
import numpy as np
# Accessing second element from second row
arr = np.array([[10,20,30,40,50], [60,70,80,90,100]])
print('2nd element on 2nd row: ', arr[1, 1])
```

Output:
[70]

Array slicing in NumPy

Slicing means accessing elements from one index position to another index position. The syntax for slicing an array is:

`<array_name>[start_index : end_index]`

It will access elements from **start_index** to **end_index-1**

`<array_name>[start_index : end_index : step]`

By default, the step value is 1. If you wish to use another step value, you may mention it.

If we do not mention **start_index**, it will be considered 0. If we do not mention **end_index**, it will be considered as the length of an array.

Example 8.5 demonstrates the concept of slicing where elements from 0 index to 4 index are accessed from the array named **arr**.

Example 8.5
```
import numpy as np
# Slicing element from index 1 to 4 of numpy array
arr = np.array([11, 12, 13, 14, 15, 16, 17])
print(arr[1:5])
```

Output:
[12 13 14 15]

Example 8.6 demonstrates the concept of slicing where elements from 0 index to 4 index are accessed from the array named **arr**. The start index is not mentioned hence the start index will automatically be assigned as 0.

Example 8.6:
```
import numpy as np
#Slicing content from 0 index to 4th index
arr = np.array([11, 12, 13, 14, 15, 16, 17])t
print(arr[:5])
```

Output:

`[11 12 13 14 15]`

Example 8.7 demonstrates the concept of slicing where elements from the 5 index to the last index are accessed from the array named **arr**. The end index is not mentioned hence the end index will automatically be assigned as the last index.

Example 8.7:

```
import numpy as np
# Slicing content from 5th index to the last index
arr = np.array([11, 12, 13, 14, 15, 16, 17])
print(arr[5:])
```

Output:

`[16 17]`

Example 8.8 demonstrates the concept of slicing where elements from 1 index to 4 index are accessed from the array named **arr**. Step value 2 is mentioned hence elements in between 1 to 4 with step value 2 are accessed.

Example 8.8:

```
import numpy as np
# Slicing content from index 1 to 4 with step value of 2
arr = np.array([11, 12, 13, 14, 15, 16, 17])
print(arr[1:5:2])
```

Output:

`[12 14]`

Traversing NumPy array

Traversing means going through all elements one by one. We can use loops to traverse all the elements of an array. *Example 8.9* demonstrates the traversal loop for single dimensional array.

Traversing single dimensional array

Example 8.9 demonstrates the concept of traversing elements from one by one from the **arr** using a for loop. The one value will be picked at a time in variable **x** and printed one by one.

Example 8.9:

```
import numpy as np
arr = np.array([11, 22, 33, 44])
#Traversing loop for single dimensional array
```

```
for x in arr:
  print(x)
```

Output:
`[11 22 33 44]`

Traversing double dimensional array

Example 8.10 demonstrates the concept of traversing elements from double dimensional array **arr** using for loop. The one row will be picked at a time in variable **x** and printed one by one.

Example 8.10:
```
import numpy as np
arr = np.array([[11, 22, 33], [44, 55, 66]])
for x in arr:
  print(x)
```

Output:
`[11 22 33]`
`[44 55 66]`

Working with Pandas

Pandas is a Python library that facilitates working with various data sets. It has various functions used for the analysis, cleaning, and manipulation of data. It helps you analyze big data and make conclusions using statistical algorithms.

The first step towards using **Pandas** is to install it using this command:
`>>pip install Pandas`

The command should be given at the command prompt.

Once the installation is complete to use **pandas**, import it using the following command:
`>>import pandas`

We can use an alias name for pandas while importing it as follows:
`>>import pandas as pd`

Handling datasets and DataFrames through Pandas

The datasets with heterogeneous datatype values can be generated and converted into DataFrames. A Pandas DataFrame is a two-dimensional data structure, like a 2-dimensional array or a table with rows and columns. Refer to *Figure 8.2* for a better understanding:

A DataFrame is a fundamental data structure used in various programming languages and libraries, particularly in data analysis and manipulation. It provides a way to organize data in a tabular form, similar to a spreadsheet or a SQL table, where data is organized into rows and columns. DataFrames are widely used in data science, statistics, and ML for handling structured data efficiently.

Example 8.11:

```
import pandas as pd
#Creating a Dataset
mydataset = {
    'Fruits': ["Orange", "Banana", "Apple", "Peer"],
    'Quantity' : [3,7,2,10]
}
#Creating DataFrame using Dataset
myvar=pd.DataFrame(mydataset)
print(myvar)
```

Output:

```
=== RESTART: D:\pvdata\book1\P4Bio\Review_done\Code\Chapter8_code\Ex_8.11.py ===
   Fruits  Quantity
0  Orange         3
1  Banana         7
2   Apple         2
3    Peer        10
>>>
```

Figure 8.2: Working with Pandas DataFrame

Loading files into a DataFrame to load files into a DataFrame, you can use **pandas** library that provides DataFrame functionality. The combination of Python and Pandas is used for data manipulation and analysis.

Pandas help in reading **.csv** files into a DataFrame. The preceding *Example 8.12* will print the data rows from the files as specified by **pd.options.display.max_rows** properties. Refer figure 8.3.

Example 8.12:

```
import pandas as pd
df = pd.read_csv("D:\\pvdata\\Python_prog\\stroke_data.csv")
print("Data rows in the file are")
print(df)
```

```
================================================ RESTART: D:/pvdata/book1
        id  gender   age  ...   bmi  smoking_status  stroke
0     9046    Male  67.0  ...  36.6  formerly smoked      1
1    51676  Female  61.0  ...   NaN    never smoked      1
2    31112    Male  80.0  ...  32.5    never smoked      1
3    60182  Female  49.0  ...  34.4          smokes      1
4     1665  Female  79.0  ...  24.0    never smoked      1
...    ...     ...   ...  ...   ...             ...    ...
5105 18234  Female  80.0  ...   NaN    never smoked      0
5106 44873  Female  81.0  ...  40.0    never smoked      0
5107 19723  Female  35.0  ...  30.6    never smoked      0
5108 37544    Male  51.0  ...  25.6  formerly smoked      0
5109 44679  Female  44.0  ...  26.2         Unknown      0

[5110 rows x 12 columns]
Maximum data rows in the file are
60
>>>
```

Figure 8.3: Printing sixty raws of dataFrame defined by max_raws property

However, to get all the records of the data file, one can use the **to_string()** function. *Example 8.13*. Refer figure 8.4.

Example 8.13:

```python
import pandas as pd
df = pd.read_csv('data.csv')
# To print all the rows of data frame
print(df.to_string())
```

```
================================================ RESTART: D:/pvdata
Data rows in the file are
        id  gender   age  ...   bmi  smoking_status  stroke
0     9046    Male  67.0  ...  36.6  formerly smoked      1
1    51676  Female  61.0  ...   NaN    never smoked      1
2    31112    Male  80.0  ...  32.5    never smoked      1
3    60182  Female  49.0  ...  34.4          smokes      1
4     1665  Female  79.0  ...  24.0    never smoked      1
...    ...     ...   ...  ...   ...             ...    ...
5105 18234  Female  80.0  ...   NaN    never smoked      0
5106 44873  Female  81.0  ...  40.0    never smoked      0
5107 19723  Female  35.0  ...  30.6    never smoked      0
5108 37544    Male  51.0  ...  25.6  formerly smoked      0
5109 44679  Female  44.0  ...  26.2         Unknown      0

[5110 rows x 12 columns]
Squeezed text (5111 lines).
>>>
```

Figure 8.4: Printing all the raws of dataFrame

The *to_string()* function will display all the records from the data file. The squeezed text bar in *Figure 8*.4 shows that all records are printed. On expanding it, all records can be viewed.

Working with Matplotlib

To get started with Matplotlib, you will need to install it first. You can install it using **pip**, the package manager for Python, by running the following command on the command line:

`pip install matplotlib`

Once you have installed Matplotlib, you can import it into your Python script or interactive session using the following import statement:

`import matplotlib.pyplot as plt`

The **pyplot** module is the primary interface for creating plots with Matplotlib.

Line plot by Matplotlib

The **plot()** function is one of the most used functions for creating plots. It allows you to plot data points and connect them with lines to visualize trends or patterns. The function can be used in different ways depending on the type of data and the desired plot style.

The general syntax of the **plot()** function is as follows:

`Plot([x],y,[format_string],**kwargs)`

This is explained below:

- **[x]**: (optional) The x-coordinates of the data points. If not provided, the indices of the y array will be used as the x-coordinates.
- **Y**: The y-coordinates of the data points.
- **[format_string]**: (optional) A format string that specifies the line style, marker style, and color of the plot.
- ****kwargs**: (optional) Additional keyword arguments that control various aspects of the plot, such as the line width, marker size, and label.

Basic plot

To draw a basic plot, we only need one data series for the y-axis. Figure 8.5 shows the runtime of *Example 8.14*:

Example 8.14

```
import matplotlib.pyplot as plt
y=[10,30,20,40,30,50]
```

```
plt.plot(y)
plt.show()
```
Output:

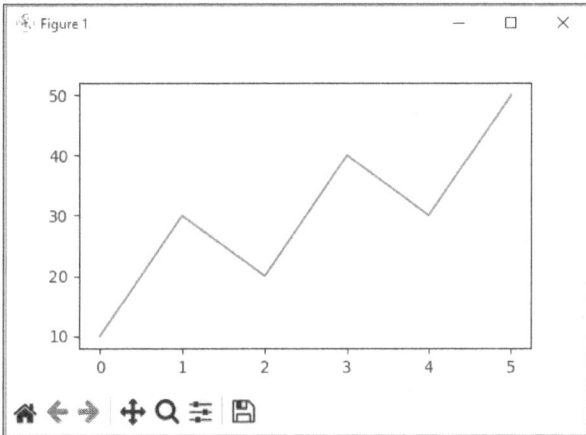

Figure 8.5: Basic line plot

Line plot with x and y values

A line plot, also known as a **line chart** or line graph, is a type of data visualization used to represent data points as a series of data connected by straight lines. Line plots are particularly useful for showing trends or changes in data over a continuous interval or time period. They are commonly used in various fields, including finance, economics, science, bioinformatics, and engineering. *Example 8.15* demonstrates the working of **plot()** function with data series at x and y axis. Refer Figure 8.6

Example 8.15:
```
import matplotlib.pyplot as plt
#Data Series for x-axis
x=[10,20,30,40,50]
#Data Series for y-axis
y=[10,30,20,40,30]
plt.plot(x,y)
plt.show()
```

Output:

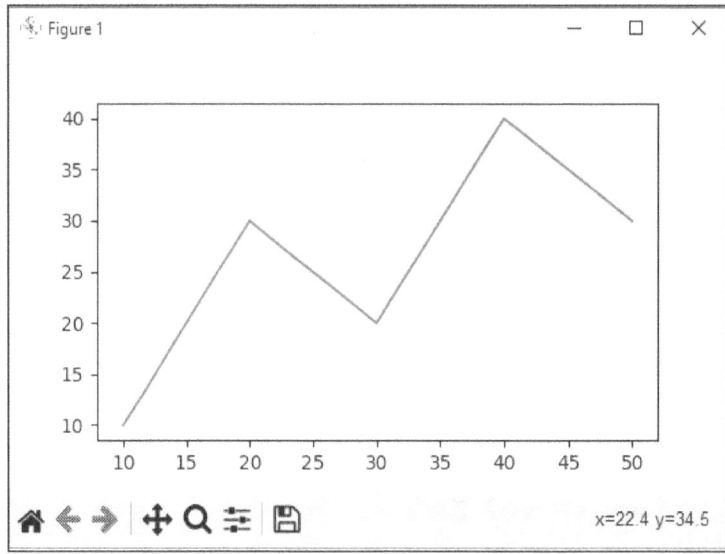

Figure 8.6: Basic line plot with x and y axis

Customizing line style and marker

You can specify the line style and marker using the **format_string** parameter. The format string consists of a combination of characters that represent the line style, marker style, and color. For *Example 8.16*, **r—** presents a red dashed line. Take a look at the following *Figure 8.7*:

Example 8.16:
```
import matplotlib.pyplot as plt
# Data for x-axis
x=[1,2,3,4,5]
# Data for y-axis
y=[1,3,2,4,5]
plt.plot(x,y,'r--')
plt.show()
```

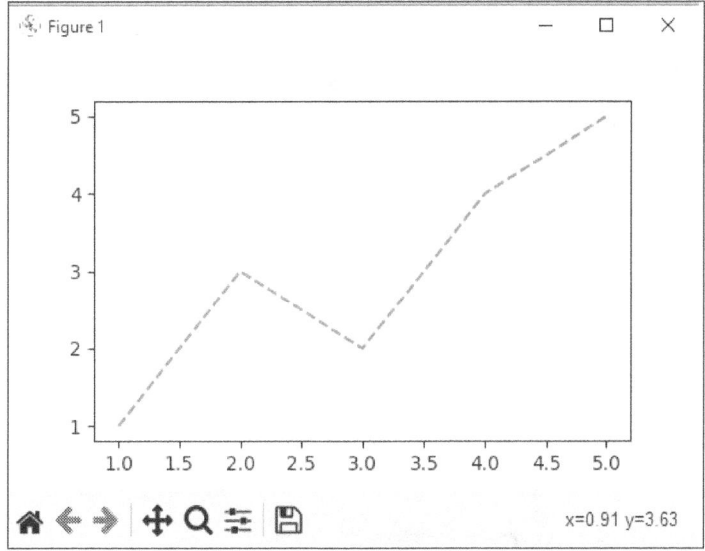

Figure 8.7: Basic line plot with line marker

Adding label and title

A label can be added to the x-axis, y-axis, and a title to your plot using the **xlable()**, **ylabel()**, and **title** functions, respectively. Look at the following *Figure 8.8* and *Example 8.17* for clarity:

Example 8.17:
```
import matplotlib.pyplot as plt
# Data for x-axis
x=[1,2,3,4,5]
# Data for y-axis
y=[1,3,2,4,5]
plt.plot(x,y,'b-o')
# Assigning labels for 'X' axis and 'Y' axis
plt.xlabel('X-axis')
plt.ylabel('Y-axis')
plt.title('My Plot')
plt.show()
```

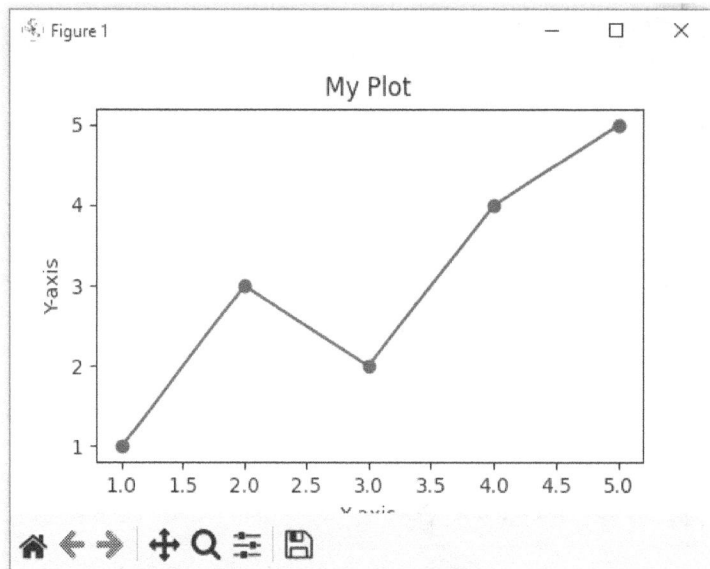

Figure 8.8: Basic line plot with label

Bar plot

In Matplotlib, you can create bar plots using the **bar()** or **barh()** functions. The **bar()** function is used for vertical plots, while the **barh()** function is used for horizontal bar plots. These functions allow you to visualize categorical or discrete data as bars, with their lengths or heights representing the values associated with each category. *Example 8.18* demonstrates the usage of a bar plot. Refer Figure 8.9

Example 8.18:

```
import matplotlib.pyplot as plt
# Prepare data
Dinucleotide = ['AT', 'GC', 'AA']
Count = [10, 15, 12]
# Create a figure and axes
fig, ax = plt.subplots()
# Plot the bar chart for count of Dinucleotide Values
ax.bar(Dinucleotide, Count)
# Customize the plot
ax.set_xlabel('Dinucleotide')
ax.set_ylabel('Count')
ax.set_title('Bar Plot')
```

```
# Display the plot
plt.show()
```

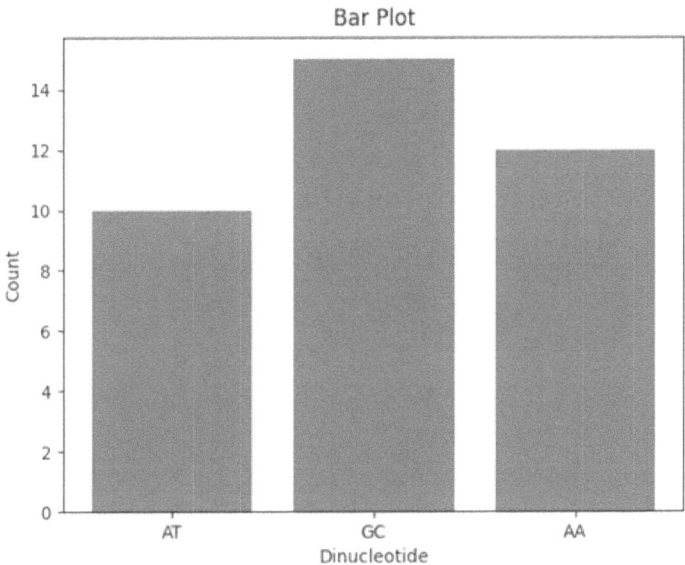

Figure 8.9: Basic bar plot

Plotting horizontal bar graph

A horizontal bar graph, also known as a **horizontal bar chart** or **horizontal bar plot**, is a data visualization that represents data using horizontal bars to compare categories or values, refer to *Figure 8.10* and *Example 8.19*:

Example 8.19:
```
import matplotlib.pyplot as plt

# Prepare data
Dinucleotide = ['AT', 'GC', 'AA']
Count = [10, 15, 12]

# Create a figure and axes
fig, ax = plt.subplots()

# Plot the bar chart for count of Dinucleotide Values
ax.barh(Dinucleotide, Count)

# Customize the plot
ax.set_xlabel('Dinucleotide')
```

```
ax.set_ylabel('Count')
ax.set_title('Bar Plot')

# Display the plot
plt.show()
```

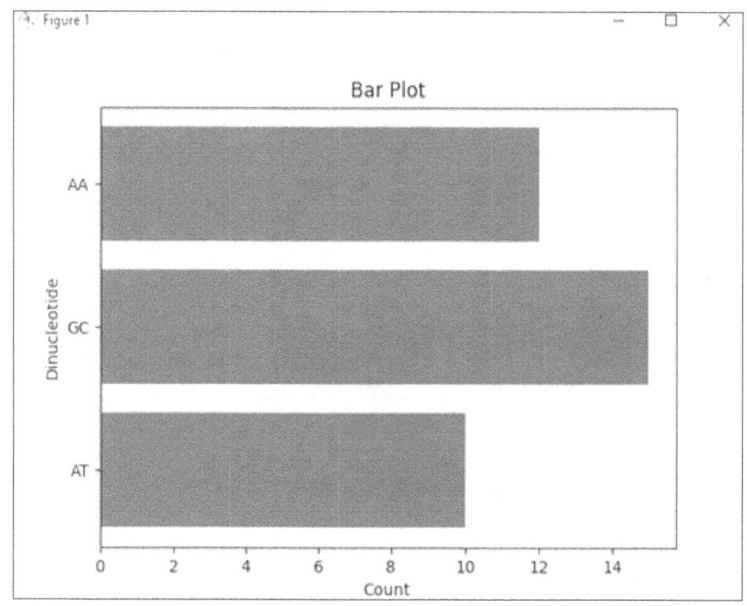

Figure 8.10: Basic horizontal bar plot

Histogram plot

In Matplotlib, you can create histograms to visualize the distribution of a continuous variable. A histogram represents the frequency or count of values falling into different bins or intervals. Matplotlib provides the **hist()** function to create histograms easily. Refer to *Example 8.20* and *Figure 8.11* for clarity:

Example 8.20:

```
import matplotlib.pyplot as plt

# Prepare data
data = [1, 1, 1, 2, 3, 3, 4, 5, 5, 6, 6, 6, 7, 8, 8, 9, 9, 9, 9]

# Create a figure and axes
fig, ax = plt.subplots()

# Plot the histogram
ax.hist(data, bins=10)
```

```python
# Customize the plot
ax.set_xlabel('Value')
ax.set_ylabel('Frequency')
ax.set_title('Histogram')

# Display the plot
plt.show()
```

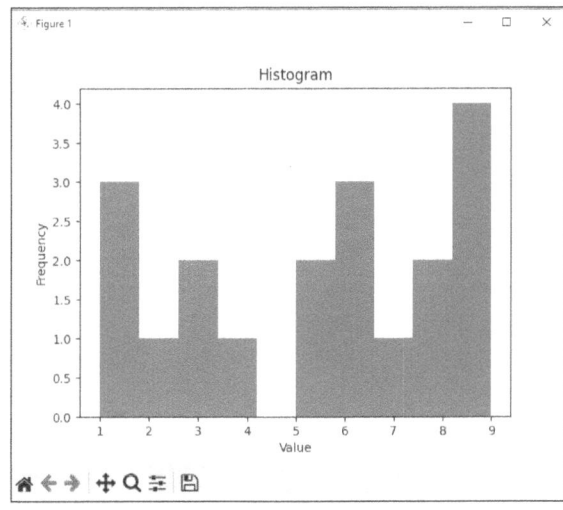

Figure 8.11: Histogram plot

Scatter plot

In Matplotlib, you can create scatter plots to visualize the relationship between two continuous variables. Scatter plots display individual data points as markers in a *Cartesian* coordinate system, with one variable represented on the x-axis and the other variable represented on the y-axis. Matplotlib provides the **scatter()** function to create scatter plots easily. Refer to *Example 8.21* and *Figure 8.12* for a better understanding:

Example 8.21:
```python
import matplotlib.pyplot as plt
# Prepare data
data_x_axis = [10, 20, 30, 40, 50]
data_y_axis = [20, 40, 60, 80, 100]
# Create a figure and axes
fig, ax = plt.subplots()
# Plot the scatter plot
ax.scatter(data_x_axis, data_y_axis)
```

```
# Customize the plot
ax.set_xlabel('X-axis')
ax.set_ylabel('Y-axis')
ax.set_title('Scatter Plot')
# Display the plot
plt.show()
```

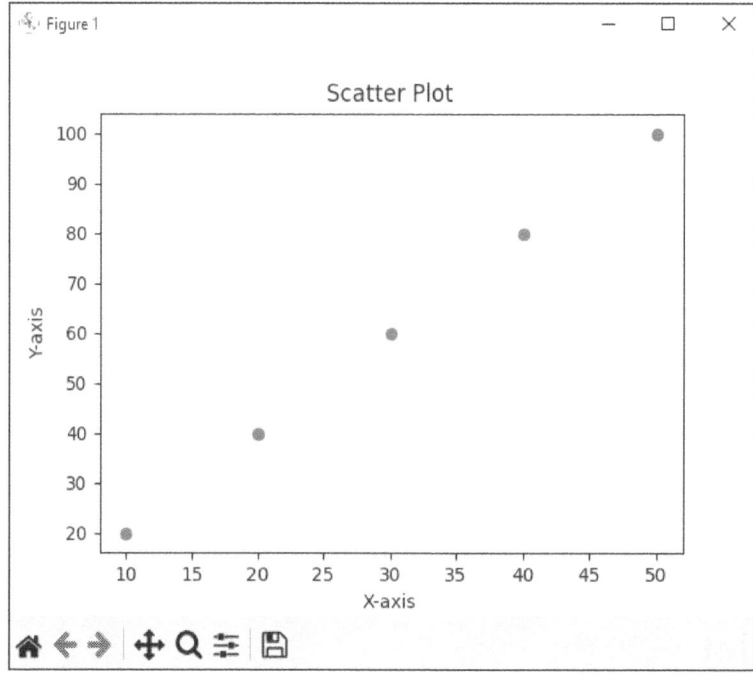

Figure 8.12: Scatter plot

Working with ggplot

We can use the **plotnine** library in Python to create data visualizations using a grammar of graphics approach, similar to **ggplot2** in R. **plotnine** provides a Pythonic way to create high-quality visualizations. It is a tool that facilitates in describing the components of a graphic. It allows us to see beyond the named graphics. To use **plotnine** library we need to install it first by using command:

```
>> pip install plotnine
```

Once it is installed import necessary modules from **plotnine**:

```
>> from plotnine import *
```

The **plotnine** library works very well with dataframes. Below is the *Example 8.22* and *Figure 8.13* that demonstrates the usage of **plotnine** library:

Example 8.22:
```
from plotnine import *
import pandas as pd

data = pd.DataFrame({
    'x': [1, 2, 3, 4, 5],
    'y': [2, 4, 1, 3, 5]
})

#Create a plot object by specifying the data and aesthetic mappings using ggplot():
#ggplot() initializes the plot and defines the aesthetics (how the data maps to visual properties).
#geom_point() adds the layer for creating a scatter plot.
#labs() sets the plot title and axis labels.

gg = (
    ggplot(data, aes(x='x', y='y')) +
    geom_point() +
    labs(title="Scatter Plot Example", x="X-axis", y="Y-axis")
)
#To display the plot, simply print the gg object:
print(gg)
```

Figure 8.13: Scatter plot

Conclusion

Data handling and visualization play crucial roles in bioinformatics, enabling researchers to gain insights from large and complex biological datasets. In bioinformatics, data can come in various forms, including genomic sequences, gene expression profiles. Protein structures etc. Effective data handling and visualization techniques help researchers analyze, interpret, and communicate their findings.

Data handling in bioinformatics involves tasks such as data preprocessing, cleaning, integration, and transformation. This often requires specialized tools and programming languages, such as Python and R, along with relevant libraries and packages. Bioinformatics researchers employ techniques like data normalization, filtering, and statistical analysis to ensure the quality and reliability of their data. Proper data handling techniques are critical for accurate and meaningful downstream analyses.

Visualization plays a crucial role in understanding complex biological data. It allows researchers to explore patterns, relationships, and trends in their data, facilitating hypothesis generation and testing. Bioinformatics researchers use various visualization techniques, including plots, charts, diagrams, and interactive visualizations, to represent and interpret their data effectively.

Matplotlib a popular plotting library in Python, is widely used for creating visualizations in bioinformatics. It offers various plot types, customization options, and interactivity. Matplotlib can be combined with other libraries, such as NumPy and Pandas, to handle and visualize biological data efficiently. In summary, data handling and visualization are essential components of bioinformatics research. They enable researchers to explore and analyze large and complex biological datasets that lead to getting meaningful information from biological systems.

Join our book's Discord space

Join the book's Discord Workspace for Latest updates, Offers, Tech happenings around the world, New Release and Sessions with the Authors:

https://discord.bpbonline.com

CHAPTER 9
Mini Applications in Bioinformatics

Introduction

Bioinformatics is an interdisciplinary field having a wide range of applications across various areas of biological research. Bioinformatics deals with a variety of applications. The chapter will cover different hands-on small coding exercises related to bioinformatics.

Structure

The chapter covers the following topics:
- Project 1: Concatenation of DNA sequences
- Project 2: Calculating AT content in the sequence
- Project 3: Searching for restriction sites/ enzymes in DNA sequences
- Project 4: Reading a Swiss-Prot file
- Project 5: Reading Swiss-Prot record from ExPASy server
- Project 6: Parsing Swiss-Prot keywords list
- Project 7: Prosite records parsing
- Project 8: Using ExPASy for parsing enzyme records
- Project 9: Reading PDB files
- Project 10: Reading GenBank file

- Project 11: Sequence alignment
- Project 12: Retrieving sequence digested by restricted enzymes

Objectives

The objective of this chapter is to explore practical applications of bioinformatics, providing learners with hands-on insights into how bioinformatics tools and techniques solve biological problems, by focusing on smaller, targeted projects. This chapter ensures readers can connect theoretical knowledge to practical uses, fostering a deeper understanding of the significance and versatility of bioinformatics in modern science.

Project 1: Concatenation of DNA sequences

Concatenating biological sequences refers to the process of combining multiple sequences into a single longer sequence. This can be done for various reasons and serves different purposes in biological research. Here are some common reasons why concatenating biological sequences may be necessary: Phylogenetic analysis, multiple sequence alignment, comparative genomics, functional annotation, barcode or tag sequences.

Let us say we have the following two sequences:
- **DNA1:** ACGTAACCGGTT
- **DNA2:** TTGGCCAATGCA

To concatenate these two sequences, we can use **+** operator. The **+** operator will only concatenate the two DNA sequences if they are string or sequence objects.

Example 9.1 demonstrates how two DNA sequences are concatenated. The two DNA sequences are taken in **DNA1** and **DNA2** string variables. The two DNA sequences are concatenated using **+** operator assigned to **DNA_CONCAT** string variable and finally printed. Refer to *Figure 9.1* for the output.

Example 9.1:

```
# Concatenation of 02 DNA sequences
DNA1 = "ACGTAACCGGTT"
DNA2 = "TTGGCCAATGCA"
# Concatenating 02 sequences using + operator.
DNA_CONCAT = DNA1 + DNA2
# Printing concatenated DNA sequence
(print ("The concatenated DNA Sequence is:: ", DNA_CONCAT)
```

```
= RESTART: D:/pvdata/book1/P4Bio/Review_done/Code/Chapter 9_code/Example9.1.py =
The concatenated DNA Sequence is::   ACGTAACCGGTTTTGGCCAATGCA
>>>
```

Figure 9.1: *DNA sequences concatenation*

Project 2: Calculating AT content in the sequence

Calculating the **Adenine-Thymine (AT)** content of a DNA sequence involves determining the proportion of nucleotides in the sequence that are either **Adenine (A)** or **Thymine (T)**. The AT content is a fundamental property of DNA sequences and can provide insights into various aspects of genetics and molecular biology.

Example 9.2 demonstrates how to calculate AT content in a DNA sequence by user-defined function `calculate_at_content()`. The function accepts a DNA sequence as a parameter and counts the occurrence of base **A** and **T** in a sequence using inbuilt function `count()`. The length of the DNA sequence is calculated using `len()` function and assigned to `total_count` variable. Finally, **AT** is calculated and assigned to a variable `at_content` and returned to the main module from where the function is called. The output is shown in *Figure 9.2*.

Example 9.2:

```
# function to calculate the AT content in a DNA sequence
def calculate_at_content(dna_sequence):
    dna_sequence=dna_sequence.upper()
    a_count=dna_sequence.count('A')
    t_count=dna_sequence.count('T')
    total_count=len(dna_sequence)
    at_content=((a_count+t_count) / total_count) * 100
    return at_content

# Example DNA sequence
sequence = "ATGCTAGCTAGCTAGCTAGCTAGCTAGCT"

# Function calcualte_at_content is called
at_content=calculate_at_content(sequence)

#Print the AT content
print("AT content :",at_content)
```

```
= RESTART: D:/pvdata/book1/P4Bio/Review_done/Code/Chapter 9_code/Example9.2.py =
AT content : 51.724137931034484
```

Figure 9.2: Calculating AT content

Project 3: Searching for restriction sites/enzymes in DNA sequences

Restriction enzymes, also known as restriction endonucleases, are enzymes that recognize specific DNA sequences and cleave the DNA at or near those recognition sites. They are essential tools in molecular biology and genetic engineering as they enable the precise manipulation of DNA molecules.

Restriction enzymes can be classified into several types based on the characteristics of their recognition sequences and cleavage patterns. The three main types are Type I, Type II, and Type III restriction enzymes. Type II restriction enzymes are the most used in molecular biology research due to their simple recognition sites and predictable cleavage patterns. Type II restriction enzymes recognize specific, short DNA sequences (usually 4-8 base pairs) and cleave the DNA at or very close to these recognition sites. This precise cutting ability allows researchers to predictably and reproducibly cut DNA into defined fragments, which is essential for cloning, mapping, and other genetic manipulations. Unlike other types of restriction enzymes, Type II enzymes do not require ATP or other cofactors (beyond magnesium ions) to function. They directly cleave DNA at the recognition site, making them more straightforward to use in the laboratory.

This small code set in *Example 9.3* demonstrates the usage of **RestrictionBatch** library. **RestrictionBatch** can give you a dictionary with the sites for all the enzymes in a batch. After creating a sequence by the name **dna_sequence**, a list of restricted enzymes is created by the name **res_enzymes**. Once the list is created, add all the enzymes in a list to an object of **RestrictionBatch** module. The next step is to search for the restriction enzymes in a sequence using **search()** function of **RestrictionBatch()** object. The search function will result into a Dictionary that holds the name of the enzyme and site index as shown in *Figure 9.3*:

Example 9.3:

```
from Bio.Seq import Seq
from Bio.Restriction import RestrictionBatch

# Define the DNA sequence
dna_sequence = Seq("ATCGATCGATCGAGTCTAGCTAGCTGAATTCGCTAGCTAGCTAGCTAGCTAGCT")

# Define the restriction enzymes of interest
res_enzymes = ["EcoRI", "HindIII"]
# Create a RestrictionBatch object and add the enzymes
rb = RestrictionBatch(res_enzymes)

# Find the restriction sites in the sequence
```

```
sites = rb.search(dna_sequence)

# Print the results
for enzyme, cut_site in sites.items():
    if cut_site:
        print(f"{enzyme} sites found at positions:", cut_site)
    else:
        print(f"{enzyme} sites not found in the sequence")
```

```
== RESTART: C:\Users\5453\AppData\Local\Programs\Python\Python38\CH9_PRO_2.py ==
EcoRI sites found at positions: [27]
HindIII sites not found in the sequence
>>>
```

Figure 9.3: Searching for restriction site

Project 4: Reading a Swiss-Prot file

A Swiss-Prot file, also known as a **UniProtKB/Swiss-Prot** file, is a text file format used to store protein sequences and associated information from the Swiss-Prot protein knowledgebase. Each entry in a Swiss-Prot file represents a specific protein and includes details such as protein name, function, sequence, post-translational modifications, and references. Here is an example of how a Swiss-Prot file entry looks:

```
ID   NU3M_BALPH              Reviewed;        115 AA.
AC   P68308; P24973;
DT   25-OCT-2004, integrated into UniProtKB/Swiss-Prot.
DT   25-OCT-2004, sequence version 1.
DT   22-FEB-2023, entry version 59.
DE   RecName: Full=NADH-ubiquinone oxidoreductase chain 3 {ECO:0000250|UniProtKB:P03897};
DE            EC=7.1.1.2 {ECO:0000250|UniProtKB:P03897};
DE   AltName: Full=NADH dehydrogenase subunit 3;
GN   Name=MT-ND3 {ECO:0000250|UniProtKB:P03897};
GN   Synonyms=MTND3, NADH3, ND3;
OS   Balaenoptera physalus (Fin whale) (Balaena physalus).
OG   Mitochondrion.
OC   Eukaryota; Metazoa; Chordata; Craniata; Vertebrata; Euteleostomi; Mammalia;
OC   Eutheria; Laurasiatheria; Artiodactyla; Whippomorpha; Cetacea; Mysticeti;
OC   Balaenopteridae; Balaenoptera.
OX   NCBI_TaxID=9770;
RN   [1]
RP   NUCLEOTIDE SEQUENCE [GENOMIC DNA].
RC   STRAIN=Isolate No. 27 / Anno 1987; TISSUE=Liver;
RX   PubMed=1779436; DOI=10.1007/bf02102808;
RA   Arnason U., Gullberg A., Widegren B.;
```

Figure 9.4: Structure of Swiss-Prot file

Here is what the different acronyms in the figure denote:
- **ID**: Entry identifier, entry name, data type, and sequence length.
- **AC**: Primary accession number.
- **DT**: Date of entry creation or last update.
- **DE**: Protein name/description.
- **GN**: Gene name.
- **OS**: Organism species (scientific name).
- **OC**: Organism classification.
- **OX**: NCBI taxonomy ID of the organism.
- **RN**: Reference number.
- **RP**: Reference position.
- **RX**: Reference cross-reference.
- **RA**: Author(s) of the reference.
- **RT**: Title of the reference article.
- **RL**: Journal name, volume, issue, and page range of the reference.
- **CC**: Free-text comments and additional information.
- **DR**: Database cross-references (e.g., EMBL, PDB, etc.).
- **//**: Entry terminator.

Swiss-Prot files can have more complex structures and additional information depending on the protein and associated annotations but the above example of Swiss-Prot entry is a simple example, Swiss-Prot files are typically downloaded from the UniProt website or obtained through various bioinformatics databases and resources.

Example 9.4:

```
from Bio import SwissProt

# Path Specification of Swiss-Prot file
swiss_file = "D:\\pvdata\\book1\\P4Bio\\P68308.txt"

# Opening a Swiss-Prot file and returning a handle
with open(swiss_file) as handle:

# Parsing records from a Swiss-Prot file through handle

    records = SwissProt.parse(handle)

# Reading records
```

```
    for record in records:
        print(record.entry_name)
        print(record.accessions)
        print(record.keywords)
        print(record.organism)
        print(record.sequence[:20] + "...")
```

```
= RESTART: C:\Users\5453\AppData\Local\Programs\Python\Python38\CH9_SWISS_PROT.p
y
NU3M_BALPH
['P68308', 'P24973']
['Electron transport', 'Membrane', 'Mitochondrion', 'Mitochondrion inner membran
e', 'NAD', 'Respiratory chain', 'Translocase', 'Transmembrane', 'Transmembrane h
elix', 'Transport', 'Ubiquinone']
Balaenoptera physalus (Fin whale) (Balaena physalus).
MNLLLTLLTNTTLALLLVFI...
>>>
```

Figure 9.5: Reading a Swiss-Prot file

The above example code *Example 9.5* demonstrates the usage of the Swiss-Prot module. Here, first, the file is opened using **open(swiss_file)** function. The function returns a file handle named **handle**. The file handle (or file object) is a reference to a file that has been opened, allowing the program to interact with the file system. It acts as a link between the program and the file, enabling reading, writing, and other file operations. The **parse()** function of the Swiss-Prot module returns the parsed records from the Swiss-Prot file. The for loop will access one record at a time from the set of records and print the details. (Here, the file **P68308.txt** consists of only a single record).

Project 5: Reading Swiss-Prot record from ExPASy server

Expert Protein Analysis System (ExPASy) is a bioinformatics resource and database developed by the **Swiss Institute of Bioinformatics (SIB)**. It provides a range of tools and databases for the analysis and annotation of protein sequences and structures. ExPASy is widely used by researchers in the fields of molecular biology and bioinformatics. It is a resource portal that provides information about genomics, proteomics, structure analysis, systems biology, evolutionary biology, population genetics, transcriptions, glycomics, and medicinal chemistry to name a few.

Example 9.5:

```
from Bio import ExPASy
from Bio import SwissProt
from Bio import SeqIO
```

```python
# Creating list of accession numbers
accessions = ["O23729", "O23730", "O23731"]

# Creating empty list to store records information
records = []

# Accessing each record by accesssion number from ExPASy server
for accession in accessions:
    handle = ExPASy.get_sprot_raw(accession)
    record = SeqIO.read(handle,"swiss")
    records.append(record)

# Printing details of each record
for record in records:
    print(record.id)
    print(record.name)
    print(record.description)
    print(repr(record.seq))
    print("Length %i" % len(record))
    print(record.annotations["keywords"])
    print("----------------------------------------")
```

Output:

```
==================== RESTART: D:\pvdata\Python_prog\ExPa.py ====================
O23729
CHS3_BROFI
RecName: Full=Chalcone synthase 3; EC=2.3.1.74; AltName: Full=Naringenin-chalcone synthase 3;
Seq('MAPAMEEIRQAQRAEGPAAVLAIGTSTPPNALYQADYPDYYFRITKSEHLTELK...GAE')
Length 394
['Acyltransferase', 'Flavonoid biosynthesis', 'Transferase']
----------------------------------------
O23730
CHS4_BROFI
RecName: Full=Chalcone synthase 4; EC=2.3.1.74; AltName: Full=Naringenin-chalcone synthase 4;
Seq('MAPAMEEIRQAQRAEGPAAVLAIGTSTPPNALYQADYPDYYFRITKSEHLTELK...GAE')
Length 394
['Acyltransferase', 'Flavonoid biosynthesis', 'Transferase']
----------------------------------------
O23731
CHS8_BROFI
RecName: Full=Chalcone synthase 8; EC=2.3.1.74; AltName: Full=Naringenin-chalcone synthase 8;
Seq('MAPAMEEIRQAQRAEGPAAVLAIGTSTPPNALYQADYPDYYFRITKSEHLTELK...GAE')
Length 394
['Acyltransferase', 'Flavonoid biosynthesis', 'Transferase']
----------------------------------------
>>>
```

Figure 9.6: Reading Swiss-Prot record from ExPASy server

The project mentioned is reading raw records from the Swiss-Prot file from ExPASy Server. The list of accession numbers of three orchid proteins for **chalcone synthase** is created as shown in *Example 9.5*. The function **get_sprot_raw()** is used to fetch records from the Swiss-Prot file using their accession numbers. The function returns the handle of the individual record against the accession number. The record is read from the handle and further appended to the empty list of records. Finally, we traverse the list of records and access specific information from each record like id, name, and description to name a few. The output is shown in *Figure 9.6*.

Accessing records directly from the ExPASy server offers several benefits, especially for researchers and professionals working in bioinformatics, molecular biology, and related fields. ExPASy (Expert Protein Analysis System) is a well-known bioinformatics resource portal operated by the SIB, providing access to a wide range of databases and analysis tools for proteins, nucleic acids, and more. ExPASy databases are regularly updated, ensuring that the data retrieved is current and accurate. This is crucial in fields like bioinformatics and molecular biology, where discoveries and updates occur frequently. ExPASy provides access to a vast array of databases, such as UniProtKB, Swiss-Prot, PROSITE, and more, offering comprehensive datasets that include protein sequences, functional annotations, post-translational modifications, and protein structure data.

Project 6: Parsing Swiss-Prot keywords list

Swiss-Prot distributes a keyword file that can be used to get information about the keywords and various categories used by Swiss-Prot. The file named **keywlist.txt** is distributed by Swiss-Prot. The entries of the file can be parsed by using the inbuilt module of Swiss-Prot **Bio.Swiss-Prot.KeyWList**. It returns every entry of the file in the form of a record which is in the format of a Python dictionary.

The file format is as follows:

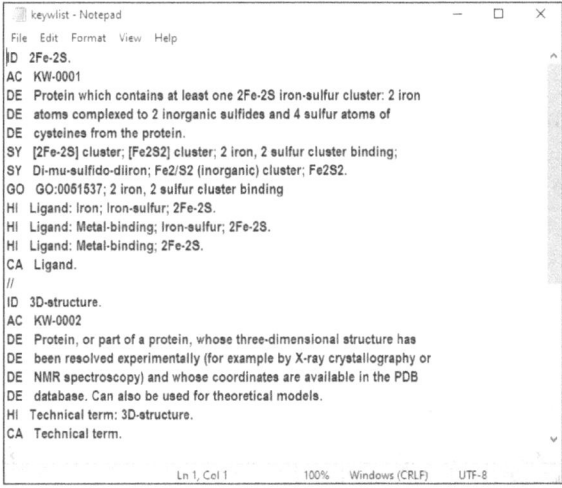

Figure 9.7: Keyword list file format

The code in *Example 9.6* can be used to access the keywords and their details in the file:

Example 9.6:
```
from Bio.Swiss-Prot import KeyWList
# Open a file with keywords list that will return a handle
handle = open("D:\\pvdata\\Python\\programs\\keywlist.txt")
# Parsing records of a handle using parse function of KeyWList module
records = KeyWList.parse(handle)
# Reading records one by one
for record in records:
    print(record['ID'])
    print(record['DE'])
    print(record['AC'])
    print("***************************")
```

```
= RESTART: D:\pvdata\book1\P4Bio\Review_done\Code\Chapter 9_code\Example9.6.py =
2Fe-2S.
Protein which contains at least one 2Fe-2S iron-sulfur cluster: 2 iron atoms com
plexed to 2 inorganic sulfides and 4 sulfur atoms of cysteines from the protein.
KW-0001
***************************
3D-structure.
Protein, or part of a protein, whose three-dimensional structure has been resolv
ed experimentally (for example by X-ray crystallography or NMR spectroscopy) and
 whose coordinates are available in the PDB database. Can also be used for theor
etical models.
KW-0002
***************************
3Fe-4S.
Protein which contains at least one 3Fe-4S iron-sulfur cluster: 3 iron atoms com
plexed to 4 inorganic sulfides and 3 sulfur atoms of cysteines from the protein.
 In a number of iron-sulfur proteins, the 4Fe-4S cluster can be reversibly conve
rted by oxidation and loss of one iron ion to a 3Fe-4S cluster.
KW-0003
***************************
>>>
```

Figure 9.8: Parsing Swiss-Prot keyword list

The example above imports **KeyWList** module from **Bio.Swiss-Prot** library. In the next statement, **open()** function is used to open the **keywlist.txt** file that is already distributed by the Swiss-Prot module. The location of the file should be mentioned properly. The **open()** function will return the file handle. The **parse()** function of **KeyWList** module helps in parsing records from the file handle and will return all records. The **for** loop can be used to traverse all records one by one and print the required information. The output is shown in *Figure 9.8*.

Project 7: Prosite records parsing

Prosite is a database of protein domains, functional sites, and motifs. It is maintained by the SIB as part of the ExPASy resource. Prosite records are descriptions of specific patterns or motifs that are characteristic of certain protein families, domains, or functional sites. These patterns are often represented using a combination of regular expressions and other notation to capture the sequence features that define a particular protein function or structure. Each Prosite record typically includes the following information:

- **Pattern**: It is a concise description of the amino acid sequence pattern or motif that is characteristic of a specific protein domain or functional site. It is often represented using a combination of letters and symbols to indicate specific amino acids and their properties.

- **Description**: A brief textual description of the protein family, domain, or functional site that the pattern represents. This description provides context and information about the biological role or significance of the pattern.

- **Documentation**: References to scientific literature or other sources that provide additional information about the protein family or domain associated with the Prosite record.

- **Examples**: Examples of protein sequences that match the pattern, along with information about the corresponding functional site or domain.

- **Taxonomic range**: Information about the taxonomic groups of organisms in which the pattern has been observed.

- **Cross reference**: Links to other databases or resources that contain additional information about the protein family or domain represented by the Prosite record.

Researchers and bioinformaticians use Prosite records to identify specific sequence features in protein sequences. This can be useful for predicting potential functional sites, understanding the evolutionary relationships between proteins, and annotating newly sequenced proteins.

Prosite patterns can be accessed and searched through the ExPASy website or through various bioinformatics tools and software that incorporate Prosite data. It is worth noting that Prosite patterns are constantly updated and refined as new information becomes available, so it is important to ensure you are using the most current version of the database for accurate analysis. *Example 9.7* demonstrates the parsing of Prosite record using parse() function of Prosite module. Parse() function will return a set of records that are further accessed one by one using a for loop. The output of the program is shown in *Figure 9.9*.

Example 9.7:

```
from Bio.ExPASy import Prosite

#Opening Prosite.dat file
handle = open('d:/pvdata/python_prog/prosite.dat')

#Parsing records of Prosite file
records = Prosite.parse(handle)
```

```
#Printing details of all records from Prosite file
for record in records:
    print("Accession number of record")
    print (record.accession)
    print("Name of Sequence")
    print(record.name)
    print("Record PDOC")
    print (record.pdoc)
    print("***********************************")
```

```
= RESTART: D:\pvdata\book1\P4Bio\Review_done\Code\Chapter 9_code\Example9.7.py =
Accession number of record
PS00001
Name of Sequence
ASN_GLYCOSYLATION
Record PDOC
PDOC00001
*******************************
Accession number of record
PS00004
Name of Sequence
CAMP_PHOSPHO_SITE
Record PDOC
PDOC00004
*******************************
Accession number of record
PS00005
Name of Sequence
PKC_PHOSPHO_SITE
Record PDOC
PDOC00005
*******************************
Accession number of record
PS00006
Name of Sequence
CK2_PHOSPHO_SITE
```

Figure 9.9: Prosite pecords parsing

Project 8: Using ExPASy for parsing enzyme records

ExPASy is a bioinformatics resource that provides a variety of tools for protein analysis. **Enzyme Commission (EC)** numbers are the primary identifier used in the Enzyme database, and they help in the classification of enzymes based on their reactions and substrates. If you have a specific enzyme record in mind, make sure you have the correct EC number of other relevant information to be accessed. Refer to *Example 9.8* for the same.

Example 9.8:

```
from Bio.ExPASy import Enzyme

# Open file
with open("lipoprotein.txt") as handle:

# Parsing Enzyme record
    record = Enzyme.read(handle)

# Printing record detail
    print(record["ID"])
    print(record["DE"])
```

```
= RESTART: D:\pvdata\book1\P4Bio\Review_done\Code\Chapter 9_code\Example9.8.py =
Record ID
*********
3.1.1.34
Record Descritption
*******************
Lipoprotein lipase.
>>>
```

Figure 9.10: ExPASy for parsing enzyme records

The enzyme record in Biopython is represented by **Bio.ExPASy.Enzyme.Record** class. The record is derived from a Python dictionary which has keys that consist of 02 letters of code used in enzyme files. To read a single record in an enzyme file use the read function in **Bio.ExPASy.Enzyme** module. The output for the same is shown in Figure 9.10.

Project 9: Reading PDB files

Bio.PDB is a module within the Biopython library, which is a collection of Python tools and libraries for computational biology and bioinformatics. The Bio.PDB module specifically focuses on working with protein structures using the PDB file format which is a standard format for representing 3D structures of biological macromolecules, such as proteins and nucleic acids. The module provides a powerful set of tools for working with protein structures and conducting various structural analyses. It is widely used by the bioinformatics community to handle and analyze protein structural data.

In the context of protein structural analysis, the term primary sequence refers to the linear sequence of amino acids in a protein. This sequence is commonly represented using the one-letter amino acid codes (e.g. **G** for glycine, **L** for leucine) and forms the foundation of a protein's structure and function. In the PDB format, the primary sequence is often included as part of the header section of the file. Here is the example PDB file:

In the example file, the **Sequence records** (**SEQRS**) provide information about the primary sequence of the protein. Each SEQRS record lists the residues in a chain along with their one-letter amino acid codes. The ATOM records contain the spatial coordinates of the atoms in the protein's three-dimensional structure. It is important to note that the SEQRS records in the PDB file might differ from the actual sequence in case there are missing residues or other modifications. The SEQRS records represent the sequence as defined by the experimenters or authors. When working with the Biopython's Bio.PDB module, you can extract the primary sequence of a protein structure using the **get_sequence()** method of the p**eptide** object. *Example 9.9* demonstrates the same. The output of the program is shown in *Figure 9.11*.

Example 9.9:

```
from Bio.PDB.PDBParser import PDBParser
from Bio import SeqIO
from Bio.PDB.Polypeptide import PPBuilder

# Creating Parser Object
parser = PDBParser()

# Accessing structure from the pdb file
structure = parser.get_structure("test", "1fat.pdb")
ppb=PPBuilder()

# Printing Sequence Object using Peptide Builder Object
print("Accessing Sequence Object using Peptide Builder Object")
for pp in ppb.build_peptides(structure):
    print(pp.get_sequence())
    print("-----------------------------------")
```

```
Accessing Sequence Object using Peptide Builder Object
SNDIYFNFQRFNETNLILQRDASVSSSGQLRLTNLN
-----------------------------------
NGEPRVGSLGRAFYSAPIQIWDNTTGTVASFATSFTFNIQVPNNAGPADGLAFALVPVGSQPKDKGGFLGLFDGSNSNFH
TVAVEFDTLYNKDWDPTERHIGIDVNSIRSIKTTRWDFVNGENAEVLITYDSSTNLLVASLVYPSQKTSFIVSDTVDLKS
VLPEWVSVGFSATTGINKGNVETNDVLSWSFASKLS
-----------------------------------
SNDIYFNFQRFNETNLILQRDASVSSSGQLRLTNLNGNGEPRVGSLGRAFYSAPIQIWDNTTGTVASFATSFTFNIQVPN
NAGPADGLAFALVPVGSQPKDKGGFLGLFDGSNSNFHTVAVEFDTLYNKDWDPTERHIGIDVNSIRSIKTTRWDFVNGEN
AEVLITYDSSTNLLVASLVYPSQKTSFIVSDTVDLKSVLPEWVSVGFSATTGINKGNVETNDVLSWSFASKLS
-----------------------------------
SNDIYFNFQRFNETNLILQRDASVSSSGQLRLTNLN
-----------------------------------
NGEPRVGSLGRAFYSAPIQIWDNTTGTVASFATSFTFNIQVPNNAGPADGLAFALVPVGSQPKDKGGFLGLFDGSNSNFH
```

Figure 9.11: Reading PDB files

Project 10: Reading GenBank file

Reading a GenBank file involves parsing the information contained within the file, which includes metadata about the sequence, features, annotations, and more. GenBank files are often used to store biological sequence data, such as DNA or protein sequences, along with associated information.

Example 9.10 demonstrates the working of reading **GenBank** file. The file **ls_orchid.gb** file is opened using **open()** function. The function will return a handle to a file. The handle is further used to retrieve accession numbers of each record and print it as well. The output is shown in *Figure 9.12*.

Example 9.10:

```
from Bio import GenBank

# Opening GenBank file and printing Accession Numbers of all records
with open("ls_orchid.gb") as handle:
    print("Printing Accession Numbers")
    for record in GenBank.parse(handle):
        print(record.accession)
```

```
>>>
================== RESTART: D:\pvdata\Python_prog\GenBank_iter.py ==================
Printing Accession Numbers
['Z78533']
['Z78532']
['Z78531']
['Z78530']
['Z78529']
['Z78527']
['Z78526']
['Z78525']
['Z78524']
['Z78523']
['Z78522']
['Z78521']
['Z78520']
['Z78519']
['Z78518']
['Z78517']
['Z78516']
['Z78515']
['Z78514']
['Z78513']
['Z78512']
['Z78511']
['Z78510']
['Z78509']
['Z78508']
```

Figure 9.12: Reading GenBank file

Project 11: Sequence alignment

Sequence alignment is a fundamental bioinformatics techniquein sequences. The goal of sequence alignment is to identify regions of similarity, which used to compare and match sequences of biological molecules, such as DNA, RNA, or protecan provide insights into evolutionary relationships, functional similarities, and structural features among different sequences. Biological sequences can vary in length and content, and they may have undergone evolutionary changes over time. Sequence alignment helps identify conserved regions (homologous regions) that might indicate shared ancestry or functional similarity, as well as variable regions that have evolved differently.

Sequence alignment has a wide range of applications in bioinformatics and molecular biology. It helps researchers extract meaningful information from biological sequences by identifying similarities, patterns, and evolutionary relationships. Here are some key applications of sequence alignment:

- **Homology detection and evolutionary analysis**: Sequence alignment is used to identify homologous sequences, which are sequences that share a common ancestry. By aligning sequences, researchers can infer evolutionary relationships, construct phylogenetic trees, and study the divergence and conservation of genes and proteins over time.

- **Protein structure and function prediction**: Aligning protein sequences can reveal conserved domains, motifs, and functional sites. Such information aids in predicting protein structures and understanding their functions. Sequence alignment can also help identify potential functional regions, active sites, and binding sites.

- **Identification of genetic variations**: Sequence alignment is used to compare DNA sequences, insertions, deletions, and other genetic variations.

- **Annotation of genomes**: Genome-wide sequence alignments are used to annotate genes and non-coding regions in newly sequenced genomes. Aligning known protein sequences against a newly sequenced genome helps identify coding regions and infer potential functions.

- **Drug design and biomarker discovery**: Sequence alignment is used to compare protein sequences associated with diseases to identify potential drug targets or disease-related biomarkers. Aligning viral or bacterial sequences can aid in designing drugs or vaccines against pathogens.

- **Structural bioinformatics**: Aligning protein sequences helps identify structural homologs and infer protein structures through homology modeling. This is crucial for understanding protein functions.

These are just a few examples of the numerous applications of sequence alignment in bioinformatics and molecular biology. Sequence alignment tools and techniques play a fundamental role in extracting valuable insights from biological sequences, advancing our understanding of genetics, evolution, and molecular interactions.

There are several sequence alignment tools available that cater to various bioinformatics needs, ranging from pairwise sequence alignment to multiple sequence alignment and more specialized tasks. Various algorithms are used for the alignment of sequences. However, it is a tedious task to write an algorithm, and it works a bit slow as well. Biopython provides us with a list of popular alignment tools that may be used. The tools are classified as follows:

Pairwise sequence alignment

There are several sequence alignment tools available that cater to various bioinformatics needs, ranging from pairwise sequence alignment to multiple sequence alignment and more specialized tasks. Here is a list of some popular sequence alignment tools provided by Biopython:

Bio.Align.PairwiseAligner module

The module is part of the Biopython package and is used for performing pairwise sequence alignments with more control and flexibility than the **Bio.pairwise2** module. This module offers a class-based approach to performing sequence alignments allowing you to customize alignment parameters and strategies. The module facilitates the alignment of two sequences by optimizing the similarity score between them. The module implements the *Needleman-Wunsch*, *Smith-Waterman*, *Gotoh (three-state)*, and *Waterman-Smith-Beyer* global and local pairwise alignment algorithms.

Example 9.11:

```
from Bio import Align
# Creating object of PairwiseAligner
aligner = Align.PairwiseAligner()


# Generating alignment using align function
alignments = aligner.align("GAACT", "GAT")
alignment = alignments[0]


# Printing Alignment
print(alignment)
```

```
========================================================== RESTART: D:\pvdata\Python_prog\pair_wise.py ====
target            0 GAACT 5
                  0 ||--| 5
query             0 GA--T 3
```

Figure 9.13: Sequence alignment using pairwise aligner module

The **PairwiseAligner** object aligner stores the alignment parameters to be used for the pairwise alignments. You may use **aligner.score()** method to calculate the alignment score between the two sequences as shown in *Example 9.11*. The output is shown in *Figure 9.14*.

Example 9.12 demonstrates the usage of the align() function of the Align model.

Example 9.12:
```
from Bio import Align
# Creating object of PairwiseAligner
aligner = Align.PairwiseAligner()
seq_1 = "AGTACGGA"
seq_2 = "AGTACC"
print("Original Sequences")
print("_____")
print("Sequence One:", seq_1)
print("Sequence Two:",seq_2)
score = aligner.score(seq_1, seq_2)
print("Alignment score::", score)

# Setting the aligner mode as local
aligner.mode="local"

# Performing Alignments
alignments = aligner.align(seq_1,seq_2)
for alignment in alignments:
    print(alignment)
```

```
= RESTART: D:\pvdata\book1\P4Bio\Review_done\Code\Chapter 9_code\Example9.12.py
Original Sequences
_____
Sequence One: AGTACGGA
Sequence Two: AGTACC
Alignment score:: 5.0
target            0 AGTAC 5
                  0 ||||| 5
query             0 AGTAC 5

target            0 AGTA-C 5
                  0 ||||-| 6
query             0 AGTACC 6

>>>
```

Figure 9.14: Calculating alignment score

We may use **aligner.align()** method to see the actual alignments and to iterate over the Pairwise alignment objects as shown in *Example 9.13* demonstrates the working. The output is shown in *Figure 9.15*.

Example 9.13:
```
from Bio import Align

# Creating object of PairwiseAligner
```

```python
aligner = Align.PairwiseAligner()
seq_1 = "AGTACGGA"
seq_2 = "AGTACC"
print("Original Sequences")
print("_____")
print("Sequence One:", seq_1)
print("Sequence Two:",seq_2)
score = aligner.score(seq_1, seq_2)
print("Alignment score::", score)
# Performing Alignments
alignments = aligner.align(seq_1,seq_2)
for alignment in alignments:
    print(alignment)
```

```
=============================== RESTART: D:/pvdata/book1/P4Bio/Review_done/Code/Chapter 9_code/Example9.13.py ===============================
Original Sequences
_____
Sequence One: AGTACGGA
Sequence Two: AGTACC
Alignment score:: 5.0
target            0 AGTACGGA- 8
                  0 |||||---- 9
query             0 AGTAC---C 6

target            0 AGTACGG-A 8
                  0 |||||---- 9
query             0 AGTAC--C- 6

target            0 AGTACG-GA 8
                  0 |||||---- 9
query             0 AGTAC-C-- 6

target            0 AGTAC-GGA 8
                  0 |||||---- 9
query             0 AGTACC--- 6

target            0 AGTA-CGGA 8
                  0 ||||-|--- 9
query             0 AGTACC--- 6

target            0 AGTACGGA  8
                  0 |||||.--  8
query             0 AGTACC--  6

target            0 AGTACGGA  8
                  0 |||||-.-  8
query             0 AGTAC-C-  6

target            0 AGTACGGA  8
                  0 |||||--.  8
query             0 AGTAC--C  6
```

Figure 9.15: Using aligner.align() method for actual alignments

By default, the **aligner** method performs global pairwise alignment however to perform local alignment we may change the mode of aligner object to **local**.

Global vs. local alignment

Global alignment aims to align the entire length of both sequences, even if that involves introducing gaps (insertions and deletions) to achieve alignment. The *Needleman-Wunsch* algorithm is often used for global alignment. This type of alignment is useful when you want to compare the two sequences that are expected to share similarities across their entire lengths. For example, you might use global alignment to compare homologous protein sequences or to find conserved regions between two DNA sequences. Refer to *Example 9.13* and *Figure 9.15 for* clarity.

Local alignment, on the other hand, aims to find the best alignment only within a specific region of the sequences. It uses the *Smith-Waterman* algorithm. This type of alignment is particularly useful when you are interested in identifying local similarities, such as functional domains or motifs, between sequences that may have significant differences in other regions. Refer to *Example 9.12* and *Figure 9.14* for a better understanding.

ClustalW

ClustalW is a widely used bioinformatics software program designed for **Multiple Sequence Alignment** (**MSA**) of biological sequences, such as DNA, RNA, and protein sequences. It was one of the pioneering tools in the field of bioinformatics and played a significant role in helping researchers analyze and understand the relationships between different sequences.

ClustalW is primarily used to align multiple biological sequences to identify regions of similarity and conversation among them. Multiple biological sequence alignment is crucial for understanding the evolutionary relationships, conserved motifs, functional domains, and structural features shared among a group of related sequences.

Typically, users input a set of sequences into ClustalW and choose alignment options such as the scoring matrix and gap penalties. The program then performs the progressive alignment, optimizing for the best alignment according to the chosen parameters.

Bio.Align.Applications module works as a wrapper for ClustalW. It is a commandline tool that works for the alignment of multiple sequences. It is quite easier to run ClustalW as a commandline. This is how we can do it:

```
>>> from Bio.Align.Applications import ClustalwCommandline
>>> help(ClustalwCommandline)
```

To use ClustalW as commandline we need to have the FASTA source file as an input. In the example below **opuntia.fasta** file is used for this purpose as an input file. The file contains 07 DNA sequences of the cactus family plant opuntia. By default, ClustalW will generate an alignment and guide tree file with names based on the input FASTA file, in this case, **opuntia.aln** and **opuntia.dnd**, but you can override this or make it explicit as mentioned in *Figure 9.16*.

Example 9.14:

```
from Bio.Align.Applications import ClustalwCommandline

# Activating Clustal command line
```

```
Cline= ClustalwCommandline("clustalw2", infile="D:\\pvdata\\Python_prog\\
opuntia.fasta")
print(cline)
```

```
>>>
= RESTART: D:\pvdata\book1\P4Bio\Review_done\Code\Chapter 9_code\Example9.14.py
clustalw2 -infile=D:\pvdata\Python_prog\opuntia.fasta
>>>
```

Figure 9.16: Using ClustalW as commandline

When ClustalW is run at the command line the output generated is redirected to the output files. ClustalW by default picks the name of the output files that are based on the name of the input **file.** In this case, the output should be in the file **opuntia.aln**. You should be able to work out how to read in the alignment using **Bio.AlignIO** as demonstrated in *Example 9.15*. The output of the same is shown in *Figure 9.17*.

Example 9.15:

```
from Bio import AlignIO
# Performing alignment using AlignIO module
align = AlignIO.read("D:\\pvdata\\Python_prog\\opuntia.aln", "clustal")

# Printing Alignment
print(align)
```

```
========================================================== RESTART: D:\pvdata\Python_prog\clust2.py ======================
Alignment with 7 rows and 156 columns
TATACATTAAAGAAGGGGGATGCGGATAAATGGAAAGGCGAAAG...AGA gi|6273285|gb|AF191659.1|AF191
TATACATTAAAGAAGGGGGATGCGGATAAATGGAAAGGCGAAAG...AGA gi|6273284|gb|AF191658.1|AF191
TATACATTAAAGAAGGGGGATGCGGATAAATGGAAAGGCGAAAG...AGA gi|6273287|gb|AF191661.1|AF191
TATACATAAAGAAGGGGGATGCGGATAAATGGAAAGGCGAAAG...AGA gi|6273286|gb|AF191660.1|AF191
TATACATTAAAGGAGGGGGATGCGGATAAATGGAAAGGCGAAAG...AGA gi|6273290|gb|AF191664.1|AF191
TATACATTAAGGAGGGGGATGCGGATAAATGGAAAGGCGAAAG...AGA gi|6273289|gb|AF191663.1|AF191
TATACATTAAAGGAGGGGGATGCGGATAAATGGAAAGGCGAAAG...AGA gi|6273291|gb|AF191665.1|AF191
>>>
```

Figure 9.17: Using Bio.AlignIO module

While ClustalW was groundbreaking and widely used for many years, it does have some limitations. It might not perform optimally for very large datasets or for sequences with extensive variations in lengths or evolutionary distances. For more complex analysis, more advanced alignment methods like *Clustal Omega* have been developed.

Basic Local Alignment Search Tool

Basic Local Alignment Search Tool (BLAST) is a powerful and widely used bioinformatics tool designed to find similarities between biological sequences. It is commonly employed to compare DNA, RNA, and protein sequences against databases to identify homologous sequences and infer functional, structural, or evolutionary databases to identify homologous sequences and infer functional, structural, or evolutionary relationships. BLAST was developed by the **National Center for Biotechnology Information (NCBI)** and has become an essential tool for various fields within biology and bioinformatics.

The primary purpose of BLAST is to quickly identify sequences in a database that are like a given query sequence. This can help researchers infer biological functions, study evolutionary relationships, identify conserved domains, and more.

BLAST can be executed at a local as well as global level. However, when we execute BLAST at the local level, it is faster as compared to global-level execution. Another benefit of executing BLAST at the local level is, that one can make its own database to search for sequences.

Using the Biopython module we can run BLAST locally as well as globally. One can also perform a BLAST search on the NCBI site save results in XML format and save the results to a file. To read contents from a file we need to get a handle that represents the source of information. We can access the information using **read()** and **readline()** functions.

To get a handle on reading BLAST records we can use **qblast()** function of the **NCBIWWW** module. After reading records from the source the records will be returned to the result handle which can be read and stored further to the XML format. Refer to *Example 9.16* which demonstrates the creation of an XML file.

The **qblast()** function is part of the Biopython library, which is a collection of tools and libraries for computational biology and bioinformatics. Specifically, **qblast** is used to perform BLAST searches programmatically from within a Python script.

We need to keep in mind that for using **qblast** you need an internet connection to access the NCBI BLAST service, and you may need to provide your own NCBI API key if you plan to use it extensively. The specific arguments and options you pass to **qblast** depend on the type of BLAST search you want to perform and your specific requirements.

Example 9.16:

```
from Bio.Blast import NCBIWWW
from Bio import SeqIO
query = SeqIO.read("D:\\pvdata\\Python_prog\\NC_005816.fna",
format="fasta")
result_handle = NCBIWWW.qblast("blastn", "nt", query.seq)
blast_file = open("my_blast.xml", "w")
# create an xml output file
blast_file.write(result_handle.read())
result_handle = open("my_blast.xml")
if (result_handle):
    print("XML file created")
# Clean up
blast_file.close()
result_handle.close()
```

Refer to the following figure for a better understanding:

```
= RESTART: D:\pvdata\book1\P4Bio\Review_done\Code\Chapter 9_code\Example9.16.py
XML file created
>>>
```

Figure 9.18: Generating XML file after reading from BLAST record

To read records from a BLAST file there are a pair of input functions, **read()** and **parse()**. The function **read()** is used when we exactly have one object and **parse()** is used as an iterator when you have multiple objects. We get BLAST record objects in return when the query is executed. An iterator allows you to step through the BLAST output, retrieving BLAST records one by one for each BLAST search result. *Example 9.17* explains the working of the parse() function. Refer to Figure *9.19* for the output of the example code.

Example 9.17:

```python
from Bio.Blast import NCBIWWW
from Bio.Blast import NCBIXML
from Bio import SeqIO
query = SeqIO.read("D:\\pvdata\\Python_prog\\NC_005816.fna", format="fasta")
# Performing Sequence Alignment using BLAST
result_handle = NCBIWWW.qblast("blastn", "nt", query.seq)

# Parsing BLAST records
blast_records = NCBIXML.parse(result_handle)

# Accessing record one by one
for blast_record in blast_records:
    for alignment in blast_record.alignments:
        for hsp in alignment.hsps:
            print(f"Alignment: {alignment.title}")
            print(f"Score: {hsp.score}")
            print(f"E-value: {hsp.expect}")
            print(f"Sequence: {hsp.sbjct}\n")
```

```
>>>
= RESTART: D:\pvdata\book1\P4Bio\Review_done\Code\Chapter 9_code\Example9.17.py
Alignment: gi|45357364|gb|AE017046.1| Yersinia pestis biovar Microtus str. 91001
  plasmid pPCP1, complete sequence
Score: 19218.0
E-value: 0.0
Squeezed text (121 lines).
Alignment: gi|45357364|gb|AE017046.1| Yersinia pestis biovar Microtus str. 91001
  plasmid pPCP1, complete sequence
Score: 55.0
E-value: 6.99378
Sequence: TACTGTACATAAAAACAGTGCTTTTATGTACAGTA

Alignment: gi|311902116|gb|HM807366.1| Yersinia pestis strain C790 plasmid pPCP1
, complete sequence
Score: 19196.0
E-value: 0.0
Squeezed text (121 lines).
Alignment: gi|311902116|gb|HM807366.1| Yersinia pestis strain C790 plasmid pPCP1
, complete sequence
Score: 55.0
E-value: 6.99378
Sequence: TACTGTACATAAAAACAGTGGTTTTATGTACAGTA

Alignment: gi|262363963|gb|CP001588.1| Yersinia pestis D106004 plasmid pPCY1, co
mplete sequence
Score: 19189.0
E-value: 0.0
```

Figure 9.19: Iterating over BLAST records

Project 12: Retrieving sequence digested by restricted enzymes

Restriction enzymes, also known as restriction endonucleases, are enzymes found in bacteria and archaea that play a crucial role in the defense mechanisms of these microorganisms against foreign DNA, such as viral DNA. These enzymes can recognize specific DNA sequences, called recognition sites, and cleave the DNA at or near these sites. This process is called restriction digestion. Restriction enzymes are important tools in molecular biology allowing scientists to manipulate and analyze DNA with precision. They are crucial for genetic research, bioinformatics, and various applications in biomedicine and biotechnology.

Here is the example *code 9.18* that will predict the fragment lengths that we will have after the sequence is digested with two made-up restriction enzymes. The two enzymes are as follows:

- **AbcI**: Its recognition site is – ANT*AAT
- **AbcII**: Its recognition site is – GCRW*TG

The asterisk here mentions the position of cut site.

The patterns themselves are relatively simple: N means any base, so the pattern for the AbcI site is **A[ATGC]TAAT**. The ambiguity code **R** means **A** or **G** and the code **W** means **A** or **T**, so the pattern for AbcII is **GC[AG][AT]TG**.

Figure 9.20 demonstrates the retrieval of digested fragments using a regular expression:

Example 9.18:
```
import re
dna = open("dna.txt").read().rstrip("\n")
print(str(len(dna)))
all_cuts = [0]

# Add cut positions for AbcI
for match in re.finditer(r"A[ATGC]AAT", dna):
 all_cuts.append(match.start() + 3)
 print(match)

# Add cut positions for AbcII
for match in re.finditer(r"GC[AG][AT]TG", dna):
 all_cuts.append(match.start() + 4)

# Add the final position
all_cuts.append(len(dna))
sorted_cuts = sorted(all_cuts)
print(sorted_cuts)
for i in range(1,len(sorted_cuts)):
 this_cut_position = sorted_cuts[i]
 previous_cut_position = sorted_cuts[i-1]
 fragment_size = this_cut_position - previous_cut_position
 print("one fragment size is " + str(fragment_size))
```

```
========================================================== RESTART: D:\pvdata\Python_prog\Double_digest.py ========
140
<re.Match object; span=(16, 21), match='AAAAT'>
<re.Match object; span=(33, 38), match='ATAAT'>
<re.Match object; span=(49, 54), match='AGAAT'>
[0, 19, 36, 52, 85, 140]
one fragment size is 19
one fragment size is 17
one fragment size is 16
one fragment size is 33
one fragment size is 55
>>>
```

Figure 9.20: Retrieval of digested fragments by restriction enzymes

Conclusion

The chapter demonstrates the usage of various Biopython libraries in the form of small projects. The various Biopython modules are used like Bio.Seq., Bio.Blast, AlignIO, Align,

GenBank, and Enzyme to name a few. These modules facilitate various bioinformatics applications in performing various tasks. These small applications of bioinformatics have significant practical applications and educational value, making them essential tools in both research and learning environments.

Join our book's Discord space

Join the book's Discord Workspace for Latest updates, Offers, Tech happenings around the world, New Release and Sessions with the Authors:

https://discord.bpbonline.com

CHAPTER 10
Mini Projects on Bioinformatics

Introduction

Bioinformatics is an interdisciplinary field that combines aspects of biology, computer science, mathematics, and statistics to analyze and interpret biological data. It involves the development and application of computational tools and techniques to address biological questions and solve problems in areas such as genomics, proteomics, transcriptomics, structural biology, evolutionary biology, and systems biology.

There are numerous applications of Python in bioinformatics like genomics, proteomics, metagenomics, phylogenetics, clustering, and drug discovery, to name a few. The chapter demonstrates the practical code aspect for the three popular applications of bioinformatics.

Structure

The chapter will cover the following topics:

- Mini project-1: Phylogenetics
- Mini project-2: Clustering
- Mini project-3: Drug discovery

Objectives

The objectives of mini projects on bioinformatics are to gain a fundamental understanding of key concepts and principles, including sequence analysis, structural biology, clustering, and computational methods. It will improve computational skills by working with bioinformatics tools, algorithms, and software packages commonly used in biological data analysis. It will make you learn how to analyze and interpret biological data, such as DNA sequences, protein sequences, gene expression profiles, and structural data, using bioinformatics techniques.

Mini project 1: Phylogenetics

Phylogenetics is the scientific field that deals with the study of evolutionary relationships among organisms. The primary goal of phylogenetics is to understand the evolutionary history and patterns of descent of different species, groups, or genes from a common ancestor. This is achieved through the analysis of shared characteristics and genetic information.

Phylogenetics has applications in various scientific disciplines, including evolutionary biology, ecology, genetics, and paleontology. It plays a crucial role in understanding biodiversity, tracing the origins of diseases, and informing conservation efforts. The development of computational methods and sophisticated software tools has further enhanced the accuracy and efficiency of phylogenetic analyses in recent years.

The evolutionary relationships between species can be inferred by molecular sequence data. Molecular data refers to information about molecules, which are the basic building blocks of matter. In biological contexts, molecular data often refers to data related to biological molecules such as DNA, RNA, proteins, and other macromolecules. This data is crucial for understanding the structure, function, and interactions of biological systems.

Phylogenetics holds significant importance across diverse scientific domains for several compelling reasons. Firstly, it provides a systematic framework for comprehending the evolutionary connections among species, unraveling the intricate tree of life, and illustrating their shared ancestry. This understanding is pivotal for effective biodiversity conservation efforts, guiding the prioritization of species preservation based on their unique evolutionary contributions. Moreover, phylogenetics plays a foundational role in contemporary taxonomy, steering the classification of organisms grounded in their evolutionary relatedness rather than solely morphological similarities. Additionally, it contributes to the study of biogeography by uncovering historical movements and connections between regions. In the medical realm, phylogenetics proves indispensable for investigating pathogen evolution, aiding in the tracking of infectious diseases, understanding their origins, and devising more efficacious prevention and treatment strategies. The discipline's reach extends to comparative genomics, agriculture, paleontology, and the realms of evolutionary biology and ecology, where it underpins critical inquiries into genetic relationships, breeding programs, historical species interactions, and adaptive radiations. In essence, phylogenetics serves as a linchpin in advancing our understanding of life's diversity, evolution, and ecological dynamics.

Phylogenetic trees depict the evolutionary relationships among a group of organisms or genes. There are several methods for generating phylogenetic trees, each with its advantages and limitations. Here are some common methods:

- **Distance-based methods**:
    - **Neighbor-Joining (NJ)**: This method constructs a tree by iteratively joining the most closely related taxa until the tree is complete. It uses a distance matrix that represents the pairwise evolutionary distances between taxa.
    - **Unweighted Pair Group Method with Arithmetic Mean (UPGMA)**: It builds a tree by successively clustering the two closest taxa based on their average distance from the rest of the taxa.

- **Character-based methods**:
    - **Maximum parsimony (MP)**: It aims to find the tree that requires the fewest evolutionary changes to explain the observed character data. It searches for the tree with the minimum number of character state changes (mutations).
    - **Maximum likelihood (ML)**: It estimates the parameters of a model of evolution and finds the tree that maximizes the likelihood of the observed data under that model. ML is based on statistical methods and can be computationally intensive.

- **Bayesian method**:
    - **Bayesian Inference (BI)**: It uses Bayesian statistics to estimate phylogenetic trees. It incorporates a prior probability distribution for the parameters and updates it based on the likelihood of the data. Markov Chain Monte Carlo (MCMC) methods are often used to sample trees and parameter values.

- **Hybrid method**:
    - **Phylogenetic networks:** Some methods combine elements of both tree and network structures to represent reticulate evolution, where different parts of a genome may have different evolutionary histories.

- **Whole-genome method**:
    - **Genome-scale phylogenetics**: These methods use entire genomes or large sets of genes to infer phylogenetic relationships. They may involve concatenation of gene sequences or co-estimation of gene trees and species trees.

- **Supertree method**:
    - **Supertree construction:** This method builds a phylogenetic tree from multiple smaller trees, each inferred from different subsets of taxa. It is useful when

dealing with large datasets or when complete data for all taxa are not available.

- **Consensus method**:
  - **Consensus trees**: These methods combine information from multiple trees to generate a consensus tree that represents the common relationships found in the input trees. Consensus trees are particularly useful when there is uncertainty in the data.
- **Phylogenetic software**:
  - **Software packages**: Various software packages are available for phylogenetic tree construction, including PAUP*, PhyML, RAxML, MrBayes, and BEAST. Each software package may implement one or more of the methods mentioned above.

The choice of method depends on the characteristics of the data, the available computational resources, and the specific goals of the analysis. Researchers often use multiple methods and compare their results to assess the robustness of the inferred phylogenetic relationships.

The project here will demonstrate the phylogenetics concept using a distance-based method that will use **the** UPGMA method for the generation of a phylogenetic tree. In phylogenetics, UPGMA is sometimes chosen over more sophisticated methods like Maximum Parsimony or Maximum Likelihood because UPGMA is a simple, straightforward algorithm that constructs phylogenetic trees based on a distance matrix, making it easy to understand and implement. It is computationally efficient, with less time complexity making it faster than Maximum Parsimony and Maximum Likelihood, which involves more complex calculations and larger computational requirements, especially for large datasets.

Project code : Phylogenetics

```
from Bio import SeqIO
from Bio import Phylo
from Bio.SeqRecord import SeqRecord
from Bio.Align import MultipleSeqAlignment
from Bio.Phylo.TreeConstruction import DistanceCalculator
from Bio.Phylo.TreeConstruction import DistanceTreeConstructor
import matplotlib.pyplot as plt

# Fetching single sequence from the fasta file
for seq_record in SeqIO.parse(open("Anolis_caro.fa",mode='r'),'fasta'):
    p1=seq_record.seq
    break
```

```python
for seq_record in SeqIO.parse(open("Balaenoptera_mus.fa",mode='r'),'fasta'):
    p2=seq_record.seq
    break

for seq_record in SeqIO.parse(open("Crocodylus_porosus.fa",mode='r'),'fasta'):
    p3=seq_record.seq
    break

for seq_record in SeqIO.parse(open("Cyclopterus_lumpus.fa",mode='r'),'fasta'):
    p4=seq_record.seq
    break

for seq_record in SeqIO.parse(open("Naja_naja.fa",mode='r'),'fasta'):
    p5=seq_record.seq
    break

for seq_record in SeqIO.parse(open("Sphenodon_punctatus.fa",mode='r'),'fasta'):
    p6=seq_record.seq
    break

for seq_record in SeqIO.parse(open("Oophaga_pumilio.fna",mode='r'),'fasta'):
    p7=seq_record.seq
    break

for seq_record in SeqIO.parse(open("Eretmochelys_imbricata.fna",mode='r'),'fasta'):
    p8=seq_record.seq
    break

#Performing MultipleSeqAlignment
align1 = MultipleSeqAlignment([SeqRecord(p1[0:143954], id="Lizard"),SeqRecord(p2[0:143954], id="Whale"),SeqRecord(p3[0:143954], id="Crocodile"),SeqRecord(p4[0:143954], id="Fish"),SeqRecord(p5[0:143954], id="Snake"),SeqRecord(p6[0:143954], id="Tuatara"),SeqRecord(p7[0:143954], id="Frog"),SeqRecord(p8[0:143954], id="Turtle"),])
# Print Sequence Alignment
print("**********Alignment Region*********")
print(align1)
```

```python
print()

# Calculating Distance
calculator = DistanceCalculator('identity')

# Generating Distance Matrix
distance_matrix = calculator.get_distance(align1)

# Print Distance Matrix
print("************Distance Matrix**********")
print(distance_matrix)

# Construct the phlyogenetic tree using UPGMA algorithm
constructor = DistanceTreeConstructor()
UPGMATree = constructor.upgma(distance_matrix)
fig = plt.figure(figsize=(20, 12), dpi=300) # create figure & set the size
matplotlib.rc('font', size=10)         # fontsize of the leaf and node labels
matplotlib.rc('xtick', labelsize=12) # fontsize of the tick labels at x axis
matplotlib.rc('ytick', labelsize=12) # fontsize of the tick labels at y axis
axes = fig.add_subplot(1, 1, 1)

# Drawing the tree
Phylo.draw(UPGMATree, axes=axes)
fig.savefig("UPGMATree")
```

Detailed description of the project

The following modules are imported to generate the phylogenetic tree:

- **from Bio import SeqIO:** The `SeqIO` module is part of the Biopython library, which is a collection of tools for computational biology and bioinformatics in Python. `SeqIO` stands for sequence input/output, and this module provides a convenient interface for reading and writing sequence data in various formats.

- **from Bio import Phylo:** The `Phylo` module in Biopython is designed to work with phylogenetic trees and evolutionary relationships. It provides functionality for reading, writing, manipulating, and visualizing phylogenetic trees. Phylogenetic trees are hierarchical structures that represent the evolutionary relationships among a group of species or genes.

- **from Bio.SeqRecord import SeqRecord:** The `SeqRecord` module in Biopython is part of the `Bio.SeqIO` package is used to represent a biological sequence along with associated metadata. It provides a way to store sequence data, annotations, and additional information in a structured manner. Each `SeqRecord` object typically corresponds to a single biological sequence, and it is a fundamental data structure when working with sequence data in the Biopython library.

- **from Bio.Align import MultipleSeqAlignment:** The `MultipleSeqAlignment` module in Biopython is designed to handle **multiple sequence alignments (MSAs)**. Multiple sequence alignments are crucial in bioinformatics for comparing and analyzing the similarities and differences among multiple biological sequences, such as DNA, RNA, or protein sequences. The `MultipleSeqAlignment` class provides a convenient way to work with and manipulate these alignments.

- **from Bio.Phylo.TreeConstruction import DistanceCalculator:** The `DistanceCalculator` module in Biopython's `Bio.Phylo.TreeConstruction` provides a convenient way to calculate distance matrices from a multiple-sequence alignment. Distance matrices are often used as input for phylogenetic tree construction methods.

- **from Bio.Phylo.TreeConstruction import DistanceTreeConstructor:** The `DistanceTreeConstructor` module in Biopython's `Bio.Phylo.TreeConstruction` provides a way to construct phylogenetic trees from distance matrices. This module is often used in conjunction with the `DistanceCalculator` module to build trees based on pairwise sequence distances.

- **import matplotlib and import matplotlib.pyplot as plt:** The `matplotlib` module is a widely used plotting library in Python. It provides a flexible and high-quality way to create visualizations for a variety of data types and formats. With `matplotlib`, you can create line plots, scatter plots, bar plots, histograms, pie charts, and more.

- **# Fetching single sequence from the fasta file:** The gene files of 08 different animal species (`Lizard`, `Whale`, `Crocodile`, `Fish`, `Snake`, `Tuatara`, `Frog`, `Turtle`) are downloaded from the online repository (**https://ftp.ncbi.nih.gov/genomes/genbank/**). The gene sequences are in the fasta file. The file may contain various gene sequences. Hence the single sequence from the file is fetched using `SeqIO.Parse()` function.

  The function will return a sequence record object. The sequence record object contains various information regarding the sequence fetched from the fasta file. The `seq_record.seq` property will retrieve the sequence only from the `seq_record` object and will store it to `p1` to `p8` variables respectively.

- **# Performing MultipleSeqAlignment:** Once the sequences of various species are stored, multiple sequence alignment is performed among all sequences to find out the alignment regions of the sequences. This will return the alignment object, and it will print the alignment sections of the sequences. Refer to the *Figure 10.1* for clarity:

```
= RESTART: D:\pvdata\book1\P4Bio\Review_done\Code\Chapter10_code1\Phylo_test_fin
al.py
**********Alignment Region*********
Alignment with 8 rows and 143954 columns
CAGAAACAAACGAAAAAAAGGTACTTTTATTATTCAAATTTGTA...GTA Lizard
GTGTCTCTCCGGCTCCGCCTGCAGCTCGGCCGGCAGGTCCGGGA...ATA Whale
AGATCAGAAGGCAATATTTTACAGTTAGGGTGGCCAAAATCTGG...TCA Crocodile
GAGACAGAGCCTCACACATGCAGTCACTCACCCTGGGATGAGAG...ACT Fish
TTGACTCAGGCTGTTAAATGCCTGCTCTTAAGATCCAGCTGTCT...NNN Snake
TATATATTATAGATATAGAATAGAGATAGATTAGAGACAGTGGA...NNN Tuatara
ttaacgtgcaaaccacccttgggggtgaaggggttaaatgattt...NNN Frog
aaccctaaccctaaccctaaccctaaccctaaccctaaccctaa...agc Turtle
```

Figure 10.1: *Alignment regions of multiple sequences*

- # **Calculating distance:** The `DistanceCalculator` class in the `Bio.Phylo.TreeConstruction` module of Biopython is used to calculate distance matrices from a multiple sequence alignment. The term *identity* refers to the percentage of identity between two sequences. The identity is a measure of similarity, representing the proportion of positions in two aligned sequences where the corresponding residues are identical.

  When you use `DistanceCalculator` with the `method='identity'` parameter, it calculates the percentage identity between pairs of sequences in a multiple sequence alignment. The resulting distance matrix will contain values ranging from 0 to 100, where 0 indicates no identity (completely different sequences), and 100 indicates complete identity (identical sequences).

- # **Generating distance matrix:** This distance matrix is then often used as input for tree construction methods. The `get_distance` function is a method of this class, and it calculates the pairwise distances between sequences in the alignment.

- # **Printing distance matrix:** Once the distance matrix is calculated it will be printed that help us assess the relationship of different species based on their similarities (*Figure 10.2*):

```
**********Distance Matrix**********
Lizard    0.000000
Whale     0.757944    0.000000
Crocodile 0.749538    0.778075    0.000000
Fish      0.765112    0.751942    0.765849    0.000000
Snake     0.848896    0.904108    0.835920    0.905643    0.000000
Tuatara   0.791593    0.802291    0.810342    0.804792    0.740035    0.000000
Frog      0.901253    0.891396    0.879614    0.897231    0.785723    0.792871    0.000000
Turtle    0.919294    0.916737    0.920259    0.916341    0.970511    0.941738    0.929075    0.000000
          Lizard      Whale       Crocodile   Fish        Snake       Tuatara     Frog        Turtle
```

Figure 10.2: *Generated distance matrix*

- **# Construct the phlyogenetic tree using the UPGMA algorithm:** Finally, the phylogenetic tree will be generated using `DistanceTreeConstructor` module. In Biopython's `Bio.Phylo.TreeConstruction` module, the `DistanceTreeConstructor` class provides a method called **UPGMA** for constructing phylogenetic trees using the **UPGMA** algorithm. **UPGMA** is a hierarchical clustering method that is commonly used for building phylogenetic trees based on distance matrices. By using the `figure()` function of matplotlib the tree generated is saved in the form of the figure. Please refer to the *Figure 10.3*:

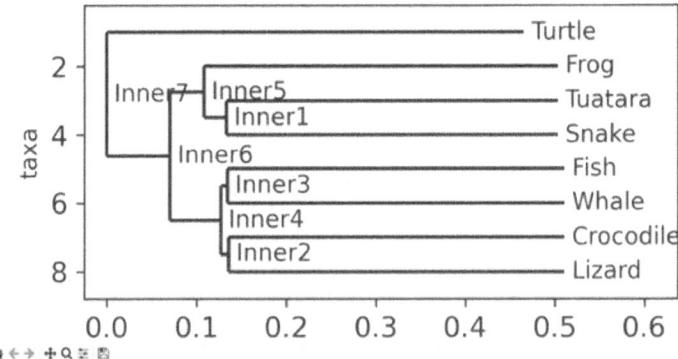

Figure 10.3: Generated phylogenetic tree

Mini poject 2: Cluster analysis

Cluster analysis is a powerful technique in bioinformatics used to explore and analyze large datasets, particularly those derived from biological experiments such as gene expression profiling, protein-protein interaction networks, and DNA sequence data. The primary goal of cluster analysis is to group similar entities based on their inherent characteristics, allowing researchers to identify patterns, relationships, and potential biological insights.

Cluster analysis, also known as clustering, is a method of grouping a set of objects or data points into subsets, or clusters, based on the similarity between them. In the context of bioinformatics, these objects could be genes, proteins, samples, or other biological entities.

The types of cluster analysis are as follows:

- **Hierarchical clustering**: Builds a hierarchy of clusters in a tree-like structure (dendrogram). Objects that are more similar are grouped together at lower levels.

- **Partitioning clustering**: Divides data into a predetermined number of clusters. Each cluster is represented by a centroid, and objects are assigned to the nearest centroid. E.g.: K-means.

- **Density-based clustering**: Identifies clusters based on dense regions in the gene expression data: Clustering genes based on their expression profiles across different conditions. E.g., DBSCAN

The following are the applications of cluster analysis:

- **Protein interaction networks**: Grouping proteins based on their connectivity and functional associations.

- **Sequence data**: Clustering sequences based on sequence similarity, aiding in functional annotation.

Project code: Cluster analysis

```
from Bio.SeqRecord import SeqRecord
from Bio import SeqIO
from Bio.Align import MultipleSeqAlignment
from Bio.Phylo.TreeConstruction import DistanceCalculator
from Bio.Cluster import kcluster
from Bio.Cluster import treecluster

# Fetching single sequence from the fasta file

for seq_record in SeqIO.parse(open("Anolis_caro.fa",mode='r'),'fasta'):
    p1=seq_record.seq
    break
for seq_record in SeqIO.parse(open("Balaenoptera_mus.fa",mode='r'),'fasta'):
    p2=seq_record.seq
    break

for seq_record in SeqIO.parse(open("Crocodylus_porosus.fa",mode='r'),'fasta'):
    p3=seq_record.seq
    break

for seq_record in SeqIO.parse(open("Cyclopterus_lumpus.fa",mode='r'),'fasta'):
    p4=seq_record.seq
    break

for seq_record in SeqIO.parse(open("Naja_naja.fa",mode='r'),'fasta'):
    p5=seq_record.seq
    break
```

```python
for seq_record in SeqIO.parse(open("Sphenodon_punctatus.fa",mode='r'),'fasta'):
    p6=seq_record.seq
    break
for seq_record in SeqIO.parse(open("Oophaga_pumilio.fna",mode='r'),'fasta'):
    p7=seq_record.seq
    break
for seq_record in SeqIO.parse(open("Eretmochelys_imbricata.fna",mode='r'),'fasta'):
    p8=seq_record.seq
    break


# Generating Multiple Sequence Alignment
align1 = MultipleSeqAlignment([SeqRecord(p1[0:143954], id="Lizard"),SeqRecord(p2[0:143954], id="Whale"),SeqRecord(p3[0:143954], id="Crocodile"),SeqRecord(p4[0:143954], id="Fish"),SeqRecord(p5[0:143954], id="Snake"),SeqRecord(p6[0:143954], id="Tuatara"),SeqRecord(p7[0:143954], id="Frog"),SeqRecord(p8[0:143954], id="Turtle"),])

#Printing Alignment
print("**************Multiple Sequence Alignment****************")
print(align1)
print()

# Calculating Distance Matrix
calculator = DistanceCalculator('identity')
distance_matrix = calculator.get_distance(align1)

# Performing K-Means clustering
print("*****************K-Means Clustering**********************")
clusterid, error, nfound = kcluster(distance_matrix)
print(clusterid,error, nfound)
print()

# Performing hierarchical clustering
print("****************Hierarchical Clustering******************")
tree = treecluster(distance_matrix)
print(tree)
```

```
= RESTART: D:\pvdata\book1\P4Bio\Review_done\Code\Chapter10_code1\Clust_analysis
_final.py
***************Multiple Sequence Alignment*****************
Alignment with 8 rows and 143954 columns
CAGAAACAAACGAAAAAAAGGTACTTTTATTATTCAAATTTGTA...GTA Lizard
GTGTCTCTCCGGCTCCGCCTGCAGCTCGGCCGGCAGGTCCGGGA...ATA Whale
AGATCAGAAGGCAATATTTTACAGTTAGGGTGGCCAAAATCTGG...TCA Crocodile
GAGACAGAGCCTCACACATGCAGTCACTCACCCTGGGATGAGAG...ACT Fish
TTGACTCAGGCTGTTAAATGCCTGCTCTTAAGATCCAGCTGTCT...NNN Snake
TATATATTATAGATATAGAATAGAGATAGATTAGAGACAGTGGA...NNN Tuatara
ttaacgtgcaaaccacccttgggggtgaaggggttaaatgattt...NNN Frog
aaccctaaccctaaccctaaccctaaccctaaccctaacccctaa...agc Turtle

*****************K-Means Clustering**********************
[0 0 0 1 1 0 0 1] 0.5681492072889873 1

***************Hierarchical Clustering*******************
(5, 4): 0.140082
(2, 0): 0.140626
(3, 1): 0.141385
(-3, -2): 0.151991
(6, -1): 0.161606
(-5, -4): 0.211878
(7, -6): 0.24467
>>>
```

Figure 10.4: Results of k-means and hierarchical clustering

Detailed description of the project

There are six modules imported into the code to perform clustering. The description of **SeqIO**, **SeqRecord,** and **MultipleSeqAlignment** modules is already discussed in the mini project - 1. The description of the modules are as follows:

- **from Bio.Phylo.TreeConstruction import DistanceCalculator:** The **Bio.Phylo.TreeConstruction** module in Biopython provides various tools for constructing phylogenetic trees from sequence data. One of the functionalities it offers is the **DistanceCalculator** class, which calculates distances between sequences or sets of sequences. These distances are often used as input for tree-building algorithms and clustering.

- **from Bio.Cluster import kcluster:** In Biopython, the **Bio.Cluster** module provides functionalities for clustering analysis, including the **kcluster** function. This function implements the k-means clustering algorithm, which is a popular method for partitioning a dataset into k clusters.

- **from Bio.Cluster import treecluster:** It is a function in the **Bio.Cluster** module of Biopython that performs hierarchical clustering. This function is used to construct a hierarchical tree (dendrogram) based on the pairwise distances between elements in a dataset. The hierarchical tree can be subsequently cut at different levels to form clusters. **treecluster** is used to perform hierarchical clustering on the **data_matrix**. The hierarchical tree (tree) is a matrix where each row corresponds to a node in the tree, and the first two columns represent the indices of the nodes that were joined at each step. The third column contains the distance at which the nodes were joined.

Keep in mind that the **treecluster** function in Biopython might have additional parameters that you can adjust according to your needs.

- **# Fetching single sequence from the fasta file:** The gene files of 08 different animal species (**Lizard**, **Whale**, **Crocodile**, **Fish**, **Snake**, **Tuatara**, **Frog**, **Turtle**) are downloaded from the online repository (**https://ftp.ncbi.nih.gov/genomes/genbank/**). The gene sequences are in the fasta file. The file may contain various gene sequences. Hence, the single sequence from the file is fetched using **SeqIO.Parse()** function.

  The function will return a sequence record object. The sequence record object contains various information regarding the sequence fetched from the fasta file. The **seq_record.seq** property will retrieve the sequence only from the **seq_record** object and store it to **p1** to **p8** variables, respectively.

- **# Performing MultipleSeqAlignment:** Once the sequences of various species are stored, multiple sequence alignment is performed among all sequences to find out the alignment regions of the sequences. This will return the alignment object, and it will print the alignment sections of the sequences. Refer to the *Figure 10.1* for a better understanding:

- **# Generating Distance Matrix:** This distance matrix is then often used as input for tree construction methods. The **get_distance** function is a method of this class, and it calculates the pairwise distances between sequences in the alignment.

- **# Performing k-means clustering:** The **kcluster** function in Biopython's **Bio.Cluster** module is a part of the Bioinformatics Python package that offers functionalities for clustering analysis, especially tailored for biological data. This function is primarily used for k-means clustering, a popular unsupervised machine-learning technique. The **kcluster** function is used to perform k-means clustering on a dataset. K-means clustering is a method of vector quantization that aims to partition a dataset into k clusters in which each observation belongs to the cluster with the nearest mean. Refer to *Figure 10.4*.

  The **kcluster()** function use the following input values:
  - **Data**: The input data should be in the form of a NumPy array or a list of lists, where each row represents an observation (e.g., a gene expression profile), and each column represents a feature (e.g., the expression level of a gene).
  - **Number of clusters (k)**: The user needs to specify the desired number of clusters to partition the data.
  - **Clustering method**: By default, the k-means algorithm is used (**method='kmeans'**), but other methods, such as hierarchical clustering (**method='a'** for average linkage, **method='m'** for maximum linkage), are also available.

The following output values are generated by **kcluster()** function:

Output values of **kcluster()** function:

- **Cluster IDs**: An array containing the cluster number assigned to each observation in the dataset.

- **Error**: The within-cluster sum of distances, which can be used as a measure of how well the data is clustered.

- **Number of times the best clustering solution found**: This indicates the number of times the algorithm found the best clustering solution.

- **# Performing hierarchical clustering:** The **treecluster** function in **Bio.Cluster** is part of the Biopython library and is used for hierarchical clustering of data, including phylogenetic data. **Bio.Cluster** is a module within Biopython that provides implementations of various clustering algorithms.

    The **treecluster** function accepts various parameters to control the clustering process, such as the distance metric to use, the clustering method, and clustering options. You can specify these parameters according to your specific needs. The output of the **treecluster** function is a tree object representing the hierarchical clustering. Refer to *Figure 10.4*.

Mini project 3: Drug discovery

Drug discovery is a multifaceted and interdisciplinary process aimed at identifying and developing new medications to treat diseases and improve human health. It involves a series of stages, from the initial identification of a therapeutic target to the development of a marketable drug product. Bioinformatics plays a critical role in modern drug discovery by leveraging computational tools, algorithms, and data analysis techniques to accelerate and enhance the drug development process. It helps in identifying potential drug targets (such as proteins, genes, or RNA molecules) associated with specific diseases by analyzing large-scale biological data, including genomic, proteomic, and transcriptomic data.

Drug discovery, as a scientific endeavor, has far-reaching applications across various fields, impacting human health, industry, and society in numerous ways. The following are the application areas of drug discovery:

- **Treatment of diseases**:
    - One of the primary applications of drug discovery is the development of medications to treat diseases. This includes the following types of diseases:
        - **Infectious diseases**: Drugs to combat bacterial, viral, fungal, and parasitic infections.
        - **Chronic diseases**: Medications for conditions like cardiovascular diseases, diabetes, cancer, autoimmune disorders, and neurological disorders.

- o **Rare diseases**: Therapies for rare genetic disorders and orphan diseases that affect a small population.
- **Improving public health**:
  - o Drug discovery contributes to improving public health by providing treatments for both common and rare diseases, thus reducing morbidity and mortality rates.
  - o Vaccines developed through drug discovery help prevent infectious diseases and contribute to disease eradication efforts.
- **Personalized medicine**:
  - o Advances in drug discovery, such as pharmacogenomics and precision medicine approaches, enable the development of personalized treatments tailored to an individual's genetic makeup, disease characteristics, and lifestyle factors.
  - o Personalized medicine allows for more effective and targeted therapies, minimizing adverse effects and optimizing treatment outcomes.
- **Drug repurposing**:
  - o Drug discovery also involves identifying new uses for existing medications, a process known as drug repurposing or drug repositioning.
  - o Repurposing drugs can lead to the discovery of novel treatments for different diseases more rapidly and cost-effectively than developing entirely new drugs.
- **Economic growth and industry**:
  - o The pharmaceutical and biotechnology industries drive innovation and economic growth through drug discovery and development.
  - o Drug discovery activities support research and development (R&D) jobs, stimulate investment in technology and infrastructure, and contribute to the economy through the sale of patented medications.
- **Drug safety and regulation**:
  - o Drug discovery research informs drug safety and regulatory practices by identifying potential risks and benefits associated with new medications.
  - o Regulatory agencies, such as the FDA, rely on scientific evidence generated through drug discovery to evaluate the safety, efficacy, and quality of pharmaceutical products.
- **Combatting drug resistance**:
  - o Drug discovery plays a critical role in addressing antimicrobial resistance, a global health threat resulting from the overuse and misuse of antibiotics.
  - o The development of new antibiotics and alternative therapies is essential for combating drug-resistant pathogens and maintaining effective treatment options.

- **Environmental and agricultural applications**:
  - Drug discovery techniques and principles are also applied in environmental and agricultural sciences to develop pesticides, herbicides, and other agrochemicals.
  - Additionally, drug discovery contributes to the development of environmentally friendly products and processes, such as green chemistry initiatives.

Overall, drug discovery has broad applications that extend beyond the healthcare sector, influencing various aspects of human life, including health, economy, environment, and agriculture. Continued innovation in drug discovery holds the promise of addressing unmet medical needs, improving health outcomes, and enhancing the quality of life globally.

Project code: Drug discovery

```python
import pandas as pd
import matplotlib.pyplot as plt
import numpy as np
import seaborn as sns
from chembl_webresource_client.new_client import new_client
from sklearn.feature_selection import VarianceThreshold
from sklearn.model_selection import train_test_split
from sklearn.ensemble import LinearRegression

# Creating an object of new_client
target_enzyme=new_client.target

# Establish a search query for an enzyme
query=target_enzyme.search("butyrylcholinesterase")

# Setting options for pandas to display maximum columns
pd.set_option('display.max_columns', None)

# Accessing targets based on target query to the dataframe
targets_retrieved=pd.DataFrame.from_dict(query)

# Printing Targets
print(targets_retrieved)

# The target protein "Butyrylcholinesterase" is selected
final_target=targets_retrieved.target_chembl_id[0]
```

```python
# Printing the final target
print("Final Target")
print("************")
print(final_target)

# Create an activity object
act=new_client.activity

# Applying filter on the final target to retreive only bioactivity data to
the dataframe
res=act.filter(target_chembl_id=final_target).filter(standard_type="IC50")
df_result=pd.DataFrame.from_dict(res)

# Converting dataframe to a csv file
df_result.to_csv("bioactive.csv", index=False)

# Data cleaning tasks
df_temp = df_result[df_result.standard_value.notna()]
df_temp=df_temp[df_temp.canonical_smiles.notna()]
df_unique=df_temp.drop_duplicates(['canonical_smiles'])

# Generating bioactivity_class
bioactive_class = []
for i in df_unique.standard_value:
  if float(i) >= 10000:
    bioactive_class.append("inactive")
  elif float(i) <= 1000:
    bioactive_class.append("active")
  else:
    bioactive_class.append("intermediate")

# Combining (molecule_chembl_id,canonical_smiles,standard_value) and
bioactive_class into a DataFrame

selection = ['molecule_chembl_id','canonical_smiles','standard_value']
df_select = df_unique[selection]
pIC50=[]
for i in df_select['standard_value']:
        molar = float(i)*(10**-9)
        pIC50.append(np.log10(molar))
```

```python
df_select['pIC50'] = pIC50

norm = []

for i in df_select['standard_value']:
        if float(i) > 100000000:
           i = 100000000
        norm.append(i)

df_select['standard_value'] = norm
bioactive_class = pd.Series(bioactive_class, name='bioactive_class')
df_combined = pd.concat([df_select, bioactive_class], axis=1)
df_combined.to_csv('bioactive_preprocessed.csv', index=False)

# Checking whether data is balanced or not
sns.countplot(x='bioactive_class', data=df_combined)
plt.show()

# Reading preprocessed data from a file
df_pre_process=pd.read_csv("bioactive_preprocessed.csv")

# Reading and processing data for X and Y coordinates
df3_X = pd.read_csv('descriptors_output.csv')
df3_X = df3_X.drop(columns=['Name'])

df3_Y = df_pre_process['pIC50']

dataset3 = pd.concat([df3_X,df3_Y], axis=1)
dataset3.to_csv('bioactive_pIC50_pubchem_fp_data.csv', index=False)

df=pd.read_csv('bioactive_pIC50_pubchem_fp_data.csv')

df.replace([np.inf, -np.inf], np.nan, inplace=True)
df=df.dropna()

X=df.drop('pIC50',axis=1)
Y = df.pIC50

selection = VarianceThreshold(threshold=(.8 * (1 - .8)))

# Dividing training and testing data
X = selection.fit_transform(X)
```

```
X_train, X_test, Y_train, Y_test = train_test_split(X, Y, test_size=0.2)

model = LinearRegression()

# Fitting the model
model.fit(X_train, Y_train)

# Finding accuracy of model
accu_score = model.score(X_test, Y_test)
print("Model Accuracy")
print("**************")
print(accu_score)
```

Detailed description of the project

The following modules are imported into the project to perform all operations:

- **import pandas as pd:** Pandas is a powerful and widely used Python library for data manipulation and analysis. It provides data structures and functions designed to make working with structured data, such as tabular or time series data, intuitive and efficient. To use **pandas**, you need to import it into your Python script or interactive session. You can import it using the conventional alias **pd**.

- **import matplotlib.pyplot as plt: matplotlib.pyplot** is a module within the **matplotlib** library, which is a popular plotting library in Python. It provides a MATLAB-like interface for creating a wide range of static, interactive, and publication-quality plots. You can import **matplotlib.pyplot** using the conventional alias **plt**.

- **import numpy as np:** The line **import numpy as np** is a common practice in Python for importing the NumPy library and giving it the alias np. NumPy is a powerful library in Python used for numerical computing. It provides support for large, multi-dimensional arrays and matrices, along with a collection of mathematical functions to operate on these arrays efficiently.

- **import seaborn as sns:** Seaborn is a popular Python visualization library based on **matplotlib**. It provides a high-level interface for creating attractive and informative statistical graphics. By executing **import seaborn**, you make all the functionalities of the Seaborn library available for use in your Python script or interactive session.

    The **as sns** part of the import statement creates an alias for the Seaborn library. An alias is an alternative name that you can use to refer to the imported module or library.

- **from chembl_webresource_client.new_client import new_client:** The line from `chembl_webresource_client.new_client import new_client` is used to import a specific function or class from the `new_client` module within the `chembl_webresource_client` package. This is a Python package that provides a client interface for accessing data from the ChEMBL database. ChEMBL is a database of bioactive molecules with drug-like properties, along with their associated targets, mechanisms of action, and pharmacological data.

  Within the `chembl_webresource_client` package, `new_client` is a module that contains the `new_client` class or function. The `new_client` class or function is typically used to create a client object that allows you to interact with the ChEMBL database and perform queries to retrieve data.

- **from sklearn.feature_selection import VarianceThreshold:** The line `from sklearn.feature_selection import VarianceThreshold` imports the `VarianceThreshold` class from the `feature_selection` module within the `sklearn` (Scikit-learn) library. `sklearn`, short for Scikit-learn, is a popular Python library for ML. It provides simple and efficient tools for data mining and data analysis and is built on top of NumPy, SciPy, and matplotlib. The `feature_selection` module in `sklearn` contains classes and functions for feature selection, which is the process of selecting a subset of relevant features (variables, attributes) for use in model construction and prediction. `VarianceThreshold` is a class provided by `sklearn` for feature selection based on variance. It removes features with low variance, assuming they contain mostly constant values and are therefore likely to be less informative for predictive modeling. This class is particularly useful for preprocessing data before fitting a machine learning model, as it can help reduce the dimensionality of the feature space and improve model performance by removing irrelevant features.

  In this case, `from sklearn.feature_selection import VarianceThreshold` imports the `VarianceThreshold` class from the `feature_selection` module, making it directly accessible without having to reference the module name.

- **from sklearn.model_selection import train_test_split:** The line from `sklearn.model_selection import train_test_split` imports the `train_test_split` function from the `model_selection` module within the `sklearn` (Scikit-learn) library.

  `sklearn`, short for Scikit-learn, is a popular Python library for ML. It provides a wide range of tools for tasks such as classification, regression, clustering, dimensionality reduction, and more.

  The `model_selection` module in `sklearn` provides functions and classes related to model selection and evaluation. This includes tools for cross-validation, hyperparameter tuning, and splitting datasets into train and test sets.

  `train_test_split` is a function provided by `sklearn` for splitting datasets into random train and test subsets. It is commonly used to prepare data for model training and evaluation. The function takes input data (features and labels) and splits them into training and testing sets according to specified proportions. By default, it randomly shuffles the data before splitting, ensuring that the train and test sets are representative of the overall dataset.

In this case, **from sklearn.model_selection import train_test_split** imports the **train_test_split** function from the **model_selection** module, making it directly accessible without having to reference the module name.

- **from sklearn.linear_model import LinearRegression:** The line from **sklearn.ensemble import LinearRegression** imports the **LinearRegression** class from the ensemble module within the **sklearn** (Scikit-learn) library.

  The **ensemble** module in **sklearn** contains classes for ensemble learning methods. Ensemble methods combine multiple individual models to improve predictive performance.

  LinearRegression is a class provided by **sklearn** for regression tasks using the concept of linear regression. Linear regression is a fundamental statistical and ML technique used to model the relationship between a dependent variable (target) and one or more independent variables (predictors). The primary goal of linear regression is to find the best-fitting linear relationship.

- **# Creating an object of new_client:** The expression **target_enzyme = new_client.target** assigns the target attribute or method from the **new_client** class to a variable named **target_enzyme**. The **new_client** is typically a class or a module within the **chembl_webresource_client** package, which provides a client interface for accessing data from the ChEMBL database, as mentioned earlier.

  target is a method or attribute of the **new_client** class that allows you to access or interact with data related to targets in the ChEMBL database. This method or attribute might provide functionality such as searching for targets, retrieving target information, or performing operations related to targets.

- **# Establish a search query for an enzyme:** The expression **query = target_enzyme.search("butyrylcholinesterase")** suggests that **target_enzyme** is an object obtained from the **new_client.target** attribute.

- **# Setting options for pandas to display maximum columns:** The statement **pd.set_option('display.max_columns', None)** is a configuration setting used with the pandas library in Python. **set_option()** is a method provided by the pandas library for setting various options that control the behavior and display of pandas objects, such as DataFrames. **display.max_columns** is a specific option that controls the maximum number of columns displayed when printing a DataFrame or other pandas object. By default, pandas will truncate the display of columns in large DataFrames, showing only a subset of the columns and replacing the rest with ellipses (...).

- **# Accessing targets based on target query to the dataframe:** The statement `targets_retrieved = pd.DataFrame.from_dict(query)` creates a pandas DataFrame from a **dictionary** object, likely obtained from the ChEMBL database query. A DataFrame is a two-dimensional labeled data structure with columns of potentially different data types. It is similar to a spreadsheet or SQL table, where data is organized in rows and columns. `from_dict()` is a method provided by the pandas library for creating a DataFrame from a dictionary object. This method takes a dictionary as input, where keys represent column names and values represent the data for each column.

- **# Target protein Bbutyrylcholinesterase is selected:** The statement `final_target = targets_retrieved.target_chembl_id[0]` assigns the value of the first element of the column named `target_chembl_id` in the DataFrame `targets_retrieved` to the variable `final_target`. The `targets_retrieved.target_chembl_id`. This expression retrieves the values from the `target_chembl_id` column of the `targets_retrieved` DataFrame. This index notation `[0]` is used to access the first element of the retrieved values. In pandas, indexing with `[0]` retrieves the value from the first row of the DataFrame.

- **# Create an activity object:** The line `act = new_client.activity` suggests that `new_client` is an object or module obtained from the `chembl_webresource_client` package, and activity is an attribute or method of this object or module. The `new_client` is likely an instance of a client class or a module within the `chembl_webresource_client` package. This package provides a client interface for accessing data from the ChEMBL database.

  The activity is an attribute or method provided by the `new_client` object or module. This attribute or method likely allows you to interact with activity data in the ChEMBL database. In the context of drug discovery, activity data typically refers to experimental measurements of a compound's biological activity, such as its potency or efficacy against a specific target.

- **# Applying filter on the final target to retrieve only bioactivity data to the dataframe:** The line `res = act.filter(target_chembl_id=final_target).filter(standard_type="IC50")` suggests that act is an object obtained from the `new_client.activity` attribute, and `filter()` is a method provided by this object to filter activity data based on certain criteria. The **act** is an object obtained from the `new_client.activity` attribute, as mentioned earlier. This object likely provides methods or attributes for interacting with activity data in the ChEMBL database. The `filter()` method is provided by the act object, which allows you to filter activity data based on specific criteria. This method accepts keyword arguments representing filtering criteria, such as target IDs and standard types, etc.

- **target_chembl_id=final_target:**
    - The first call to **filter()** filters the activity data based on the **target_chembl_id** attribute. **final_target** is likely a variable containing the ChEMBL ID of a specific target, as obtained earlier.
    - This filter operation selects activity data associated with the specified target.
- **standard_type="IC50":**
    - The second call to **filter()** further refines the filtered activity data based on the **standard_type** attribute. In this case, **"IC50"** is specified as the standard type.
    - This filter operation selects activity data with the specified standard type, which typically represents the assay measurement type (e.g., IC50, EC50, Ki).
- **Assignment to res:**
    - By using the assignment operator =, the result of chaining the **filter()** method calls is assigned to the variable **res**.
    - This suggests that the filtered activity data obtained from the **filter()** operations will be stored in the variable res for further processing or analysis.

    Finally, data is stored in a dataframe name **df_result**.

- # **Converting dataframe to a csv file:** The dataframe named **df_result** is converted to .**csv** file.
- # **Data cleaning tasks:** Data cleaning, also known as **data cleansing** or **data preprocessing**, is a crucial step in any data analysis, data science, or ML project. In this project, the drug discovery process is using a linear regression model. This model is based on ML. The performance of any model used in the ML approach depends on the quality of data used for training a model. Hence, regress data cleaning is required to provide correct data to the model. It involves identifying and correcting errors, inconsistencies, and inaccuracies in the data to ensure it is high quality, reliable, and suitable for analysis.

    The line **df_temp = df_result[df_result.standard_value.notna()]** is used to create a new **DataFrame (df_temp)** by filtering rows from an existing **DataFrame (df_result)** where the **standard_value** column is not null.

    The line **df_unique = df_temp.drop_duplicates(['canonical_smiles'])** is used to create a new DataFrame (**df_unique**) by removing duplicate rows from an existing DataFrame (**df_temp**) based on the values in the **'canonical_smiles'** column.

- **# Generating bioactivity_class:** The **bioactivity** class is generated. The bioactivity data is in the **IC50** unit. Compounds having values of less than 1000 nM will be active while those greater than 10,000 nM will be considered to be inactive. As for those values between 1,000 and 10,000 nM will be referred to as intermediate.

- **# Combining features with bioactivity class and generating dataframe:** The 03 features **['molecule_chembl_id','canonical_smiles','standard_value']** are selected and further normalized. Finally, features and the **bioactivity** class is combined and converted into a DataFrame, which is finally converted into a CSV file.

- **# Checking whether data is balanced or not:** The line **sns.countplot(x='bioactivity_class', data=df_combined)** is a Seaborn function used to create a count plot, which is a type of bar plot that shows the count of observations in each category of a categorical variable. Refer to *Figure 10.5* for clarity:

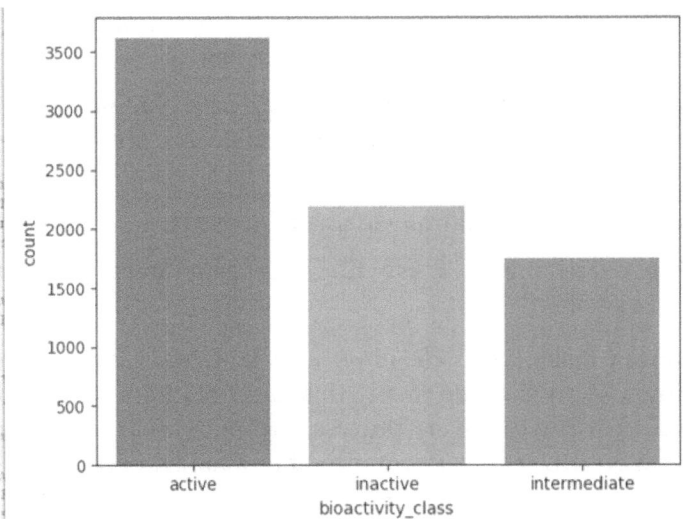

Figure 10.5: Result of data biasness

- **# Reading preprocessed data from a file:** The statement will read data from a CSV file named **preprocessed_bio_active.csv** file.

- **# Reading and processing data for X and Y coordinates:** The data is read for X and Y coordinates. The data for Y coordinate is read from the dataset generated as **df_pre_process** and data for Y coordinate are read from the dataset generated as **df3_X**. Finally, the concatenated **dataset3** is generated. **dataset3** is used to generate the CSV file **bioactivity_class_data.csv**. Data is read from **bioactivity_class_data.csv** file to **df**.

- **# Dividing training and testing data:** This step will divide data into train and test data and then the object model of linear regression is created.

- **# Fitting the model:** The fitting of the model is performed using the **fit()** function.

- **# Finding the accuracy of the model:** Finally, the accuracy of the model is calculated using **score()** function. The model gives 42.8 % of accuracy. Further investigation by application of other models can be done and verified. Refer *Figure 10.6* for clarity:

```
>>> 
===== RESTART: D:/pvdata/book1/P4Bio/Review_done/Code/Chapter10_code1/t.py =====
Model Accuracy
**************
0.4286832522408649
>>> 
```

Figure 10.6: Accuracy level of the applied model

Conclusion

In conclusion, mini projects on bioinformatics offer valuable opportunities for students to gain practical experience in applying computational and analytical techniques to solve biological problems. These projects provide a platform for students to develop essential skills in data analysis, programming, and scientific research while exploring the fascinating intersection of biology and computer science. The three projects discussed in this chapter help the readers in a basic understanding of the role of bioinformatics in various applications like phylogenetics, clustering, and drug discovery.

Join our book's Discord space

Join the book's Discord Workspace for Latest updates, Offers, Tech happenings around the world, New Release and Sessions with the Authors:

https://discord.bpbonline.com

Index

A

abstraction 110
acute myeloid leukemia (AML) 16
adeno-associated viral vectors
    (AAVs) 14
adenoviral vectors (ADV) 13
ADMET 19
agricultural genomics 31-33
antiretroviral therapy (ART) 31
applications of bioinformatics
  Adenine-Thymine (AT) content in
      sequence, calculating 181
  DNA sequences, concatenating 180
  ExPASy, for parsing enzyme records
      190, 191
  GenBank file, reading 193
  PDB files, reading 191, 192
  Prosite records parsing 188-190
  restriction enzymes, searching in
      sequences 182
  sequence alignment 193, 194
  sequence retrieving 202, 203
  Swiss-Prot file, reading 183-185
  Swiss-Prot keywords list, parsing 187,
      188
  Swiss-Prot record, reading from ExPASy
      server 185-187
arithmetic operators 56
arrays in NumPy 161
  double dimensional array, traversing
      165
  multi-dimensional array 162, 163
  single dimensional array 162
  single dimensional array, traversing 164
  slicing 163, 164
  traversing 164
assignment operator 57
asterisk quantifier 146
attributes 110

B

bar plots 172
  horizontal bar plot 173
Basic Local Alignment Search Tool
      (BLAST) 199-201
binary files 101
  closing 102, 103
  data reading 102
  data writing 102
  opening 101, 102
  seeking and position 102
binary type 52
biochemical pathway 160
bioinformatics 2, 4
  applications 2-4
  data structures 4, 5
  dynamic data structures 6
  priority queues 6
  sparse data structures 6
  spatial data structures 6
  structural databases 6-8
  tools and techniques 8-10
Biopython module 119
  installing 120
  mutable sequence 127-129
  sequence object 121
  sequence object operations 123
  sequence, working as string 121, 122
Boolean data type 52
Breadth-First Search (BFS) 6
break statement 70, 71

C

character classes 145
Chimeric antigen receptor (CAR)
      T-cell therapy 14
class 110
  defining 111-113
clinical genomics 29-31
ClustalW 198
  using 198, 199

cluster analysis 213
  density-based clustering 213
  hierarchical clustering 213
  partitioning clustering 213
  project code 214
  project description 216, 217, 218
comma-separated values (CSV) files 103
  reading 103
  reading, with headers 103
  writing 104
  writing, with headers 104, 105
comments 58, 59
  docstrings syntax 59
complementary DNA (cDNA) 23
conditional statements 62
  if-elif-else statement 64, 65
  if...else statement 64
  if statement 62, 63
cryo-electron microscopy (cryo-EM) 6
curly braces quantifier 148-150

D

DataFrame 166
data handling 157-159
  tools, using 160
data mining 9
data structures, bioinformatics
  alignment matrices 5
  graph 5
  graph algorithms 6
  hash tables 5
  lists and arrays 5
  sequence databases 5
  sequences 5
  stacks and queues 5
  trees 5
data structures, Python
  dictionaries 87
  lists 82
  sets 87
  strings 88

data types 48
  binary type 52
  Boolean data type 52
  mapping type 50
  numeric data type 48-50
  sequence data type 50
  set type 51, 52
  text data type 48
data visualization 10, 157, 159
  expression profile 160
  Genome annotation 159
  molecular pathway 160
  phylogeny and taxonomy 160
  sequence analysis 159
  tools, using 160
definite loop 66-70
density-based clustering 213
Depth-First Search (DFS) 6
dictionaries 87
directed acyclic graphs (DAGs) 5
directories
  working with 107-109
docstrings 59
drug discovery 18-20, 218
  application areas 218-220
  project code 220
  project description 223-229
duck typing 116
  example 116, 117

E

ecogenomics 4
embryonic stem cells 15
encapsulation 89, 110
Enzyme Commission (EC) 190
Expert Protein Analysis System
    (ExPASy) 185
explicit type casting 55
expression 53

F

FAIR principles 159
FASTA files 105
  reading 105, 106
  writing 106, 107
files
  appending to 98
  audio files 101
  binary data files 101
  binary files 100, 101
  binary files, working with 99
  closing 99
  comma-separated values (CSV) files 100
  common modes 98
  compressed files 101
  configuration files 101
  Excel files 100
  existence, checking 99
  HTML files 100
  image files 101
  iteration 99
  JSON files 100
  log files 101
  opening 98
  PDF files 101
  reading from 98-100
  shapefiles 101
  SQLite databases 101
  text files 100
  writing to 98
  XML files 100
  YAML files 100
frozenset 52
functional annotation 9
functions 88-92

G

Gene Ontology (GO) 5
gene therapy 12, 13
genome assembly and annotation 8
genomic data analysis 20-22

Genomic Data Commons
        (GDC) 159
Genomic Data Sharing
        (GDS) policy 159
geographic information system
        (GIS) applications 101
ggplot
  working with 176
graft-versus-host disease
        (GVHD) 17
group() function 152, 153

H

Hematopoietic stem cell transplantation
        (HSCT) 16
hierarchical clustering 213
histogram 174
homologous structures 7
horizontal bar chart 173
Hypertext Markup Language
        (HTML) files 100

I

identifier 46
if-elif-else statement 64, 65
if…else statement 64
if statement 62, 63
implicit type casting 54
indentation 60
  expected an indented block 61, 62
  unexpected indent 61
inheritance 110, 113
  benefits 114, 115
  example 113, 114
input statement 60

J

Joint Center for Structural Genomics
        (JCSG) 7
jump statements 70
  break statement 70-73
  continue statement 72, 73

pass statement 73

K

keywords 55

L

lentiviral vectors 13
line chart 169
line plot, by Matplotlib 168
  basic plot 168
  label and title, adding 171
  line style and marker, customizing 170
  with x and y values 169
Lipid Nanoparticles (LNPs) 14
lists 82
  concatenation 83
  creating 82
  elements, accessing 82
  elements, modifying 83
  length 83
  methods 84
  repetition 83
  slicing 83, 84
logical operators 57
loops
  definite loop 66, 67
  indefinite loop 68
  nested loop 68-70

M

machine learning 9
mapping type 50
match position
  obtaining, with regular
        expression 153, 154
Matplotlib 160
  bar plot 172
  histogram plot 174
  line plot 168
  scatter plot 175
  working with 168

Membrane Protein Data Bank (MPDB) 8
messenger RNA (mRNA) 23
metabolic pathway 160
metagenomics 9, 27-29
method overriding 115
　example 115
methods 110
modular programming 88, 89
　examples 89, 90
module 88
MODULES 92
Multiple Sequence Alignment (MSA) 198
mutable sequence 127, 128
　functions 128, 129
　multiplying 130

N

National Center for Biotechnology Information (NCBI) 136, 199
nested if-elif-else statement 65, 66
next-generation sequencing (NGS) 23, 29
non-viral vectors 14
Nucleic Acid Database (NDB) 6
nucleic acid sequence 123
numeric data type 48
NumPy 160
　arrays 161
　working with 161

O

object 110
object-oriented programming (OOP) 98, 109
　concepts 110
operators, Python 56
　arithmetic operators 56
　assignment operator 57
　logical operators 57
　relational operators 56
　special operator 58

P

packages 89, 92-95
Pairwise sequence alignment 195
Pandas 160, 165
　DataFrames, handling 165-167
　datasets, handling 165-167
　working with 165
partitioning clustering 213
pattern recognition 139
patterns in bioinformatics sequences 140, 141
Phylogenetics 9, 206, 207
　methods 207, 208
　project code 208
　project description 210-213
plus sign quantifier 147
polymorphism 110, 115
　duck typing 116
　method overriding 115, 116
position anchors 151, 152
Protein Data Bank (PDB) 6
proteomics 25-27
Python 37, 38
　comments 58
　data structures 82
　data types 48
　downloading 41
　evolution 38, 39
　features 40
　file types 100
　history 38
　indentation 60
　input statement 60
　installing 41, 42
　jump statements 70
　keywords 55
　loops 66
　modes 43, 44
　operators 56

script mode 44-46
string basic 76
variables 46

Q

qblast() function 200
quantifiers 146
  asterisk quantifier 146, 147
  curly braces quantifier 148-150
  plus sign quantifier 147
  question mark quantifier 148
Quantitative Structure-Activity Relationship (QSAR) 19
question mark quantifier 148

R

regular expression 141-143
  alternation feature 144, 145
  character groups 145, 146
  for obtaining match position 153, 154
  for searching pattern 143, 144
  for string splitting 155, 156
  group function 152, 153
  multiple matches, finding 154, 155
  positions 151
  quantifiers 146
relational operators 56

S

scatter plot 175
Scikit-Learn 161
sequence alignment 193, 194
  global, versus local alignment 197, 198
  Pairwise sequence alignment 195-197
sequence analysis 8
sequence data type 50
sequence input-output module 131, 132
sequence iterators 132
  for FASTA file 132-135
  for GenBank file 136
sequence object 121

sequence object operations
  back transcription 124
  reverse complement function 123
  sequence, complementing 123
  transcribe function 124
  translation 125-127
SequenceRecord object 130
  creating 130, 131
Sequence records (SEQRS) 192
sequences
  filtering, from FASTA file 135
sets 51, 87
special operator 58
stem cell therapy 15, 16
string methods 79
  find() 81, 82
  lower() 80
  replace() 81
  split() 81
  strip() 80, 81
  upper() 79, 80
strings 48, 76, 88
  characters, accessing 76
  concatenation 77
  length 76
  slicing 77-79
  splitting, with regular expression 155, 156
structural bioinformatics 8
Structural Classification of Proteins (SCOP) 7
structural databases
  drug-target interaction database 7
  genomics database 7
  molecular modeling database 7
  Protein Data Bank (PDB) 6
  protein membrane database 8
  protein structure classification databases 7
  virus structure database 8

Structural Genomics Consortium (SGC) 7
Structure-Activity Relationship (SAR) analysis 19
Swiss Institute of Bioinformatics (SIB) 185
systems biology 33-35

T

three-dimensional (3D) structural information 6
transcriptomics 23-25
tuples 84
  creating 85
  elements, accessing 85
  immutable nature 86
  length 85
  packing 86
  unpacking 86
type casting 55
type conversion 53, 54
  explicit type casting 55
  implicit type casting 54

V

variables 46, 47
viral vectors 13
  adeno-associated viral vectors (AAVs) 14
  adenoviral vectors (ADV) 13
  lentiviral vectors 13

W

web resources 10

Y

YAML Ain't Markup Language (YAML) files 100

Made in United States
Cleveland, OH
06 June 2025

17551312R00142